The age of community care has brought with it an increasing awareness of the right of all people with a learning disability to inclusion in mainstream society. Asserting these rights brings increasing challenges to community services to meet the needs of a significant number of people whose behaviour represents a challenge. The combination of intellectual and behavioural disabilities which encompass a wide range of activities involving aggression and self-injury through to bizarre mannerisms and the eating of inappropriate objects can easily jeopardise the health, safety and welfare of the affected and their carers.

This book provides a concise overview of current practice in behavioural approaches to understanding, assessing and treating challenging behaviour. It discusses criticisms of these approaches, and draws attention to recent developments which have implications for future practice. Also covering the social context and epidemiology, neurobiological models and psychophar-macological approaches to intervention, it will be an invaluable resource to clinical and educational psychologists, psychiatrists and all practitioners involved in the assessment and treatment of challenging behaviour.

CHALLENGING BEHAVIOUR:
analysis and intervention in people
with learning disabilities

....

CHALLENGING BEHAVIOUR:
analysis and intervention in people with learning disabilities

Eric Emerson

Hester Adrian Research Centre
School of Psychiatry and Behavioural Science
University of Manchester, UK

CAMBRIDGE
UNIVERSITY PRESS

Published by the Press Syndicate of the University of Cambridge
The Pitt Building, Trumpington Street, Cambridge CB2 1RP
40 West 20th Street, New York, NY 10011-4211, USA
10 Stamford Road, Oakleigh, Melbourne 3166, Australia

First published 1995

Printed in Great Britain at the University Press, Cambridge

A catalogue record for this book is available from the British Library

Library of Congress cataloguing in publication data
Emerson, Eric.
Challenging behaviour: analysis and intervention in people with
learning disabilities/Eric Emerson.
    p.   cm.
Includes bibliographical references.
ISBN 0-521-40485-1 (hc). – ISBN 0-521-40665-X (pbk.)
1. Mentally handicapped – Mental health.   2. Mentally handicapped
– Behavior modification.   I. Title
[DNLM: 1. Social Behaviour Disorders.   2. Learning Disorders.
3. Mental Disorders. WM 600 E53c 1995]
RC451.4.M47E44   1995
362.2'7–dc20
DNLM/DLC
for Library of Congress   95–10509   CIP

ISBN 0 521 40485 1 hardback
ISBN 0 521 40665 x paperback

VN

CONTENTS

FOREWORD

This is a very timely text for a number of reasons. The development of community care for people with learning disabilities is now a well-established policy in the majority of English-speaking countries and a broadening theme in the policies of others. Initially, community care in many countries was not felt to be appropriate for people with challenging behaviour but, with an increasing emphasis on the rights of all people with learning disabilities to inclusion in mainstream society, the rights of people whose behaviour challenges services have been asserted and acknowledged. This shift in policy has brought with it increasing challenges to community services to meet the needs of people whose behaviour represents a challenge. It is clear that, if services fail, community care could be progressively eroded as pressure for segregated provision builds for this, and other, marginalised groups of people with learning disabilities. As a consequence, it is important that services are equipped with the knowledge and skills which will allow them to meet their responsibilities.

Against this background, methods of working with people with challenging behaviour have developed in a piecemeal and often erratic way. Professionals faced with problems, which are both urgent and puzzling, have often turned to out-moded methods or methods for which unsubstantiated claims have been made. Part of the problem stems from the history of the development of methods of management of challenging behaviour. Adaptations of applied behaviour analysis were introduced in the early 1960s under the banner of 'behaviour modification'. At that time, there was an urgent need to 'do something' against the context of all pervasive inaction in managing challenging behaviour in a constructive way. Such was the extent of the neglect of the rights of people with learning disabilities to learn new skills and to live more satisfactory lives, that behaviour modification had to be a simple easy-to-learn set of strategies which could be used by often poorly educated front-line staff. As such, behaviour modification fell prey to the argument that 'an easily understood, workable, falsehood, is more useful than a complex incomprehensible truth' (*Thumb's Second Postulate*). Unfortunately, beyond relatively minor challenging behaviour the 'easily understood' has not proved workable.

During the last two decades, behaviour modification techniques have significantly affected techniques for skill-building in work with people with learning disabilities, and have been substantially incorporated in practice.

However, the application of the techniques in managing challenging behaviour has led to abuse and controversy. Meanwhile, applied behaviour analysis as a theoretically and empirically based discipline has developed in ways which have led to increased understanding of the mechanisms underlying challenging behaviour and, as a result, to the promise of more effective methods through which behaviour may be understood and managed.

This book has been written with the purpose of redressing these imbalances. It presents a scholarly and imaginative account of current ways of conceptualising, assessing and intervening in the challenging behaviour of people with severe learning disabilities and challenging behaviour. Although the author has a solid professional grounding in working with people with learning disabilities and challenging behaviour, it is not intended as a 'how to do it' text. It is arguable that challenging behaviour, especially when it is severe and well established, is never simple. The text faces this problem. It provides the serious reader with a well-thought through framework from which informed and imaginative analyses and interventions may be developed, which stem from rational, theoretically and empirically based formulations. As such, it makes a significant contribution to thinking which is critical to the future of people with learning disabilities and challenging behaviour and to the people who live and work with them.

CHRIS KIERNAN
Hester Adrian Research Centre
University of Manchester
December, 1994

1 INTRODUCTION

Over one million of the citizens of Europe, North America and Australasia who have a severe learning disability also show additional problematic or challenging behaviours. These include such behaviours as aggression, self-injury, destructiveness, overactivity, inappropriate social or sexual conduct, bizarre mannerisms and the eating of inappropriate objects. This combination of intellectual and behavioural disabilities can blight the lives of those affected, and place the health, safety and welfare of those who care for them in jeopardy. They also represent a significant challenge to agencies involved in the purchase or provision of health and welfare services.

Over the past three decades the discipline of behavioural psychology has been particularly influential in guiding thinking and practice with regard to the assessment and treatment of such behaviours. Behavioural models have provided coherent accounts of various forms of challenging behaviour and have guided practice in assessment and treatment. Behavioural interventions have repeatedly been shown to be effective in bringing about rapid and clinically significant decreases in challenging behaviour. They have also, however, attracted considerable controversy. In recent years, concerns have been expressed both within and outside of the discipline regarding the direction the field has taken. These have included reservations about the restricted focus, theoretical backwardness, ethical acceptability and social significance of the effects and side-effects of behaviourally orientated intervention procedures (Guess *et al.*, 1987; National Institute of Health, 1991; Repp & Singh, 1990).

The goals of this book are twofold. First and foremost, to attempt to provide a relatively concise introduction to the area and, in so doing, to give a balanced overview which addresses some of the criticisms outlined above. Secondly, to draw attention to some of the more recent developments in the area of behaviour analysis, which will need to be incorporated into practice if behavioural approaches are to continue to contribute to the struggle to help people with severe disabilities to overcome their challenging behaviours and become more fully participating members of our communities.

This is not, however, a 'how-to-do-it' book. Rather, it will place emphasis on describing those developments in basic and applied research which are likely to have important implications for clinical practice. Those with more pressing practical needs are referred to any one of the number of excellent books and guides which are currently available (e.g. Carr *et al.*, 1993; Donnellan *et al.*, 1988; Durand, 1990; Evans & Meyer, 1985; Konarski, Favell & Favell, 1992; McBrien & Felce, 1994; Meyer & Evans, 1989; Zarkowska & Clements, 1994).

TERMS AND DEFINITIONS

The terminology used to identify and describe people with severe disabilities has undergone numerous revisions over the last century. Scientific and lay terminologies also vary between English-speaking countries. Lay and technical terms themselves reflect deeply rooted cultural beliefs regarding the nature of disability. As the prominence of different beliefs change within a culture, their associated terminologies are likely to become outdated and unhelpful. Thus, for example, use of the term 'mongol' with its racist overtones arising from its association with the notion of 'atavistic regression' (Clarke & Clarke, 1974) has, quite rightly, fallen from contemporary usage. Furthermore, as technical terms enter the common vocabulary, they themselves can quickly acquire disparaging connotations. Today's terminology quickly becomes tomorrow's terms of abuse. 'Idiots', 'imbeciles', 'morons', 'subnormals' and 'retards' are, nowadays, nothing more than terms of denigration.

Two recent changes in terminology in the UK are relevant to the content of this book: the replacement of the term 'mental handicap' with 'learning disability', and the emergence of the concept of 'challenging' behaviour.

Learning disability

Throughout this book, the term learning disability will be used in preference to the UK terms mental handicap and learning difficulties, the North American terms mental retardation and mental deficiency, and the Australasian term intellectual impairment. This choice reflects current practice within health and social services in the UK.

At times, however, two related terms will be employed which are based on the terminology of the World Health Organisation. First, the term *intellectual or cognitive impairment* will be used to refer to any underlying loss or disturbance of basic psychological functions which may result in the person experiencing a learning disability. This learning disability will itself be reflected in the person experiencing difficulty in acquiring the skills or attaining levels of performance characteristic of their non-impaired peers. In most social contexts, of course, a learning disability will result in a *social handicap*. That is, the person with a learning disability is likely to experience difficulty in fulfilling the requirements of the social roles expected of someone of such an age and gender within their society. Indeed, in most, if not all, societies individuals will, as a result of their learning disabilities, be prescribed abnormal or deviant social roles as well as being excluded from normative roles (Wolfensberger, 1975). Reducing the impact of impairments upon disabilities and of disabilities upon handicaps are, of course, the manifest objectives of health and welfare agencies.

The use of the term learning disability should, however, be regarded as being synonymous with the terms mental handicap and mental retardation. Mental retardation has been defined as referring to

significantly subaverage general intellectual functioning [IQ< 70] resulting in or associated with concurrent impairments in adaptive behaviour and manifested during the developmental period' (Grossman et al., 1983). More recently this definition has been amended to

substantial limitations in present functioning. It is characterised by significantly subaverage intellectual functioning [IQ< 75], existing concurrently with related limitations in two or more of the following applicable adaptive skill areas: communication, self-care, home living, social skills, community use, self-direction, health and safety, functional academics, leisure and work. Mental retardation manifests itself before age 18. (Luckasson et al., 1992, p.5; for discussion of the implications of these changes see MacMillan, Gresham & Siperstein, 1993; Schalock et al., 1994).

People with a *severe* learning disability (severe or profound mental handicap/mental retardation) will, in addition to the above general characteristics, score below IQ 50 on standardised tests of intelligence, show clear signs of significant disabilities in the acquisition of adaptive behaviours from early in life, and will need considerably more support than their peers to successfully participate in everyday activities. Most of them will show some evidence of damage to their central nervous system and many of them will have additional physical or sensory handicaps.

Challenging behaviour

Over the past few years, the term 'challenging behaviour', initially promoted in North America by The Association for People with Severe Handicaps, has come to replace a number of related terms including abnormal, aberrant, disordered, disturbed, dysfunctional, maladaptive and problem behaviours. These terms have previously been used to describe a broad class of unusual or odd behaviours shown by people with severe learning disabilities. They include aggression, destructiveness, self-injury, stereotyped mannerisms and a range of other behaviours which may be either harmful to the individual (e.g. eating inedible objects), challenging for carers and care staff (e.g. non-compliance, persistent screaming, disturbed sleep patterns, overactivity) and/or objectionable to members of the public (e.g. regurgitation of food, the smearing of faeces over the body).

The term challenging behaviour has been defined as

behaviour of such an intensity, frequency or duration that the physical safety of the person or others is likely to be placed in serious jeopardy, or behaviour which is likely to seriously limit or deny access to and use of ordinary community facilities (Emerson et al., 1988).

The term challenging behaviour will be used throughout the remainder of the book for a number of reasons. First, it is free from implicit assumptions regarding the psychological characteristics of the behaviour in question. A number of alternative terms have unhelpful connotations regarding either the organisation of behaviour (e.g. disordered behaviour) or the nature of the relationship between the behaviour and ongoing events (e.g. dysfunctional or maladaptive behaviour). As we shall see, considerable evidence suggests that 'challenging' behaviours may be both orderly, in being integrated within an individual's behavioural repertoire in a coherent fashion, and adaptive, in that they may be functionally related to important events occurring in the person's social environment. Indeed, many challenging behaviours can be construed as (at least in the short term) coherently organised adaptive responses to 'challenging' situations.

Secondly, the term is specific to a socially significant subclass of abnormal, odd or unusual behaviours. Challenging behaviour only refers to behaviours which involve significant risks to people's physical well-being or act to markedly reduce access to community settings. This consequently excludes behaviours which may be either statistically or culturally infrequent but have minimal physical or social impact. Implicit in the use of the term challenging behaviour is a notion that the behaviours in question also contravene important social or cultural norms or expectations. Thus, for example, both cigarette smoking and long-distance running meet formal definitions of self-injurious behaviour in that they are repetitive behaviours which commonly result in physical harm or tissue damage (Fee & Matson, 1992). They would also meet the definition of challenging behaviour proposed by Emerson *et al.*, (1988). Such behaviours have yet, however, to be included in studies of the epidemiology of challenging behaviour. They are also unlikely to be construed as providing legitimate targets for intrusive intervention (Romanczyk, Lockshin & O'Connor, 1992). The issue of the social construction of challenging behaviour will be discussed in greater detail in the next chapter.

In light of the above discussion, however, the definition of challenging behaviour provided by Emerson *et al.* (1988) will be amended to

culturally abnormal behaviour(s) of such an intensity, frequency or duration that the physical safety of the person or others is likely to be placed in serious jeopardy, or behaviour which is likely to seriously limit use of, or result in the person being denied access to, ordinary community facilities.

Culturally abnormal behaviours shown by people with severe learning disabilities, which are likely to place the physical safety of the person or others in serious jeopardy, include serious physical aggression, destructiveness and self-injury as well as such health-threatening behaviours as the smearing of faeces over the body and the eating of inedible objects. Behaviours which are likely to seriously limit or prevent them gaining access to ordinary community facilities include, in addition to all the behaviours listed above, behaviours such as less serious forms of physical aggression, verbal abuse, tantrums, minor self-injury and stereotypy, i.e. behaviours which may lead to significant levels of avoidance by members of the public (e.g. Jones, Wint & Ellis, 1990). In the main, however, the focus throughout this book will be on more seriously challenging behaviours, i.e. those behaviours which represent a major threat to the physical well-being or safety of individuals.

It should be noted that challenging behaviour is not synonymous with psychiatric disturbance. Not all psychiatric disorders (e.g. anxiety, mild depression) place the safety of the person or others in jeopardy, or lead to the person being denied access to community settings. On the other hand, many challenging behaviours appear to be functional adaptive responses to particular environments rather than the manifestations of any underlying psychiatric impairment.

Finally, the use of the term 'challenge' may help to focus our attention on the process by which social problems are defined. That is, it may help to broaden the focus of enquiry by placing individual pathology in the important interpersonal context in which certain acts may be deemed problematic. As Blunden and Allen (1987) point out, the term challenging behaviour

emphasises that such behaviours represent challenges to services rather than problems which individuals with learning disabilities in some way carry around with them (Blunden & Allen, 1987, p.14).

To construe a situation as a challenge rather than a problem may encourage more constructive responses, although it would, of course, be mistaken to believe that minor changes in terminology are capable of bringing about major changes in practice.

AN OVERVIEW

Much has been written over recent years on some of the general issues involved in providing community-based services for people with challenging behaviours (e.g. Allen, Banks & Staite, 1991; Blunden & Allen, 1987; Department of Health, 1989, 1993; Emerson, McGill & Mansell, 1994; Fleming & Stenfert Kroese, 1993; Kiernan, 1993; Lowe & Felce, 1994a; Mansell *et al.*, 1994a; Russell, 1995). The purpose of this book, however, is to address technical or clinical issues relating to the assessment and treatment of challenging behaviours.

Clinical activities can not, of course, exist in a vacuum. Rather, they need to be seen as one (important) component of a comprehensive strategy for supporting people with challenging behaviours. Such a strategy can be seen as comprising four overlapping components (see also Department of Health, 1993; Mansell, McGill & Emerson, 1994c).

☐ The *prevention* of challenging behaviour through, for example, targeting resources at those considered at greatest risk and ensuring that people with severe learning disabilities live, learn and work in enriched environments in which they receive appropriate help and encouragement to develop adaptive and socially appropriate behaviours.

☐ *Early detection and intervention* to ensure that potential problems are identified and responded to as they arise. This applies equally to the emergence of challenging behaviour in young children and the identification of signs of potential breakdown in families, residential settings and day services.

☐ The provision of *practical, emotional and technical support* to people in the places in which they normally live, learn, work and enjoy their leisure to help them overcome their challenging behaviours. This will also require effective approaches for the management of crises.

☐ For a few people, the *development and support of new places for them to live, learn or work* which will maximise their quality of life while continuing to strive (possibly over many years) to understand and respond appropriately to their challenging behaviour. Such specialised community-based services are likely to require very high levels of practical, emotional and technical support over extended periods of time.

In the remainder of this book the focus, in the terms of the above framework, will be on the content of the types of *technical support* which should be available to people with severe learning disabilities. Before doing so, however, it will be necessary to provide a context within which to place such discussion.

In Chapter 2, *The social context of challenging behaviour*, some of the social processes, which are involved in defining behaviour as challenging will be highlighted, and some of the personal and social consequences which arise from having a severe learning disability and challenging behaviour will be examined. Throughout these discussions it will be argued that challenging behaviour must be seen as a social construction. The implications of this perspective will then be explored in relation to approaches to assessing the social validity of behavioural interventions. Chapter 3, *Epidemiology*, will look at some of the available evidence regarding the prevalence, incidence and natural history of challenging behaviours. This information will add to our understanding of the social significance of challenging behaviour and will also provide a backdrop against which the successes and failures of intervention may be judged. In addition, the research which has attempted to identify factors which place people at risk of developing challenging behaviour will be reviewed. Such information is important if approaches to the prevention of challenging behaviour are to be appropriately targeted.

In Chapter 4, *Models and theories*, the models and concepts which underlie behavioural approaches to analysis and intervention will be discussed. Attention will be drawn to some of the more recent developments in applied behaviour analysis which are likely to significantly strengthen the effectiveness of behavioural approaches. In addition, the more prominent neurobiological models of challenging behaviour will be briefly reviewed prior to discussion of the possibilities for the integration of behavioural and neurobiological approaches. The discussion of the concepts which underlie behavioural approaches will be continued in Chapter 5, *The bases of intervention*. Here consideration will be given to some of the broad perspectives and issues which should guide behavioural (and other) approaches to intervention.

In Chapter 6, *Approaches to assessment*, the aims of a behavioural assessment will be discussed in terms of identifying the social impact of the person's challenging behaviour and understanding its behavioural function. This will involve an evaluation of informant-based, descriptive and experimental approaches to assessment.

In Chapter 7, *Behavioural approaches*, the main behavioural approaches to reducing challenging behaviour will be examined. In doing so, particular attention will be paid to some of the more recent developments in the emerging technology of 'nonaversive' behavioural support (Horner *et al.*, 1990*a*). These include the modification of setting events to alter the motivational bases of challenging behaviour and the use of functional displacement and skill building to provide the person with more socially appropriate alternatives to challenging behaviour. In Chapter 8, *Psychophar-macology*, further consideration will be given to the integration of behavioural and neurobiological approaches by discussing and briefly reviewing the evidence in support of psychopharmacological approaches to reducing challenging behaviour.

In Chapter 9, *Longer-term management*, some of the issues involved in the longer-term management of persistent challenging behaviour will be highlighted. These include the use of protective devices and the management of staff motivation during intensive and prolonged interventions. Finally, Chapter 10, *Challenges ahead*, will summarise and draw together the conclusions arising from the previous chapters. In addition, consideration will be given to the implications of these conclusions for behavioural practice in the remainder of the 1990s and beyond.

As will be seen, most of the evidence cited in this book has been drawn from studies undertaken in the UK and North America. This obviously raises questions regarding the applicability of the issues raised to other societies and cultures. This issue will be addressed at appropriate points throughout the book.

2 THE SOCIAL CONTEXT OF CHALLENGING BEHAVIOUR

In the last chapter, a definition was proposed which defined challenging behaviour as culturally abnormal behaviour of such an intensity, frequency or duration that the physical safety of the person or others is likely to be placed in serious jeopardy, or behaviour which is likely to seriously limit use of, or result in the person being denied access to, ordinary community facilities.

This amendment to the definition made by Emerson *et al.* (1988) helps make explicit the importance of social and cultural expectations and contextual factors in defining behaviour as challenging. Indeed, the phenomenon of challenging behaviour can only be fully understood when viewed as a social construction, a position which is highly consistent with the 'contextualist' world view of behaviour analysis (Morris & Midgley, 1990).

The operation of social and cultural influences may take a number of forms. As suggested above, socially condoned behaviours which may result in serious physical harm to the person themselves (e.g. smoking) or to others (e.g. automobile driving) are unlikely to be construed as examples of challenging behaviour, even though they may meet the formal characteristics of contemporary definitions. Whether a behaviour is defined as challenging in a particular context will be dependent upon such factors as:

☐ the norms and expectations concerning appropriate social behaviour in that setting;

☐ the ability of the person to give a plausible account for their behaviour;

☐ the beliefs held by other participants in the setting about the nature of learning disabilities; and

☐ the capacity of the setting to manage any disruption caused by the person's behaviour.

Behaviour in social settings is, in part, governed by implicit and explicit rules and expectations regarding appropriate conduct and the contingencies which may be brought to bear on those who transgress these expectations. In general, the more formal the setting, the more explicit the rules. Indeed, context is essential in giving meaning to any behaviour. Particular behaviours can only be defined as challenging in particular contexts. For example, loud shouting and the use of 'offensive' language is likely to be tolerated (if not condoned) on the factory floor, in a steel mill or at a football match. The same behaviour would certainly be 'challenging' during a church service. Physical aggression is positively valued in the boxing ring. Severe self-directed aggression, however, is likely to be seen as challenging behaviour when shown by a person with learning disabilities, but may be viewed as a mark of religious piety when shown by a flagellant. At a more mundane level, stereotypy is less likely to be tolerated in public places than in an institution for people with learning disabilities.

Expectations concerning the appropriateness of particular behaviours are also determined by cultural beliefs and general role expectations. Enabling a young man to enjoy an alcoholic drink in the local pub may be seen as a positive achievement by young white staff in a residential service for people with learning disabilities, as unremarkable by other customers in the local pub, and as highly problematic by the young man's devout Muslim family. Similarly, physical aggression may be seen as being more deviant (in terms of involving a greater discrepancy between performance and cultural expectations) when shown by a woman with learning disabilities than when shown by a man.

As well as transgressing social conventions, people with disabilities are also likely to be cast in deviant or abnormal social roles. These may serve to modify the operation of contextual rules which ascribe social meaning to behaviour. Thus, for example, viewing people with learning disabilities as 'eternal children' (Wolfensberger, 1972, 1975) may be associated with a tendency to fail to attribute personal responsibility to challenging behaviour shown by people with learning disabilities (cf. Hastings, 1993). In a similar vein, if a person is labelled 'mentally retarded', observers tend to ascribe their success at a task to external factors (e.g. the ease or simplicity of the task), while ascribing failure to internal factors (e.g. their cognitive impairments) (Severence & Gastrom, 1977).

These processes may have a number of consequences including an increased tolerance for deviant behaviour *as long as the person is clearly identified as belonging to a defined deviant group.* Indeed, the expectations surrounding group membership may include a positive expectation that the person will behave in unusual or odd ways. So, for example, members of the public may show greater tolerance of minor aggression or stereotypic rocking when shown by a person whom they can clearly label as having a learning disability than they would of an 'ordinary' member of the public.

The capacity of a setting to cope with any disruption caused by a person's challenging behaviour is also likely to contribute to determining whether they will be excluded. So, for example, the increased pressure in the UK on mainstream schools to demonstrate academic achievement, while at the same time being deprived of external support for pupils with special needs, is likely to increase the pressure to exclude pupils with learning disabilities who show challenging behaviour. Similarly, fluctuations in the levels of experience, competence, stress, stability and fatigue among members of a staff team are likely to determine their capacity to cope with the disruption caused by someone who shows severe self-injury.

Of course, none of these factors is static. The social acceptability of particular behaviours changes over time within and across cultures (note, for example, the increase in social disapproval for smoking in the UK). Expectations and norms governing behaviour within settings vary over time and across locations. The meaning of having a learning disability is currently undergoing significant changes. As has been discussed above, the capacity of settings to manage the social disruption caused by challenging behaviour is likely to be influenced by factors ranging from public policy to local fluctuations in staff sickness.

While contextual factors are crucial to defining behaviour as challenging, it would be surprising if there were no commonalities between settings in their tendency to perceive particular behaviours as more or less challenging. Emerson *et al.* (1988) asked service agencies in the South East of England to identify the two or three individuals with a learning disability who presented the greatest challenge to services in each administrative area covering 200 000–300 000 people. Of the 31 people identified in this process (total population base 1.6 million), 25 (81%) showed aggressive behaviour, 16 (52%) showed destructive behaviour and 8 (26%) showed self-injurious behaviour. More recently, Lowe and Felce (1994*b*) summarised the results of two studies which suggested that the level of social disruption caused by a behaviour was integral to its definition as 'challenging' by carers and care staff. In the first study, analysis of carer and staff ratings over a four-year period for a cohort of 92 people with learning disabilities indicated that behaviours which caused the greatest social disruption (e.g. aggression) or had significant implications for the duty of care exercised by carers or care staff, were rated as creating the most severe management problems. In the second study, they reported that the probability of referral to specialised challenging behaviour services was significantly increased if the person showed high levels of behaviours which were likely to be socially disruptive (e.g. aggression, non-compliance).

Similarly, Kiernan and Kiernan (1994) employed discriminant function analysis to identify factors which distinguished more difficult from less difficult pupils with severe learning disabilities in a survey of segregated special schools in England and Wales. The first ten factors, in order of significance for mobile pupils ($n = 321$ more difficult; $n = 549$ less difficult), identified in this analysis were: physical aggression involving significant risk to others; persistent interruption of activities of other pupils; social disruption (e.g. screaming); violent temper tantrums occurring weekly; unpredictability of challenging behaviour; breakage of windows, fixtures and fittings; aggression toward other pupils; lack of understanding of the emotions of others; non-compliance.

Consideration of the range of social issues involved in defining behaviour as challenging is important for a number of reasons. First, it highlights the importance of explicitly acknowledging the operation of such factors in the definition of challenging behaviour, including operational definitions of challenging behaviour employed in epidemiological research. As has already been noted, many existing definitions (e.g. of self-injurious behaviour) are clearly incomplete, in that socially normative behaviours which do meet the formal properties of the definition are nevertheless excluded from consideration in the resulting literature. Unless we acknowledge the importance of social and cultural factors in defining challenging behaviour, we may be tempted to search for ever more refined mechanical and physical definitions of inherently social processes. Such a course of action would, of course, be doomed to failure. Recognising the important role played by social and contextual factors in defining behaviour as challenging does, however, cause considerable problems for epidemiological studies of challenging behaviour.

Secondly, viewing challenging behaviour as a social construction illustrates the complexity of the phenomenon and helps to begin to identify some possible approaches to intervention. Thus, for example, if a person's minor stereotypy has been defined as challenging primarily due to the avoidance behaviours it elicits in others, intervention may be most appropriately aimed at reducing such avoidance, rather than eliminating stereotypy.

Finally, there has been considerable concern expressed over recent years regarding the *social validity* of behavioural interventions. An intervention which is socially valid should (a) address a socially significant problem, (b) be undertaken in a manner which is acceptable to the main constituencies involved and (c) result in socially important outcomes or effects (Fuqua & Schwade, 1986; Kazdin & Matson, 1981; Schwartz & Baer, 1991; Wolf, 1978). Re-conceptualising challenging behaviour as a complex social phenomenon, rather than simply a problem of aberrant behaviour, has considerable implications for evaluating the social significance of the outcomes of intervention. Prior to discussing this point in more detail, it will be necessary to examine the social impact of challenging behaviours.

THE SOCIAL IMPACT OF CHALLENGING BEHAVIOURS

The social significance of challenging behaviours results from the interaction between their prevalence and their consequences or impact. By definition, seriously challenging behaviours may significantly impair the health and/or quality of life of the persons themselves, those who care for them and those who live or work in close proximity.

Thus, for example, self-injurious behaviours can result in damage to the person's health. Indeed, repeated self-injury may lead to such problems as secondary infections, permanent malformation of the sites of repeated injury through the development of calcified haematomas, loss of sight or hearing, additional neurological impairments and even death (cf. Borthwick-Duffy, 1994). Similarly, serious aggression may result in significant injury to others as well as to the person themselves as a result of the defensive or restraining action of others (e.g. Spreat *et al.*, 1986).

However, the consequences of challenging behaviours go far beyond their immediate physical impact. Indeed, the combined responses of the community, carers, care staff and service agencies to people who show challenging behaviours may prove significantly more detrimental than the immediate consequences of the actual behaviours. These social responses can include abuse, inappropriate treatment, exclusion, deprivation and systematic neglect.

Abuse

It is, perhaps, not surprising that the difficulties involved in caring for people with challenging behaviours and, in particular, the management of episodes of challenging behaviour, may, at times, lead to inappropriate reactions from carers and care staff. Some of these reactions include physical abuse. Thus, for example, Rusch, Hall and Griffin (1986), in an analysis of documented instances of abuse in a North American institution, identified challenging behaviour as the major predictor of who was likely to be abused. Similarly, Maurice and Trudel (1982) reported that 1 in 40 ward staff in Montreal institutions for people with learning disabilities indicated that their *typical* response to an episode of self-injury was to hit the resident.

Inappropriate treatment

The challenge posed by severe problem behaviours has, not unnaturally, led services to develop methods of control, not all of which can be considered beneficial to the persons themselves. North American studies suggest that between 26% and 40% of all residents of community-based facilities, and between 38% and 50% of all residents of institutional facilities, receive psychotropic medication for challenging behaviour, of which the major tranquillisers haloperidol, chlorpromazine and thioridazine are the most common (Buck & Sprague, 1989; Pary, 1993; Stone *et al.*, 1989). Between one-half and two-thirds of people with severe learning disabilities and challenging behaviour receive such medication (Altmeyer *et al.*, 1987; Davidson *et al.*, 1994; Meador & Osborn, 1992) and are likely to be maintained on it over some considerable time (Chadsey-Rusch & Sprague, 1989). In the UK, the results of a large-scale survey undertaken in 1987 by Kiernan and colleagues indicated that antipsychotic medication was prescribed for 52% of people with challenging behaviour (Kiernan & Qureshi, 1993; Qureshi, 1994; see also Oliver, Murphy & Corbett, 1987).

The widespread use of such powerful psychopharmacological agents raises a number of concerns as: (1) there is little evidence that neuroleptics have any specific effect in reducing challenging behaviours (see Chapter 8); (2) such medication has a number of well-documented serious side-effects including sedation, blurred vision, nausea, dizziness, weight gain, opacities of the cornea, grand mal seizures and a range of extrapyramidal syndromes including Parkinsonian syndrome, akathisia, acute dystonic reaction and tardive dyskinesia (Aman & Singh, 1988; Gadow & Poling, 1988; Thompson, Hackenberg & Schaal, 1991); (3) prescription practices for people with learning disabilities and a clearly diagnosed psychiatric illness have been judged to be inappropriate in between 40% to 55% of instances (Bates, Smeltzer & Arnoczky, 1986); and (4) drug use in institutions has been substantially reduced through peer review processes with no apparent negative effects (Briggs, 1989; Fielding *et al.*, 1980; Findholt & Emmett, 1990; LaMendola, Zaharia & Carver, 1980). As Singh and Repp (1989) point out, while the results of drug reduction programmes 'are heartening, they suggest that much of the medication was unnecessary when either originally prescribed or by the time the reduction programme was instituted' (Singh & Repp, 1989, p. 273–274).

Similarly, the use of mechanical restraints and protective devices to manage challenging behaviours, including up to 50% of cases of self-injury (Griffin, Ricketts & Williams, 1986*a*), gives cause for serious concern. Such procedures can lead to muscular atrophy, demineralisation of bones and shortening of tendons as well as resulting in other injuries during the process of the restraints being applied (Griffin *et al.*, 1986*a*; Luiselli, 1992*b*; Richmond, Schroeder & Bickel, 1986; Spreat *et al.*, 1986).

Finally, people with severe learning disabilities may be at risk of exposure to unnecessarily degrading or abusive psychological treatments (e.g. Altmeyer, Williams & Sams, 1985; G. Allan Roeher Institute, 1988). Freagon (1990), for example, reported that procedures for eliminating challenging behaviours employed at the Behavior Research Institute, Inc. included spanking, pinching, taste aversion, inhalation of ammonia, loosely tying students to another student they find aversive, ankle cuffs secured by an 11-inch chain and standing for up to 2 hours in an Automatic Vapour Spray Station. This latter procedure involved the student standing with ankles and wrists retrained, while wearing an American football helmet incorporating an opaque screen to occlude vision and white noise to mask external sounds with an attachment for squirting a mixture of compressed air and water to the back of the student's neck.

Exclusion, deprivation and systematic neglect

People with challenging behaviours are significantly more likely to be excluded from community-based services and to be admitted or re-admitted to institutional settings (Borthwick-Duffy, Eyman & White, 1987; Eyman & Call, 1977; Hill & Bruininks, 1984; Intagliata & Willer, 1982; Lakin *et al.*, 1983; Schalock, Harper & Genung, 1981). They are also less likely to be placed from institutional settings into the community (Hill & Bruininks, 1984). Once admitted to institutional care they are likely to spend most of their time in materially deprived surroundings (cf. Emerson & Hatton, 1994), disengaged from their world and avoided by staff (Emerson *et al.*, 1992; Mansell, 1994). They are also at risk of having their needs neglected. Most episodes of inappropriate client behaviours occurring in institutions are ignored by staff (Cullen *et al.*, 1983; Felce *et al.*, 1987) and the low levels of attention which are provided are likely to be disproportionately negative in character (Grant & Moores, 1977).

People with challenging behaviours are also likely to be excluded from services provided *within* institutional settings. Oliver *et al.*, (1987), for example, reported that nearly half of institutional residents with self-injury in the South East Thames region of England received no programmed day activity. Once institutionalised they are also unlikely to receive specific psychological help for their challenging behaviours (Griffin *et al.*, 1986*a*; Oliver *et al.*, 1987; Qureshi, 1994) but are, as noted above, likely to be medicated or restrained. Some of the *socially* undesirable effects of medication and restraint procedures include the general sedative effects of neuroleptic medication (Gadow & Poling, 1988), the impact of mechanical restraints in precluding the person's participation in many everyday activities and the effect of restraints in setting the occasion for reduced levels of interaction with carers (Luiselli, 1992*b*). The little evidence that is available also suggests that, at least for frequent or severe self-injury, the psychological interventions which are provided are more likely to be of a punitive nature (Altmeyer *et al.*, 1987).

Within the community, challenging behaviours may serve to limit the development of social relationships (Anderson *et al.*, 1992), reduce opportunities to participate in community-based activities (Bromley & Emerson, 1993; Hill & Bruininks, 1984) and prevent access to health and social services (Jacobsen, Silver & Schwartz, 1984). They are also, of course, a major cause of stress experienced by carers (Quine & Pahl, 1985; Qureshi, 1992) and care staff (Bersani & Heifetz, 1985), particularly those behaviours which are wearing over time (Bromley & Emerson, in press). Care staff also report that they and significant numbers of their colleagues experience strong emotional reactions such as anger, despair, sadness, fear and disgust in response to episodes of challenging behaviour (Bromley & Emerson, in press; Hastings, 1993). Given that services provided to young adults with challenging behaviours living at home with their parents are often insufficient, especially in the area of providing advice or assistance within the parental home to effectively manage episodes of challenging behaviour (Kiernan & Alborz, 1994; Qureshi, 1992), it is hardly surprising to find that the presence of challenging behaviours is one of the main predictors of whether parents will seek a residential placement for their son or daughter (e.g. Tausig, 1985).

THE SOCIAL VALIDITY OF INTERVENTION OUTCOMES

So far this chapter has highlighted some of the social processes involved in establishing behaviour as challenging and, in the section above, has drawn attention to aspects of the potential personal and social impact of challenging behaviours. In addition, the notion of social validity has been introduced. To recap, it has been proposed that an intervention which is socially valid should (a) address a socially significant problem, (b) be undertaken in a manner which is acceptable to the main constituencies involved and (c) result in socially important outcomes or effects.

The concept of social validity was introduced into behavioural practice in order to address two issues which were considered to underlie the apparent failure of services to implement behavioural procedures which had been 'demonstrated' to be effective (Wolf, 1978). These were:

☐ conflict between applied behaviour analysts and other stakeholders in the intervention process (e.g. the person with disabilities, their families, staff in service settings, the general public) regarding the appropriateness or acceptability of the intervention procedures themselves;

☐ discrepancies between stakeholders regarding the actual significance of any changes brought about through intervention.

Issues concerning the social acceptability of intervention *procedures* will be discussed in Chapter 5.

It is clear from the discussion so far in this chapter that challenging behaviour must be considered as a complex social phenomenon, both in terms of the processes which lead to particular behaviours being defined as challenging and in terms of its social consequences. This suggests that any attempt to evaluate the successes and failures of behavioural, or any other, approaches to intervention will need to take account of the range of outcomes of significance to all the major stakeholders in the intervention process (Emerson, Cambridge & Harris, 1991).

Unfortunately, behavioural research and practice has largely failed to live up to this task (Meyer & Evans, 1993*a*; Meyer & Janney, 1989; Schwartz & Baer, 1991). Instead, applied behavioural research has tended to focus solely upon demonstrating functional relationships between intervention processes and changes in the rate or duration of the targeted challenging behaviours. Thus, for example, analysis of the content of the five most recent issues of the *Journal of Applied Behavior Analysis**, the premier journal for applied behaviour analysts, indicates that, of the 22 separate papers addressing the issue of challenging behaviour in people with severe learning disabilities, only six (27%) reported data on outcomes other than changes in the rate or duration of the targeted challenging behaviour itself. Other outcomes which were reported were confined to changes in such aspects of the participant's behaviours as appropriate or desirable behaviour (Foster-Johnson, Ferro & Dunlap, 1994; Northup *et al.*, 1994), correct task performance (Kennedy, 1994), pro-social behaviours (Day, Horner & O'Neill, 1994) and positive affect or vocalisations (Fisher *et al.*, 1994; Kennedy, 1994).

Evans and Meyer (1985) have argued the case for expanding current practice to include the assessment of the 'meaningful outcomes' of intervention (see also, Emerson *et al.*, 1991; Horner, 1991; Meyer & Evans, 1989, 1993*a*; Meyer & Janney, 1989). These include the assessment of change in:

☐ the targeted challenging behaviour and other challenging behaviours shown by the person;

☐ replacement skills and behaviours, including, for example, the development of self-control strategies to support behaviour change and the development of alternative communicative responses;

☐ procedures for managing the person's challenging behaviour including use of medication, restraint and crisis management techniques;

☐ health-related consequences of the person's challenging behaviour such

* Volume 26, Issue 3 to Volume 27, Issue 3.

as trauma, skin irritations (e.g. Iwata *et al.*, 1990*b*);

☐ the restrictiveness of the person's residential and vocational placement (e.g. Pratt, Luszcz & Brown, 1980);

☐ broader aspects of the person's quality of life including physical and social integration, personal life satisfaction, affect and the range of choices available to the individual (e.g. Heal *et al.*, 1993; Schalock & Kieth, 1993);

☐ the perceived significance of the person's challenging behaviour by others (e.g. family, staff, public).

The importance of such a multifaceted approach to evaluating the impact of intervention is, in many ways, self-evident once the significance of social processes in the definition and response to challenging behaviour has been recognised. Thus, for example, a reduction in the rate of a person's self-injury by 75% is unlikely to be of social significance if they remain at risk of losing their sight, continue to be mechanically and psychopharmacologically restrained, and are still avoided by most people and excluded from community settings and activities.

In adopting broader criteria against which to judge the impact of intervention, however, it is important to ensure that a plausible association exists between the person's challenging behaviour and these wider dimensions of outcome. Thus, for example, it would be inappropriate to assess the effectiveness of an intervention to reduce challenging behaviour in terms of changes in the person's participation in community-based activities unless evidence existed to suggest that their behaviour did, in fact, act as a significant barrier to such participation. While such a relationship may be assumed to operate in general, other factors (e.g. physical isolation of the setting; service policies, resources and orientation) may be much more important in specific situations.

This points to the importance of tailoring the measurement of 'meaningful outcomes' to particular social contexts and, by implication, to conducting an evaluation of the social significance of a person's challenging behaviour prior to intervention. These two issues will be discussed further in Chapter 6.

3   EPIDEMIOLOGY

In this chapter, a number of issues will be addressed which relate to the epidemiology of challenging behaviour. These include:

☐ the number of people with learning disabilities who show challenging behaviour;

☐ the prevalence of particular forms or topographies of challenging behaviour;

☐ the co-occurrence of different forms of challenging behaviour;

☐ the personal and environmental correlates or 'risk factors' associated with challenging behaviour;

☐ the emergence and persistence of challenging behaviour.

In addressing these issues, the research evidence which is relevant to either furthering our understanding of challenging behaviour or to the planning and organising of interventions will be highlighted.

Epidemiological studies of challenging behaviours have focused, almost exclusively, on attempting to identify the *prevalence* of particular behaviours and to investigate the relationship between prevalence and other personal or environmental variables (cf. Emerson, 1992; Johnson & Day, 1992). That is, they have attempted to identify the number of individuals in the population under study (e.g. total population of Manchester) who, at a given point in time, show challenging behaviour and, through the use of correlational methods, to identify those personal and environmental characteristics associated with people being at increased risk of exhibiting these behaviours.

Prevalence rates vary as a function of the incidence and duration (or persistence) of a particular disorder (Kiely & Lubin, 1991). Incidence is a measure of the number of new 'cases' appearing within a given population within a specified period of time (e.g. number of live births per year of children with Down's syndrome in Manchester, number of people *developing* self-injurious behaviour per year in Cardiff). Duration or persistence is a measure of the length of time a condition is present (e.g. life expectancy of people with Down's syndrome, mean number of years a person will show self-injurious behaviour). As Kiely and Lubin point out, in the hypothetical case in which neither incidence nor duration vary, prevalence (P) may be calculated as the product of incidence (I) and duration (D) (i.e. $P = I \times D$).

Unfortunately, there would appear to be few, if any, studies which directly address the issue of the incidence of challenging behaviours among people with learning disabilities (see, for example, the review of the incidence and prevalence of self-injurious behaviour provided by Johnson & Day, 1992) and only an extremely limited number of studies which address the issue of the duration or persistence of challenging behaviour (see below).

THE PREVALENCE OF CHALLENGING BEHAVIOURS

In the last chapter, stress was placed on the importance of social processes in leading to particular behaviours being seen as challenging. One implication of this approach is that attempts to measure the prevalence of challenging behaviour must themselves be seen as bound by the constraints and expectations of particular social contexts and cultures. Estimates of the prevalence of challenging behaviour will also, of course, be influenced by such methodological factors as the selection of operational definitions, methods of case identification (e.g. review of case notes vs interview with care staff) and the overall sampling strategy adopted within the study (e.g. total administratively defined population of people with learning disabilities vs children with learning disabilities at school).

Relatively few studies have attempted to identify the prevalence of multiple forms of challenging behaviour among all people with learning disabilities in a defined area. More commonly, studies have focused on either specific topographically defined subtypes of challenging behaviour, such as self-injurious behaviour (e.g. Oliver, Murphy & Corbett, 1987) or aggression (e.g. Harris, 1993) in total populations, or have restricted sampling to specific sub-populations of people with learning disabilities, for example, those living in institutional settings (e.g. Griffin et al., 1987; Maurice & Trudel, 1982), community settings (e.g. Rojahn, 1986) or children attending schools (e.g. Kiernan & Kiernan, 1994).

The results of two relatively large-scale studies, both of which were undertaken in 1987, will be used in order to illustrate some of the issues involved in the epidemiological study of challenging behaviour. One of these studies was undertaken in the North West of England (Kiernan & Qureshi, 1993; Qureshi, 1994; Qureshi & Alborz, 1992) and the other in California (Borthwick-Duffy, 1994). Both studies sought to identify the prevalence of various forms of challenging behaviour among the total population of people with learning disabilities in a defined geographical area. In both studies 'people with learning disabilities' were operationally defined as those people receiving services from provider agencies.

Qureshi, Kiernan and colleagues conducted their survey in seven administrative areas (District Health Authorities) in the North West of England with a total *general* population of 1.54 million. They screened approximately 4200 people with learning disability, and identified people as showing serious challenging behaviours if they had either:

☐ at some time caused more than minor injury to themselves or others, or destroyed their immediate living or working environment; or

☐ showed behaviours at least once a week that required the intervention of more than one member of staff to control, or placed them in danger, or caused damage which could not be rectified by care staff, or caused more than one hour's disruption;

☐ or showed behaviours at least daily that caused more than a few minutes' disruption.

Using this definition, 1.91 people per 10 000 of the general population (range 1.41 to 2.55 per 10 000 across the seven areas) were identified as having a learning disability and serious challenging behaviour. This translates to an estimated prevalence rate of 5.7% of all people within these areas who had been administratively defined as having a learning disability. More recently, Emerson and Bromley (in press), using closely parallel methods in another area of North West England, identified 3.33 people per 10 000 of the general population as having a learning disability and serious challenging behaviour (equivalent to approximately 7.8% of the people with learning disabilities who were screened). Combining these studies gives an overall prevalence of 2.08 per 10 000 of the general population or 6.1% of people administratively defined as having a learning disability.

Borthwick-Duffy (1994) examined the prevalence of challenging behaviours among 91 164 people with learning disabilities served by the California Department of Developmental Services. People were identified as showing one or more of four possible types of challenging behaviour on the basis of data derived from their annual Client Development Evaluation Report. These were:

☐ *aggressive behaviour*, defined as one or more violent episodes causing serious physical injury (requiring immediate medical attention) to others within the last year;

☐ *frequent and severe self-injurious behaviour*, defined as behaviour causing severe self-injury and requiring a physician's immediate attention at least once a month and/or behaviour causing minor self-injury and requiring first aid at least once per week;

21

□ *frequent self-injurious behaviour*, defined as self-injurious behaviour occurring at least once per week;

□ *property destruction*, defined as serious property destruction within the past year and/or minor property damage on six or more occasions within the past year (Borthwick-Duffy, 1994, p.9).

On the basis of this exercise, 18 826 people were identified as showing challenging behaviour. This is equivalent to 14% of the population of people with learning disabilities who were screened or 6.33 per 10 000 of the general population.

The discrepancy in overall prevalence rates between these studies may be due to a number of factors including differences in the operational definitions employed to identify people as showing challenging behaviour and differences in the populations studied. In particular, the inclusion of the category 'frequent self-injurious behaviour' in the Californian study is likely to have led to people being identified in that study who would not have been identified in the UK study. While behaviours in this category were markedly more prevalent than behaviours in other categories (Table 3.1), the data does not allow for the identification of those people who only showed frequent self-injury (see discussion below on the co-occurrence of different forms of challenging behaviour).

TYPES OF CHALLENGING BEHAVIOURS

Table 3.1 summarises the data from these studies to provide general prevalence estimates for physical aggression, self-injury, property destruction and, for the English studies only, other forms of challenging behaviour.

Of course, each of these broad groups of challenging behaviours is likely to contain a range of specific behavioural topographies. Studies which have focused on the prevalence of particular forms of challenging behaviour provide a more detailed breakdown of topographical variants of general classes of challenging behaviours. Harris (1993), for example, reports that the most prevalent forms of aggression shown in the past month by 168 people with learning disabilities identified in one administratively defined area were: punching, slapping, pushing or pulling (51% of people showing aggression); kicking (24%); pinching (21%); scratching (20%); pulling hair (13%); biting (13%); headbutting (7%); using weapons (7%); choking, throttling (4%).

Similarly, Oliver *et al.* (1987) reported that the most common topographies of self-injurious behaviour shown by 596 people with learning disabilities identified through a total population survey carried out in the South East

Table 3.1. *Prevalence of different forms of challenging behaviours*

	Kiernan, Qureshi & Alborz; Emerson & Bromley (base $n = 5200$)	Borthwick-Duffy (base $n = 91\ 164$)
	Behaviour rated as	
	present and serious management problem (%)	*present* (%)
Physical aggression	1.9	2.1
Self-injury (frequent and severe)	1.3	2.2
Self-injury (frequent)	–	9.3
Property destruction	1.4	7.1
Other	3.3	–

Thames Regional Health Authority were: skin picking (39%); self-biting (38%); head punching/slapping (36%); head-to-object banging (28%); body to object banging (10%); other (10%); hair removal (8%); body punching or slapping (7%); eye poking (6%); skin pinching (4%); cutting with tools (2%); anal poking (2%); other poking (2%); banging with tools (2%); lip chewing (1%); nail removal (1%); teeth banging (1%).

It should be noted that, in both studies, the totals add up to more than 100% owing to the co-occurrence of different forms of challenging behaviour in the same individual, an issue which will be discussed in more detail below. Rojahn (1994) examined inter-relationships between different types of self-injurious behaviour. He identified five general forms of self-injury on the basis of a factor analytic study of results obtained from the *Behavior Problems Inventory* for 431 people with self-injurious behaviour (Rojahn, 1986). These were: hitting (e.g. head punching, body hitting); inserting (e.g. fingers or objects in body cavities, pica); biting, scratching, pinching and hair pulling; teeth grinding; vomiting and rumination.

An illustration of the range of behaviours which may be defined as challenging in a particular type of setting is provided by Kiernan and Kiernan (1994). In a postal survey of a sample of day-schools for children with severe learning disabilities in England and Wales, they identified 22.2% of the school population as presenting some degree of challenge, including 8.2% of the school population who were identified as presenting a significant challenge. The forms of challenging behaviour shown by the 'more' and 'less' challenging groups are presented in Table 3.2.

Table 3.2. *Challenging behaviours shown by 'more' and 'less' challenging pupils of segregated day schools for children with severe learning disabilities in England and Wales*

	'More' challenging $n = 367$ (%)	'Less' challenging $n = 662$ (%)
Aggression	42	17
Social disruption	36	12
Temper tantrums	34	10
Self-injurious behaviour	33	15
Physical disruption	31	8
Destructive behaviours	27	7
Non-compliance	27	10
Rituals	24	14
Stereotypy	19	15
Wandering	18	6
Masturbation in public	13	8
Average number of behaviours shown per child	4.1	1.7

THE CO-OCCURRENCE OF CHALLENGING BEHAVIOURS

As has been indicated, people may show more than one form or type of challenging behaviour. Thus, in the Kiernan, Qureshi and Alborz survey, 43% of the people identified as showing challenging behaviours which were rated as presenting a serious management problem did so in two or more of the four possible areas of aggression, self-injury, property destruction and 'other' behaviour (Qureshi, 1994).

Similarly, analysis of the Californian data indicated that, once the two categories of self-injurious behaviour were collapsed, 10.8% of the population sampled showed just one form of challenging behaviour, 3% two forms and 0.6% all three forms (Borthwick-Duffy, 1994). Thus, of those identified as showing challenging behaviour, 25% did so in more than one of the three possible areas (aggression, self-injury, property destruction). Murphy *et al.* (1993) report that, of the people with self-injurious behaviour identified in the South East Thames Regional Health Authority study who wore protective devices, 40% showed physical aggression and 36% property destruction.

In addition to the co-occurrence of challenging behaviour across broadly defined categories, people are also likely to show multiple forms of challenging behaviour within categories. Thus, for example, Oliver *et al.* (1987) report that

54% of the people identified as showing self-injurious behaviour engaged in more than one form of self-injury. Indeed, 3% (20 of the 596) engaged in five or more different forms of self-injury. This rose to 7% for people whose self-injury was sufficiently severe to justify the use of protective devices (Murphy *et al.*, 1993).

Emerson and Bromley (in press) used the *Behavior Problems Inventory* to provide a more detailed breakdown of the co-occurrence of challenging behaviours among all people with learning disabilities in a defined administrative area who met the definition of challenging behaviour used in the Kiernan, Qureshi and Alborz study ($n = 70$). They reported that 36% of service users had shown two or more forms of aggression, and 47% of users had shown two or more forms of self-injury in the past month. Overall, only 7% (5/70) of users had shown just one form of challenging behaviour in the past month.

PERSONAL AND ENVIRONMENTAL RISK FACTORS

One of the most important potential contributions of epidemiological research is to identify those personal and environmental factors which are associated with variation in the prevalence of a particular disorder. The identification of such 'risk factors' is obviously important if preventative interventions are to be appropriately targeted and may, in addition, point to possible social and/or biological causal mechanisms. Provided below, is a brief summary of the evidence regarding some of the better established correlates of challenging behaviour among people with learning disabilities.

Gender

In general, boys and men are more likely to be identified as showing challenging behaviour than girls and women. This relationship appears to be more pronounced:

☐ for aggression and property destruction than for self-injury (Borthwick-Duffy, 1994; Johnson & Day, 1992; Oliver *et al.*, 1987; Rojahn, 1994);

☐ in institutional settings (Qureshi, 1994);

☐ for more severe challenging behaviour (Kiernan and Kiernan, 1994).

Thus, for example, 73% of the people identified as showing both property destruction and aggression in the Californian survey were men, compared to 53% of people who showed frequent self-injury and 49% of those who showed no challenging behaviour. There is, however, some evidence to suggest that women may be more likely to show multiple topographies of self-injurious behaviour (Maurice & Trudel, 1982; Maisto, Baumeister & Maisto, 1978).

Age

The overall prevalence of challenging behaviours increases with age during childhood, reaches a peak during the age range 15–34 and then declines (e.g. Borthwick-Duffy, 1994; Kiernan & Kiernan, 1994; Oliver et al., 1987; Rojahn, 1994). When comparisons are made with the age structure of the total population of people with learning disabilities, it is apparent that challenging behaviours appear to be particularly over-represented in the 15–24 age group (Kiernan & Qureshi, 1993). This progression is more complicated, however, when the prevalence of particular forms of challenging behaviour is examined. Oliver et al., (1987), for example, report that while multiple topographies, head-to-object banging, head punching and finger chewing are significantly more prevalent in younger people with self-injurious behaviour, skin picking and cutting with tools are more prevalent among older people.

Specific syndromes and disorders

An increase in the prevalence of some particular forms of challenging behaviour has been reported to occur in association with specific syndromes associated with learning disabilities. These include:

☐ occurrence of self-injurious behaviour, specifically hand and lip biting, among *all* people who have Lesch–Nyhan syndrome (Harris, 1992; Nyhan, 1994);

☐ very high prevalence of self-injurious hand-wringing in Rett syndrome (Harris, 1992);

☐ greater than expected prevalence of various forms of self-injurious behaviour in the Cornelia de Lange, Riley–Day and Fragile-X syndromes (Harris, 1992);

☐ greater than expected prevalence of hyperkinesis, attention deficits and stereotypy in Fragile-X syndrome (Borghgraef et al., 1990; Lachiewicz et al., 1994);

☐ very high prevalence of food-related challenging behaviours in Prader–Willi syndrome (Murphy, 1994).

In addition, an increased prevalence of challenging behaviour has been reported among people with epilepsy, both in general (cf. Kiernan & Kiernan, 1994) and in relation to specific forms of epilepsy (e.g. Gedye, 1989a, b).

26

Level of intellectual impairment

In general, the prevalence of aggression, property destruction, self-injurious behaviour and other forms of challenging behaviours are positively correlated with degree of intellectual impairment (e.g. Borthwick-Duffy, 1994; Johnson & Day, 1992; Kiernan & Kiernan, 1994; Kiernan & Qureshi, 1993; Oliver *et al.*, 1987; Oliver, 1993; Qureshi, 1994; Rojahn, 1994). Thus, for example, in the Californian survey, 7.6% of people with mild mental retardation, 13.6% of people with moderate mental retardation, 22.0% of people with severe mental retardation and 32.9% of people with profound mental retardation showed one or more forms of challenging behaviour (Borthwick-Duffy, 1994). People with more severe intellectual impairment are also likely to show multiple forms of challenging behaviour (Borthwick-Duffy, 1994; Oliver *et al.*, 1987; Rojahn, 1986, 1994) and, if self-injurious, are more likely to be restrained (Oliver *et al.*, 1987).

Additional disabilities

In addition to the overriding effects of level of intellectual impairment, challenging behaviours are more likely to be seen in people who:

☐ have additional impairments of vision or hearing (e.g. Kiernan & Kiernan, 1994; Maisto, Baumeister & Maisto, 1978; Schroeder *et al.*, 1978);

☐ are non-verbal or who have particular difficulty with receptive or expressive communication (e.g. Borthwick-Duffy, 1994; Kiernan & Kiernan, 1994; Schroeder *et al.*, 1978);

☐ are reported to have periods of disturbed sleep (Kiernan & Kiernan, 1994);

☐ have mental health problems (e.g. Borthwick-Duffy, 1994).

Self-injury, in particular, is markedly more prevalent among people with severe learning disabilities who have significant impairments of mobility (Kiernan & Kiernan, 1994; Kiernan & Qureshi, 1993).

Setting

The prevalence of challenging behaviour is also positively related to the level of restrictiveness in the person's residential placement (Borthwick-Duffy, 1994; Bruininks *et al.*, 1994; Emerson, 1992; Johnson & Day, 1992; Harris, 1993). Again, data from the Californian survey indicate that 3.0% of people living independently, 8.0% of people living with their families, 8.8% of people living in smaller (1–6 place) community facilities, 24.4% of people living in larger community-based facilities and 48.8% of people living in institutions were identified as showing one or more forms of challenging behaviour (Borthwick-Duffy, 1994). However, the prevalence of challenging behaviour in institutional settings varies considerably across individual States in North America ranging from a low of 23.5% in Montana to a high of 90.0% in Alaska (Bruininks *et al.*, 1994). There is also evidence to suggest that the prevalence of challenging behaviour in institutional settings may be increasing as institutions come to serve an increasingly disabled population (cf. Emerson, 1992).

The interpretation of the relationship between setting and challenging behaviour is problematic owing to the important role played by challenging behaviour in increasing the risk of admission and re-admission to more restrictive settings (Borthwick-Duffy *et al.*, 1987; Eyman & Call, 1977; Hill & Bruininks, 1984; Intagliata & Willer, 1982; Lakin *et al.*, 1983; Schalock *et al.*, 1981). Indeed, since studies of the effects of deinstitutionalisation have failed to identify any consistent effects of a move to less restrictive settings on challenging behaviour reported by key informants (Emerson & Hatton, 1994; Larson & Lakin, 1989), it would appear that such behaviours lead to institutionalisation, rather than institutional environments leading to challenging behaviour.

Summary

A number of interlinked personal and environmental characteristics have been associated with variations in the prevalence of challenging behaviour. Unfortunately, due to methodological limitations and the use of relatively simplistic approaches to analysis, it is not possible to identify the unique contribution made by individual factors. For example, such factors as increased mortality among people with challenging behaviour (cf. Borthwick-Duffy, 1994) and among people with more severe learning disabilities may account, in part, for the noted decline in the prevalence of challenging behaviour during adulthood. Hopefully, future research will help untangle this and other issues. Nevertheless, the existing data do provide a basis for identifying those populations most at risk and are suggestive of some possible underlying mechanisms, an issue to which we shall turn in the next chapter.

THE NATURAL HISTORY OF CHALLENGING BEHAVIOURS

As noted above, little is known about the natural history of challenging behaviours. The information which is available, however, suggests that seriously challenging behaviours are likely to have their onset in childhood and may be highly persistent over time. Murphy *et al.* (1993), for example, report that the mean age of onset for people whose severe self-injurious behaviour was managed by protective devices was 7 years of age, and that their self-injury had a mean duration of 14 years. During the period of a two-year follow-up of this group, only two of the 54 individuals were reported to have stopped self-injuring; staff reports on one of these two people being invalidated by the observation of self-injury during the follow-up study itself (Murphy *et al.*, 1993). Similarly, Emerson *et al.* (1988) reported that, of the 29 individuals (mean age 28.1) identified by service agencies as being the 'most challenging', 27 were placed outside their natural families. On average, this group had been first admitted to institutional care at 9.6 years of age, often for the same challenging behaviours they were displaying nearly two decades later (see also Special Development Team, 1988).

Very few studies have examined the course of challenging behaviour over time. Windahl (1988) followed up residents of a Swedish special hospital who had been identified as showing severe self-injury. He reported that 87% of people who remained in the special hospital, and 97% of people who had been discharged (primarily to other institutions), were still showing self-injurious behaviours 10 years later. Leudar, Fraser and Jeeves (1984) in a two-year follow up of 118 adults with learning disabilities reported extremely high degrees of persistency of aggression (see also Eyman, Borthwick-Duffy & Miller, 1981). On a more modest scale, Stenfert-Kroese and Fleming (1993) reported that only 1 of a group of 17 children with challenging behaviour showed no challenging behaviour over each of the following three years.

Evidence from the long-term follow-up of intervention studies provides a similarly bleak picture. Schroeder, Bickel and Richmond (1986) report that *all* of the 52 individuals who had received treatment in a specialised facility for people with severe self-injurious behaviour (Schroeder *et al.*, 1982) still required 'high level behaviour management programmes' eight years later. Similarly, Griffin *et al.* (1986b) reported that 60% of institutional residents with severe self-injury who were subject to aversive behavioural programmes still had problems up to 7 years later. Murphy and Wilson (1980) reported 75% relapse rates within 2 years for individuals whose severe self-injury had been initially treated by contingent electric shock.

While caution must be taken in extrapolating from such a restricted database (see, for example, Foxx, 1990; Jensen & Heidorn, 1993; Williams, Kirkpatrick-Sanchez & Crocker, 1994) the available evidence does suggest that severe self-injurious behaviours can be highly persistent *despite* discharge from specialised congregate care settings or significant changes in staffing resources and the quality of the physical environment. The possible chronicity of severe self-injurious behaviours points to the need for services to develop the capacity to effectively manage the physical, personal and social consequences of severe self-injurious behaviours over considerable periods of time, an issue which will be discussed in more detail in Chapter 9.

4　MODELS AND THEORIES

The previous chapters have concentrated on delineating the social significance of challenging behaviour on the basis of its prevalence and its social and personal impact. Attention has also been drawn to some of the personal and environmental factors which are associated with a person having an increased risk of showing challenging behaviour. In this chapter, behavioural and neurobiological approaches to understanding challenging behaviour will be discussed.

Behavioural and neurobiological approaches have, for some time, been the dominant approaches within the scientific and applied communities. As such, they have generated voluminous amounts of basic and applied research and have lead directly to the development of approaches to intervention which have been repeatedly empirically validated. That is not to say that other approaches – other 'ways of knowing' – have no contribution to make to furthering our understanding of challenging behaviour (see, for example, Meyer & Evans, 1993*b*; and commentaries by Baer, 1993; Evans & Meyer, 1993; Ferguson & Ferguson, 1993; Kaiser, 1993; Morris, 1993). Rather, it would appear that research within alternative paradigms have either been largely unproductive (e.g. psychoanalytic interpretations of challenging behaviour: see Carr, 1977, Romanczyk *et al.*, 1992) or are still in their relative infancy.

In the final section of the chapter, attempts to develop more comprehensive bio-behavioural models of challenging behaviour will be reviewed (e.g. Guess & Carr, 1991; Murphy, 1994; Oliver, 1993).

BEHAVIOURAL MODELS

Since the late 1940s psychologists have sought to apply principles derived from learning theory to the solution of important social problems, including performance deficits and challenging behaviours shown by people with learning disabilities. These attempts have been accompanied by, and have themselves made a significant contribution to, a revolution in our approach to severe learning disabilities. Early demonstrations of the power of simple behavioural techniques helped to debunk the prevailing ideas that people with serious disabilities had little potential for change (e.g. Azrin & Foxx, 1971; Bailey & Meyerson, 1969; Lovaas *et al.*, 1965; Tate & Baroff, 1966; Ullman & Krasner 1965).

Tate and Baroff (1966), for example, describe the use of brief (three second) time-out from social contact to reduce the severe self-injurious behaviour of a nine year-old boy with learning disabilities. His self-injury, which consisted of 'banging his head forcefully against floors, walls, and other hard objects, slapping his face with his hands, punching his face with his fists, hitting his shoulder with his chin, and kicking himself', had resulted in partial detachment of his right retina and the development of a 7 cm firm haematoma on his forehead. His self-injury had been treated, for the previous four years, by individual and group psychotherapy and drugs but without success. Intervention (in the first phase of the study) consisted of the withdrawal of all social contact for three seconds following each self-injurious act. This resulted in his self-injurious behaviour rapidly reducing from an average of one hit every 9 seconds to one hit every 10 minutes.

The explicit focus of behavioural approaches on the *environmental control of behaviour* stood in stark contrast to the existing pre-occupation with internal pathology. The growing influence of the behavioural model drew attention to the impact of the environment on the behaviour of people with severe disabilities, including the types of environments provided within institutional services (e.g. Bijou, 1966).

Initial successes in the use of behavioural approaches led to their increasing use. In 1968 the emerging discipline of applied behaviour analysis was marked by the launch of the *Journal of Applied Behaviour Analysis*. In its first issue Baer, Wolf and Risley (1968) described the basic nature of applied behaviour analysis as it ought to be practised. They suggested, and reiterated 20 years later (Baer, Wolf & Risley, 1987), that applied behaviour analytic studies should be:

☐ *applied* – in that the behaviours and events studied should be of importance to society;

☐ *behavioural* – in that studies should be concerned with what people actually do;

☐ *analytic* – in that studies should provide a 'believable demonstration', usually through demonstrating experimental control, that changes in behaviour are linked to the environmental events postulated;

☐ *technological* – in that the techniques used to change behaviour are identified and described in a manner that allows their replication;

☐ *conceptually systematic* – in that the procedures used are shown to be related to basic behavioural principles;

☐ *effective* – in that socially significant changes in behaviour are achieved; and,

☐ *general* – in that the behavioural change achieved 'proves durable over time ... appears in a wide variety of possible environments or ... spreads to a wide variety of related behaviours'.

Since then, the practice of applied behaviour analysis has steadily advanced both in its traditional areas of application and in many new fields (see, for example, *Journal of Applied Behavior Analysis*, issues **20**(4), **24**(1), **24**(4), **25**(3), **26**(4) and **27**(1)).

The application of applied behaviour analysis in the field of severe learning disabilities has focused on enhancing people's competence to become participating members of society as well as the remediation of challenging behaviours (see Bailey *et al.*, 1987; Matson, 1990; Remington, 1991 *a*). Many studies have demonstrated the success of behavioural approaches in teaching skilled behaviour and in motivating people's participation (e.g. Bellamy, Horner & Inman, 1979; Gold, 1980). Increasingly, these techniques are being developed to support the generalised use of community living skills in integrated settings (Danforth & Drabman, 1990; Felce, 1991; Horner, Dunlap & Koegel, 1988; Rusch & Hughes, 1989). More importantly within the context of the present book, applied behavioural approaches have revolutionised thinking about the causes and management of seriously challenging behaviours (Carr, 1977).

The dominant approach within applied behaviour analysis has been to view challenging behaviour as an example of *operant behaviour*. That is, to see it as behaviour which is shaped and maintained by its environmental consequences. In this approach, challenging behaviour is seen as functional and (in a general sense) adaptive. It is behaviour which has been 'selected' or shaped through the person's interaction with their physical and, perhaps more importantly, social world. In lay terms it can be thought of as behaviour through which the person exercises control over key aspects of their environment. In the sections below, this approach will be explored in some detail. In addition, two other behavioural approaches to understanding challenging behaviour will be briefly discussed. In these alternative approaches, challenging behaviour is seen as an example of *respondent behaviour* (learned reflexive behaviour which is elicited by environmental stimuli) or *schedule-induced behaviour* (behaviour which occurs as a 'side-effect' of other behaviour–environment relationships).

Operant behaviour

This section of the book will be concerned with some of the key issues involved in applying the operant model to challenging behaviour. It will first be necessary, however, to define some terms and introduce some technical concepts.

As indicated above, operant behaviour is behaviour which is maintained or shaped by its environmental consequences. Consequences which shape or maintain behaviour are termed reinforcers. Two types of contingent relationship between behaviour and reinforcers are important in *establishing and maintaining* operant behaviour.

☐ *Positive reinforcement* refers to an increase in the rate of a behaviour as a result of the contingent *presentation* of a reinforcing stimulus (positive reinforcer).

☐ *Negative reinforcement* refers to an increase in the rate of a behaviour as a result of the contingent *withdrawal* (or prevention of occurrence) of a reinforcing stimulus (negative reinforcer).

Common examples of positive reinforcement include pressing a light switch to activate the lights in a room (positive reinforcer: light), smiling and saying hello to a colleague to initiate further conversation (positive reinforcer: conversation) and requesting a drink when thirsty (positive reinforcer: drink). Similarly, common examples of negative reinforcement include completion of a piece of work to *escape* from the demands of your manager (withdrawal of negative reinforcer: demands) and the *avoidance* of potential crashes and fines by stopping at red lights when driving (negative reinforcer: fines and/or crashes).

Similarly, two types of contingent relationship between behaviour and reinforcers are important in *reducing or eliminating* operant behaviour.

☐ *Positive punishment* refers to a decrease in the rate of a behaviour as a result of the contingent *presentation* of a (negatively) reinforcing stimulus (positive punisher).

☐ *Negative punishment* refers to a decrease in the rate of a behaviour as a result of the contingent *withdrawal* of a (positively) reinforcing stimulus (negative punisher).

Common examples of positive punishment include the use by parents of reprimands or (for some) smacking to reduce the unruly behaviour of their children. Examples of negative punishment include the use of fines to prevent inappropriate parking (negative punisher: loss of money) and the withdrawal of attention to reduce the overbearing or rude behaviour of colleagues.

Figure 4.1 provides a schematic representation of these four types of relationship.

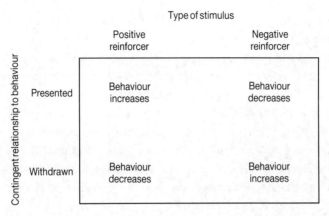

Fig. 4.1. Contingencies of reinforcement and punishment of operant behaviour.

This approach to understanding behaviour has three important charac-teristics:

☐ it is primarily concerned with the discovery of *functional relationships* between behaviours and between behaviour and environmental variables;

☐ it places a strong emphasis on the importance of the *context* in which behaviour occurs;

☐ it views the behaviours shown by a person as the product of a *dynamic system* of elements which may interact in complex and unforeseen ways.

The importance of function

The behavioural approach is based on the analysis of functional relationships between events. This is illustrated in the definitions of reinforcing and punishing stimuli, response classes, and in the nature of credible evidence within behaviour analysis.

In behavioural theory, reinforcing and punishing stimuli are defined functionally. That is, they are defined solely in terms of the impact which their withdrawal or presentation has upon subsequent behaviour. Positive reinforcers, for example, are those stimuli which increase the rate of a behaviour when presented contingently. They cannot be defined or identified independently of their function. That is, no *a priori* assumptions are made regarding whether particular types or classes of stimuli are reinforcing or punishing. Instead, the capacity of a particular stimulus or event to act as a reinforcer or punisher in a particular context must be demonstrated.

This reliance on functional definitions leads to behavioural theory appearing highly circular or tautological. Behaviour changes owing to the contingent presentation or withdrawal of reinforcers. Reinforcers are those events which, when presented or withdrawn contingent upon behaviour, bring about change. As Remington (1991b) points out, the lack of 'independent criteria on which to decide in advance whether a given event will act as a reinforcer or punisher has long been a theoretical embarrassment' (p. 11)*.

The concern within the behavioural approach regarding the analysis of functional relationships also extends to the way in which behaviour is classified. So far, we have used the term operant behaviour. It would be more accurate, however (from the perspective of behavioural theory) to talk about behaviours which are members of an operant *response class*. That is, in a behavioural analysis, attention is normally directed to determining the effect (or function) that a person's behaviour may have upon their environment, rather than the particular form (or topography) of behaviour. For example, a behaviour analyst would be interested in understanding the conditions under which you pressed a light switch rather than on how you pressed it (e.g. with your fingers, elbow or arm). Behaviours which result in the same environmental effects are classified as members of the same response class. In most experimental research the focus of attention lies in the environmental selection or control of response classes (e.g. lever pressing). Historically, little attention has been paid to examining the inter-relationships between the actual behaviours which may be members of a particular response class (Mace, 1994a). As we shall see, this attention to function rather than form is both a blessing and a curse in applied studies.

Finally, the concern of behaviour analysts with the study of functional relationships and their reliance on functional definitions has implications with regard to what is seen as credible evidence in behavioural studies. As we have seen, one implication of defining reinforcement contingencies functionally is

---

* One relatively recent way round this problem has been to conceptualise reinforcement contingencies as constraints imposed on the preferred distribution of behaviour in a particular context. Imagine you were locked in a room with this book and nothing else to do but to pace up and down. If you were free to do as you wished (technically, under conditions of a free operant baseline), you might choose to distribute your time between reading for 80% of your time and pacing for the remaining 20% (for the sake of simplicity we will ignore all the other creative activities you could invent in such a situation). It would be possible to introduce constraining relationships which would lead to either reading or pacing to act as reinforcers for each other. For example, pacing could be used to reinforce reading if you had to read for 90 minutes before being allowed to pace for 10 minutes. Alternatively, reading could be used to reinforce pacing if you had to pace for 30 minutes before being allowed to read for 70 minutes. The key here is that the constraining relationship will act as a reinforcer if it results in an imbalance in your preferred or optimal distribution of activities. Specifically, a reinforcing contingency will exist if the ratio of reinforcer to response in the constrained condition is less than the ratio of reinforcer to response under free operant baseline. In the first example, above, 10/90 is less than 20/80. In the second, 70/30 is less than 80/20. Similarly, punishment contingencies through 'response satiation' could be implemented by ensuring that the ratio of reinforcer to response in the constrained condition is *greater* than the ratio of reinforcer to response under free operant baseline. For a fuller discussion of this complex issue, see Konarski et al. (1981), Realon and Konarski (1993) and Remington (1991b).

that such relationships need to be demonstrated, preferably through the direct manipulation of contingencies. The notion that credible evidence requires experimental manipulation is reflected in the suggestion that applied behaviour analysis should provide a 'believable demonstration', *through demonstrating experimental control*, that observed changes in behaviour are linked to the suggested environmental events (Baer *et al.*, 1968, 1987). Thus, *the analysis of behavior, as the term is used here, requires a believable demonstration of the events that can be responsible for the occurrence or non-occurrence of that behavior. An experimenter has achieved an analysis of a behavior when he can exercise control over it.* (Baer *et al.*, 1968, p.93–94).

The contextual control of behaviour

Consideration of the context in which behaviour occurs, including its biological and historical context, is fundamental to the behaviour analytic perspective. Contextual factors may operate in two very general ways. First, they may provide or establish the motivational base which underlies behaviour. Secondly, the context in which behaviour occurs may provide important information or clues to the individual concerning the probability of particular behaviours being reinforced.

As has just been discussed, reinforcers and punishers are functionally defined. Moreover, the behavioural approach makes no assumptions regarding the capacity of a particular stimulus to function as a positive or negative reinforcer. Indeed, behavioural theory would suggest that the reinforcing or punishing power of stimuli needs to be *established* by constraining relationships, or historical and contextual variables. Thus, for example, food will only operate as a positive reinforcer if the person is denied free access to it and also if, among other things, they have not recently eaten. Specific food preferences are likely to reflect the effects of previous experience. Indeed, food could in a different context (e.g. immediately after a very large meal or during a stomach upset) operate as a negative reinforcer (increasing behaviours which lead to the withdrawal or postponement of food) or a positive punisher (decreasing behaviours which are 'rewarded' by the presentation of food).

Similarly, a particular classroom task may only become aversive (and consequently become established as a negative reinforcer) for a child when repeated many times over a short period or when presented in a noisy or stressful setting (cf. Winterling, Dunlap & O'Neill, 1987). Social contact with adults may become aversive (and hence act as a negative reinforcer) after the experience of sexual abuse. That is, personal, biological, historical and environmental contexts influence the motivational basis of behaviour by determining or establishing the reinforcing and punishing potential of otherwise neutral stimuli. In light of the discussion above, they would alter the person's preferred distribution of activities under a free operant baseline. The behavioural terminology for dealing with such operations is currently evolving but includes the concepts of setting factors (Kantor, 1959), setting events (Bijou & Baer, 1978; Wahler & Fox, 1981), establishing operations and establishing stimuli (Michael, 1982, 1993).

In addition to this motivational influence, aspects of contexts may gain 'informational value' as a result of their previous association with variations in the probability with which particular behaviours have been reinforced. That is, contextual *discriminative stimuli* distinguish between situations in which specific consequences for a given behaviour are more or less likely. So, for example, an 'out of order' notice on a lift provides information regarding the operation (or not) of a particular contingency, i.e. the probability of button pressing being followed by the appearance of a lift. An oncoming driver flashing their lights may have informational value in signifying the operation of a police radar trap (contingency: behaviour = speeding; consequence = fine). The difference between these two general classes of antecedent or contextual stimuli is crucial. In lay terms, establishing operations and stimuli change *people's behaviour by changing what they want ... [as opposed to discriminative or conditional stimuli, which change] ... their chances of getting something that they already want* (Michael, 1982, p.154).

These basic arrangements between A(ntecedent):B(ehaviour):C(on-sequence) comprise what is commonly described as the *three-term contingency* which defines *discriminated operant behaviour,* that is operant or 'voluntary' behaviour which shows contextual sensitivity to informational as well as motivational factors.

In recent years, the experimental analysis of complex human behaviour has lead to an expansion of interest in the informational value of stimuli in order to encompass the area of conditional relations, i.e. contextual control over the 'meaning' of discriminative stimuli (Sidman, 1986), and the role of verbal rules in regulating much human behaviour (Hayes, 1989).

The latter issue is crucial to our understanding of human behaviour. Skinner (1966) suggested that, while the operant behaviour of animals is *directly* shaped by contingencies, much human behaviour is *rule governed.* That is, verbal rules (instructions and self-instructions) play an important role in mediating between environmental contingencies and behaviour.

A classic example of the importance of verbal rules is provided by the comparison of the performance of people and non-humans on a simple experimental task. On a fixed-interval schedule of reinforcement, the reinforcer (e.g. food, money, points) becomes available after a *fixed* period of time has elapsed since it was last presented (e.g. 30 seconds). The next appropriate response (e.g. bar press, button push) after the reinforcer becomes available will, therefore, be reinforced. In this situation it does not matter at all what the person does in the intervening period. The most efficient strategy would be simply to wait for the fixed period of time to finish, respond in order to earn the reinforcer and then start waiting again. Non-humans rarely do this. Typically, their rate of responding (e.g. lever pressing) will increasingly accelerate during the interval. Adults who are not briefed regarding the nature of the task, however, usually do one of two things. Either they show the type of efficient pattern of responding described above (wait – respond – wait – respond), or they show a consistently high rate of responding throughout, a remarkably inefficient strategy. The most plausible explanation of these differences lies in the types of verbal rules people have formulated about the task (Lowe, 1979). People who show the (efficient) low rate of responding will, when debriefed, tend to describe the nature of the task reasonably accurately (e.g. being able to earn points after waiting for a while). People who show the (inefficient) high rate of responding, however, tend to describe the task (inaccurately) as one in which points are earned on the basis of *how many times* they respond.

While rather trivial in itself, this example does illustrate two important points. First, verbal rules (or self-instructions) formulated by people mediate between the actual contingency and performance. Secondly, such rules may lead to inefficient (or inaccurate) performance. Indeed, one of the characteristics of rule-governed behaviour is its tendency to make people insensitive to changes in the actual contingencies operating on our behaviour (Hayes, 1989).

A key question given our current interests in accounting for the behaviour of people with severe learning disabilities concerns the level of language development necessary for the emergence of rule-governed behaviour. Unfortunately, there is no clear-cut answer to this question. Initial evidence suggested that, on the type of simple experimental task described above, the performance of preverbal infants showed no evidence of rule governance, the performance of children over five years of age appeared to be predominantly rule governed, and the performance of children in an intermediate age range of two and a half to four years showed a mixed and confusing pattern of responding (Bentall, Lowe & Beasty, 1985). More recent evidence, however, has described performance assumed to be characteristic of rule governance in preverbal infants (Darcheville, Rivière & Wearden, 1993). The only safe assumption, it would appear, is that the concept of rule-governed behaviour *may* have some relevance to the explanation of the challenging behaviours shown by people with severe learning disabilities who are likely to have restricted verbal repertoires. As Hastings and Remington (1994a) point out, however, it is likely to be highly relevant to understanding the behaviour of carers and staff toward people with challenging behaviour. This latter point will be discussed in more detail in Chapter 9.

A systems approach

In the real world, we live, work and play in settings in which we could potentially engage in an enormous range of behaviours, *all* of which will be under the control of different reinforcement contingencies. As a result, what we actually do needs to be seen as the product of a complex and dynamic behavioural system, rather than reflecting the operation of one discrete contingency on a particular behaviour (Schroeder & MacLean, 1987; Scotti *et al.*, 1991*a*; Voeltz & Evans, 1982; Willems, 1974). The study of variables influencing choice between competing alternative behaviours has been at the forefront of experimental research for many years (Davison & McCarthy, 1988; Mace, 1994*a*). In addition, there has been a long-standing interest within both experimental and applied research regarding the 'side-effects' of particular contingencies of reinforcement or approaches to intervention (e.g. Balsam & Bondy, 1983; Hutchinson, 1977; Newsom, Favell & Rincover, 1983; Staddon, 1977). This issue will be given further consideration at a number of points in the following chapters.

Viewing the challenging behaviours shown by people with learning disabilities as examples of operant behaviour has opened up two avenues of approach. First, in primarily analytic studies, it led to the search for the contextual factors and environmental consequences responsible for maintaining challenging behaviours. Secondly, it opened up the possibility of developing intervention or treatment techniques based upon either the modification of naturally occurring contingencies or the introduction of new contingencies in order to reduce the rate of the challenging behaviours or increase the rate of competing and more appropriate behaviours.

In the section below, evidence relevant to the idea that challenging behaviours shown by people with severe learning disabilities may be maintained by their environmental consequences will be reviewed (e.g. Carr, 1977). Following this, a parallel notion, that challenging behaviours may be maintained by their internal consequences or by processes of automatic or perceptual reinforcement, will be discussed (Carr, 1977; Lovaas, Newsom & Hickman, 1987; Vollmer, 1994).

Positive and negative reinforcement hypotheses

These complementary approaches suggest that challenging behaviour may be maintained by a process of either positive or negative reinforcement. This idea is represented schematically (and rather simplistically) in Fig. 4.2. First,

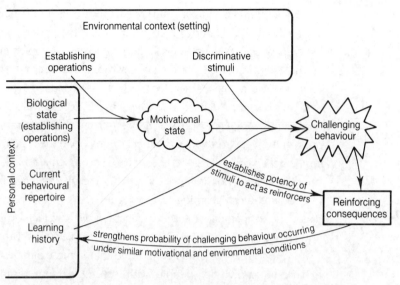

Fig. 4.2. Schematic representation of the reinforcement of challenging behaviour.

aspects of the personal and environmental context interact to produce a particular motivational state. This, in effect, establishes the reinforcing potential of previously neutral stimuli. It is also, when matched with a particular learning history and the presence of discriminative stimuli which signal the availability of reinforcement, likely to precipitate an episode of challenging behaviour. Reinforcement of the challenging behaviour will contribute to the person's learning history (one aspect of the personal context) by increasing the probability that such behaviour is likely to occur in the future in response to similar motivational and environmental conditions.

For example, let us assume that a young man with severe learning disabilities has not eaten for a number of hours and is experiencing hunger pangs (personal context: biological state). He is sitting in the lounge of a small community residence with little to do, but with no obvious threats to his immediate safety (environmental context). He would quite like something to eat (motivational state: food becomes established as a potential positive reinforcer). He does not have the skills (personal context: current behavioural repertoire) or opportunity (environmental context) to prepare his own food. A member of staff wanders in with a hamburger (environmental context: discriminative stimulus indicating the presence of food and the presence of someone capable of providing food). As a result of previous learning (personal context: learning history), he begins to moan, cry and bite his hand. The member of staff, who is trying to eat his hamburger, correctly guesses that he is 'communicating' his desire to have something to eat and yells through to a colleague in the kitchen to bring the young man a biscuit (positive reinforcement).

In another scenario, a young woman with severe learning disabilities is feeling irritable and jumpy. She is about to start her period (personal context: biological state). She is being asked to complete a complex task in her noisy and hot supported work placement (environmental context). The combination of these factors makes her feel very stressed indeed (motivational state: demands become established as a negative reinforcer). She does not have the negotiating skills (personal context: current behavioural repertoire) or opportunity (environmental context) to postpone the task to another day. A sympathetic work colleague comes over (environmental context: discriminative stimuli indicating possibility of escape). As a result of her previous experience (personal context: learning history) she begins to moan, cry and bite her hand. The sympathetic colleague notices her distress, feels upset at the sight of it and persuades her job coach to let her have a break (negative reinforcement).

Four sources of evidence indicate that some examples of challenging behaviours shown by people with severe learning disabilities may be maintained by their environmental consequences. These are:

☐ descriptive studies which have examined the context in which challenging behaviours occur (e.g. Edelson, Taubman & Lovaas, 1983; Emerson *et al.*, in press *a, b, c*; Hall & Oliver, 1992; Maurice & Trudel, 1982);

☐ experimental studies which have demonstrated the contextual control of challenging behaviour (e.g. Carr, Newsom & Binkoff, 1976; Iwata *et al.*, 1982; Iwata *et al.*, 1994*a*; Mace *et al.*, 1986);

☐ experimental studies which have directly manipulated the contingencies hypothesised to maintain challenging behaviour (e.g. Lovaas *et al.*, 1965; Lovaas & Simmons, 1969);

☐ experimental studies which have directly manipulated the contingencies operating on competing members of the response class containing challenging behaviour (e.g. Carr & Durand, 1985*a*).

At the simplest level, a number of purely descriptive studies have examined aspects of the social context in which challenging behaviours occur. Edelson and colleagues, for example, observed 20 young people with learning disabilities residing in a state institution in North America. They recorded, for approximately five hours for each participant, occurrences of self-injurious behaviour and various staff behaviours directed towards the young person (e.g. demands, denial, punishment, praise). Their results indicated that, for 19 of the 20 participants, rates of self-injury escalated markedly immediately following staff demands, denials or punishment (Edelson *et al.*, 1983). Whilst other explanations cannot be ruled out, such results are certainly consistent

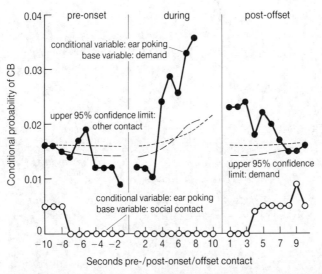

Fig. 4.3. The conditional probability of Susan's self-injurious ear poking prior to, during and following, teacher demands and other forms of teacher contact.

with the notion that the participant's self-injury may have been maintained by a process of negative reinforcement. That is, the presentation of a potential negative reinforcer (staff contact) elicited the behaviour (self-injury) which may have been associated in the past with its subsequent withdrawal (escape from contact).

More recently, Emerson *et al.*, (in press *a*) and Emerson *et al.*, (in press *c*) employed the statistical technique of lag sequential analysis (Sackett, 1987) to examine the relationship between staff behaviour and the severe challenging behaviours shown by five children and one young adult with severe learning disabilities. Analysis of eight hours of videotape per participant taken in their everyday settings indicated that 28 of the 34 separate forms of challenging behaviour shown by the participants occurred in situations which were consistent with them being maintained by a process of either positive or negative reinforcement. Figures 4.3 to 4.5 illustrate the (apparent) operation of social contingencies in maintaining challenging behaviour.

Figure 4.3 shows the relationship between teacher demands to complete an academic task, other forms of teacher contact (e.g. general conversation) and ear poking shown by Susan, a 13 year-old girl with multiple and severe self-injurious behaviour. As can be seen, the onset of demands (but not other forms of contact) is associated with a marked and statistically significant escalation in the probability of her ear poking (i.e. the conditional probability of ear poking rises above the upper 95% confidence limit surrounding the behaviour's chance level of occurrence). After demands are withdrawn, her self-injury gradually returns to normal levels. Again, this is consistent with the

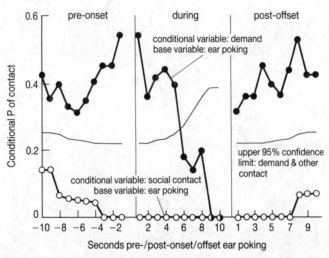

Fig. 4.4. The conditional probability of teacher demands prior to, during and following, Susan's self-injurious ear poking.

idea that her self-injury is a member of a discriminated operant response class maintained by a process of negative reinforcement involving escape from teacher demands. If this were the case, we would also expect that the *onset* of ear poking would be associated with the contingent *withdrawal* of demands. This is illustrated in Fig. 4.4.

As can be seen, the onset of Susan's ear poking is associated with the complete cessation of teacher demands which were occurring at higher than chance levels before the onset of her self-injury.

A pattern of results consistent with challenging behaviour being maintained by positive (social) reinforcement is provided in Fig. 4.5.

This shows the probability of teacher demands and other forms of contact prior to, and following, spitting shown by Sabiha, an eight year-old Asian girl with severe learning disabilities. As can be seen, the probability of Sabiha receiving 'other' forms of contact from her teacher increases markedly in the period immediately following her spitting. Teacher demands then increase significantly in the period six to ten seconds following her spitting.

More convincing evidence in support of the operant hypothesis is provided by the experimental *demonstration* of the contextual control of challenging behaviour. Carr *et al.* (1976) demonstrated in two different locations that the self-injurious head hitting shown by Tim, an eight year-old boy with learning disabilities and childhood schizophrenia, was reliably elicited by adult requests (compared with other types of interaction and free time). Interestingly, they then went on to show that changing the context in which the requests were made brought about dramatic changes in Tim's behaviour (see Fig. 4.6).

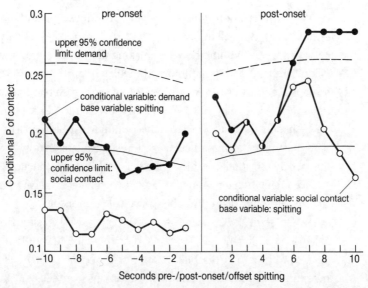

Fig. 4.5. The conditional probability of teacher demands and other forms of teacher contact prior to, during and following, Sabiha's spitting.

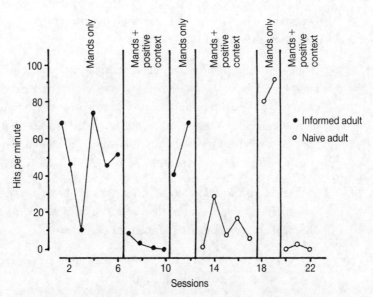

Fig. 4.6. Number of hits per minute, over sessions, for the Mands versus Mands Plus Positive Context conditions. The filled circles are the data for the informed adult and the open circles, the data for the naive adult. (From Carr, *et al.*, 1976).

When interaction consisted solely of requests (mands in behavioural terminology) his self-injury occurred, as previously, at very high rates. However, when the time between making the same requests was filled with telling Tim a story, his self-injury immediately dropped to near zero levels. Perhaps the most plausible explanation of these results is that adult requests functioned, in certain contexts, as a negative reinforcer for Tim's self-injury (i.e. he had in the past learned that his self-injury would lead to the withdrawal of requests). What is particularly interesting in this study, however, is the dramatic demonstration of the contextual control of this functional relationship. Relatively small changes in the situation (telling a story) appeared to be capable of totally disrupting this powerful relationship.

Iwata *et al.* (1982), in a now classic paper, used an alternating treatment design to examine the effect of context on the self-injurious behaviour of nine children with learning disabilities. They recorded the rates of self-injury shown under four different conditions. The conditions were selected as representing three general cases of the types of contexts under which self-injury maintained by operant processes may occur, and one control condition.

☐ In the *social disapproval* condition an adult was present throughout but did not interact with the child except to express concern or mild disapproval (e.g. 'don't do that') on the occurrence of self-injury. This condition was assumed to be discriminative for the occurrence of self-injury maintained by positive social reinforcement.

☐ In the *academic demand* condition an adult was present throughout and encouraged the child to complete an educational task using a graduated (ask – show – guide) prompting procedure. However, the adult withdrew their attention for 30 seconds contingent on the child's self-injury. Such a condition was assumed to be discriminative for self-injury maintained by negative social reinforcement.

☐ In the *alone* condition no adults or materials were present. Such a condition was assumed to be discriminative for behaviours maintained by automatic or perceptual reinforcement (see below).

☐ The *control* condition consisted of a stimulating environment in which social attention is delivered contingent upon the non-occurrence of self-injury.

Each child was observed under each condition for 15 minutes on at least four occasions. The order of presentation of the conditions was random. Of the nine children, two showed their highest rates of self-injury under conditions of academic demand, one under conditions of social disapproval and three whilst alone. The remaining three children showed undifferentiated responding across conditions. Thus one-third of the children showed patterns of self-injury which were consistent with their behaviour being maintained by environmental consequences.

Recently, Iwata *et al.* (1994*a*) have summarised the results of such analyses for 152 people with learning disabilities who showed self-injurious behaviour. Of these, 93% (142) had a severe learning disability. Of the 152 people:

☐ 38% ($n = 58$) showed patterns of responding consistent with their self-injury being maintained by *negative reinforcement*;

☐ 26% ($n = 40$) showed patterns of responding consistent with their self-injury being maintained by *positive reinforcement*;

☐ 21% ($n = 32$) showed patterns of responding consistent with their self-injury being maintained by internal or *automatic reinforcement*;

☐ 5% ($n = 8$) showed patterns of responding consistent with their self-injury being maintained by multiple controlling variables (e.g. positive and negative reinforcement);

☐ 10% ($n = 14$) showed undifferentiated or unpredictable patterns of responding.

Similarly, Derby *et al.* (1992) reported that similar brief analytic procedures conducted on various forms of challenging behaviour shown by 79 people with learning disabilities indicated that the behaviours of 23 (29%) were maintained by negative reinforcement, 17 (22%) by positive reinforcement and 12 (15%) by automatic reinforcement. The controlling variables for the remaining 27 (34%) were unclear.

Similar approaches have been used to demonstrate the contextual control of aggression in people with learning disabilities (e.g. Derby *et al.*, 1992; Emerson, 1990; Mace *et al.*, 1986; Paisey, Whitney & Hislop, 1991). Other types of experimental conditions (and hence types of potential reinforcers) employed in these studies have included continuous social attention (Oliver, 1991), delayed access to food (Durand & Crimmins, 1988), noise (Iwata *et al.*, 1994*b*), contingent access to individually defined reinforcers (Day *et al.*, 1988), medical examination (Iwata *et al.*, 1990*a*), adults talking to each other (Mace *et al.*, 1986) and response cost (Steege *et al.*, 1989).

The strongest evidence in support of the operant model is provided by those studies which have demonstrated control over the challenging behaviour by manipulating its maintaining consequences. If a behaviour is maintained by a process of positive reinforcement, preventing the reinforcer occurring contingent on the behaviour should lead to the cessation or *extinction* of the behaviour. Similarly, if a behaviour is maintained by a process of negative reinforcement, preventing the withdrawal of the reinforcer contingent on the behaviour should lead to the extinction of the behaviour. (The latter technique is often referred to as negative or escape extinction.)

Some of the earliest evidence supporting the operant model used this approach. Lovaas and Simmons (1969), for example, demonstrated that the consistent withholding of adult attention led to the extinction of the severe self-injurious behaviour shown by two boys with severe learning disabilities. They then went on to re-instate, before finally eliminating, the self-injury shown by one of the boys by providing 'comforting' attention contingent on his self-injury. The 'comforting' attention, which led to a rapid *worsening* of his self-injury, consisted of such natural responses as holding his hand and re-assuring him that everything was OK. Lovaas has subsequently referred to such 'humane' reactions as an example of 'benevolent enslavement', in that the good intentions of carers in comforting the child appeared themselves primarily responsible for maintaining the self-injury (Lovaas, 1982). More recently, Zarcone *et al.* (1993) demonstrated the use of escape extinction to reduce the self-injurious behaviours of three women with severe learning disabilities, which appeared to be maintained by a process of negative reinforcement.

Finally, a number of studies have provided strong evidence in support of the operant model by demonstrating functional control over challenging behaviour by *differentially reinforcing* a more socially appropriate member of the same response class. That is, they have identified the behavioural function of the person's challenging behaviour (e.g. to escape from teacher demands, to elicit teacher attention). They have then taught and systematically reinforced a *functionally equivalent* response (e.g. to request a break as an alternative to escape motivated challenging behaviour). Under conditions which are themselves predictable from behavioural theory, this approach can lead to rapid and significant reductions in the person's challenging behaviour (e.g. Carr & Durand, 1985*a*; Durand, Berotti & Weiner, 1993).

These studies, in combination, provide strong evidence to support the proposition that some examples of challenging behaviours shown by people with severe learning disabilities may be maintained by processes of either positive or negative reinforcement. All the examples of negative reinforcement which have been discussed have involved the person's challenging behaviour acting as an *escape* behaviour (i.e. leading to escape from, or withdrawal of, the negative reinforcer). Given that this particular behavioural function appears to be the most prevalent (see above), it is probable that some examples of challenging behaviours may also function as *avoidance* behaviours. That is, they may serve to prevent, postpone or delay the presentation of (aversive) negative reinforcers. Thus, for example, carers may have learned to avoid presenting negative reinforcers (e.g. social demands) under conditions in which the person with learning disabilities appears distressed (e.g. by exhibiting self-injurious behaviour). In such a situation, self-injurious behaviour would serve to avoid (postpone or prevent) the occurrence of demands.

If this were the case, then we would expect (assuming the avoidance behaviour was under some form of discriminative control) that the behaviour would occur under conditions in which the negative reinforcer (demands) was more likely to occur. If it operated as a *successful* avoidance behaviour, however, we would not see *any* environmental consequences of the behaviour as the maintaining contingency involves the non-occurrence of a potential event (the negative reinforcer). To an observer, therefore, the person's challenging behaviour would appear to have no consequence and, unless very precise discriminative control had been established, to have no clear antecedents. Nevertheless, it would still be an example of operant behaviour maintained by its environmental consequences.

Processes of negative reinforcement can also be used to account for the unhelpful behaviour of carers in socially reinforcing the challenging behaviour of the person with learning disabilities (Carr, Taylor & Robinson, 1991; Hastings & Remington, 1994a, b; Hastings, 1993; Oliver, 1993; Taylor & Carr, 1993, 1994). In both of the hypothetical examples with which we started this section, the cessation of an individual's challenging behaviour may be thought of as negatively reinforcing the action of care staff. In these examples, the person's challenging behaviour may act as a negative reinforcer which is withdrawn contingent upon the helping behaviours of care staff (providing food, withdrawing demands). The staff behaviour which reinforces the person's challenging behaviour is itself reinforced by the termination of the challenging behaviour. Thus, carer and user get locked in a vicious circle (or negative reinforcement trap) which perpetuates the person's challenging behaviour.

If this is the case, then we may expect two further things to happen. First, carers and care staff are likely to habituate (get used to) particular intensities or forms of challenging behaviour over time. Thus, they may only respond (and hence provide contingent reinforcement) intermittently unless the person shows *more intense* or *more complex* forms of challenging behaviour. This is, of course, the basis of all shaping procedures in which new behaviours are taught by differentially reinforcing particular aspects of the behaviour which the person already shows. In this case, however, the possibility of carers and care staff habituating to 'ordinary' levels of challenging behaviour may lead to the systematic (but unplanned) shaping of more and more intense or complex forms of the behaviour. Such a process may partially account for the development of challenging behaviour (cf. Guess & Carr, 1991; Oliver, 1993).

In addition, if the termination of challenging behaviour acts as a negative reinforcer, we may also expect carers and care staff to develop strategies for *avoiding* the occurrence of such behaviours. So, people may come to avoid interacting with users whose challenging behaviours are maintained by processes of negative social reinforcement (e.g. escape from demands, escape from social attention), while increasing their rates of interaction with users whose challenging behaviour is maintained by processes of positive social reinforcement (e.g. access to social attention). Taylor and her colleagues have demonstrated that such a pattern is quite rapidly established and is sufficiently robust to be used to predict the functions served by a user's challenging behaviour (Carr *et al.*, 1991; Taylor & Carr, 1993, 1994; Taylor & Romanczyk, 1994).

Automatic reinforcement

It is clear that not all behaviour is shaped by environmental consequences. Some behaviours are innate (e.g. salivating at the sight of food when hungry). Others are learned reflexive behaviours which are elicited by environmental stimuli (e.g. salivating at the sound of a dinner bell when hungry). Others may appear to be maintained by private events or consequences internal to the person (e.g. clenching your teeth may attenuate the pain from a sprained ankle, scratching an insect bite may temporarily relieve the sensation of itching).

It has been suggested that this latter class of behaviours may be thought of as examples of operant behaviour maintained by a process of automatic or perceptual reinforcement, in which the reinforcing stimuli are private or internal to the person (Berkson, 1983; Carr, 1977; Lovaas *et al.*, 1987; Vollmer, 1994). Potential internal or automatic reinforcers include perceptual feedback from the response itself (e.g. visual effects of eye poking, kinaesthetic feedback from rocking, auditory feedback from spinning toys), modulation of levels of arousal, relief from itching and the attenuation of pain (see below).

This approach is not without its problems for behaviourists. Mace, Lalli and Shea (1992) point out that, if the (internal) reinforcer is integral to the response (as would be the case if the reinforcer was perceptual feedback from the behaviour), discriminative control of the behaviour is unlikely to develop as the reinforcer is *always* present*. In addition, if the maintaining stimuli are internal and private, they will not be amenable to manipulation. Given the lack of discriminative control and inability to manipulate the hypothesised

---

* It is important to keep in mind that discriminative control develops through the association of (discriminative) stimuli with *variations* in the probability of a response being reinforced. Thus, if the response is always reinforced, discriminative control simply cannot develop. The behaviour would, however, be expected to vary across contexts owing to (motivational) variation in the extent to which the perceptual feedback was reinforcing.

contingencies, how are we to provide a 'believable demonstration' that these unknowable events really are responsible for maintaining behaviour? Circumstantial support for the notion of automatic or perceptual reinforcement is provided by a number of studies.

First, studies have indicated that the probability of occurrence of some forms of challenging behaviour (primarily stereotypy and self-injury) varies with the level of general environmental stimulation. As has been discussed above, a significant proportion of challenging behaviours occur at their highest rates under conditions of social and material deprivation. In Iwata's large-scale study, 21% of people showed their highest rates of self-injury in the 'alone' condition. Of the 79 people in the Derby study, 15% showed their highest rates of challenging behaviour in this condition. Similarly, a number of studies have shown that increasing the level of environmental stimulation may lead to reductions in stereotypic and other forms of challenging behaviour (e.g. Favell, McGimsey & Schell, 1982; Horner, 1980; Steege *et al.*, 1989). These results are consistent with predictions made from the study of behavioural choice if we assume that the challenging behaviours in question are maintained by (positive) automatic reinforcement (Mace *et al.*, 1992; Vollmer, 1994).

Interestingly, however, exactly the opposite results have been obtained in other studies. Duker and Rasing (1989), for example, found that *decreasing* the level of stimulation in the classroom by removing furniture, pictures and extraneous materials led to a *reduction* in stereotyped behaviour (and increase in on-task behaviour) of three young adults with severe learning disabilities and autism. These results are consistent with an alternative explanation – that some forms of challenging behaviour may be maintained by a process of (negative) automatic reinforcement in that they serve to actively dampen (aversive) levels of overarousal (cf. Isaacson & Gispin, 1990; Murphy, 1982).

This notion is akin to viewing the challenging behaviour as a *coping response* which reduces the aversiveness of extraneous sources of stimulation. If this is the case, then we would expect such behaviours to occur at their highest rates under conditions of stressful external stimulation (e.g. the 'academic demand' condition in Iwata's analogue situations). Thus, evidence of contextual control can only ever provide circumstantial evidence in support of operant hypotheses. The key difference between coping and escape responses is that a coping response would reduce the aversiveness of an external event. An escape response would remove the event itself.

Further circumstantial evidence for the operation of automatic reinforce-ment is provided by the impact of sensory extinction in reducing some forms of challenging behaviour (e.g. Iwata *et al.*, 1994a; Rincover & Devany, 1982;

Rincover *et al.*, 1979*a*; Rincover, Newsom & Carr, 1979*b*). This procedure involves masking the sensory consequences arising from the behaviour. Rincover and Devany (1982), for example, used foam padding to mask the sensory consequences arising from head banging. Unfortunately, as well as masking the sensory consequences, such procedures may also exert discriminative control over behaviours maintained by external consequences, lead to changes in environmental contingencies or reduce challenging behaviour through punishment (e.g. Mazaleski *et al.*, 1994). Let us, for the sake of argument, make the alternative assumption that the person's head banging had been maintained by a process of positive social reinforcement. If this were the case, it is plausible to suggest that their previous experience with self-injuring in different environments may have taught them that head-banging against foam padding was unlikely to be reinforced (i.e. foam padding exerts discriminative control over self-injury). Alternatively, the foam padding may directly alter the behaviour of others by reducing the aversiveness of the person's self-injury and hence reducing the probability of them intervening. In this case the foam padding initiates the unplanned extinction of a socially reinforced behaviour.

Of course, none of this evidence is particularly convincing, owing to the inability or failure to independently measure the hypothesised internal consequences of the challenging behaviour. While, in some situations, this is clearly either impossible or pointless, in that the internal consequence is guaranteed to occur (e.g. independent measurement of the perceptual feedback from the behaviour), in other cases it is both viable and necessary to provide independent measures of potential processes of automatic reinforcement (Romanczyk *et al.*, 1992). While the physiological monitoring of levels of arousal is itself a highly complex area, Romanczyk and his colleagues discussed some of the relatively simple approaches to monitoring levels of arousal, which are commonly used in the analysis of issues related to anxiety in non-disabled people.

Respondent behaviour

Respondent behaviours are those reflexive or conditioned behaviours which are primarily 'involuntary' in nature (e.g. blinking, salivating, changes in heart rate, skin conductance). A considerable amount of behavioural theorising about issues of arousal and anxiety in non-disabled people has viewed them as examples of acquired or conditioned respondent behaviours. Phobic fear, for example, has been viewed as a form of conditioned response acquired through previous association between the feared object (the conditioned stimulus) and another aversive event (Marks, 1987; Rachman, 1990).

As Romanczyk *et al.* (1992) point out, however, there has been remarkably little attention paid to issues of anxiety and arousal among people with severe learning disabilities (see also Benson, 1990). Romanczyk and his colleagues have suggested that anxiety and arousal may play some role in the maintenance of self-injurious behaviour (Romanczyk, 1986; Romanczyk *et al.*, 1992). They suggest that self-injury may be elicited as a reflexive response to high levels of arousal generated by environmental stressors. They also point out that self-injury can itself generate high levels of arousal. Similarly, evidence from basic research has indicated that aggression may be elicited as a reflexive response by punishment (e.g. Hutchinson, 1977).

These are not presented as models of challenging behaviour which stand on their own, but as additional processes within complex models (Romanczyk, 1986; Romanczyk *et al.*, 1992). We will return to them in the concluding section of this chapter.

Schedule-induced behaviour

The occurrence of a particular class of abnormal stereotypic behaviours has been studied in basic experimental behavioural research for a number of years. Under conditions involving the repetitive delivery of food on fixed schedule, or under some examples of fixed-interval schedules of reinforcement, schedule-induced behaviours may appear. These are behaviours which occur in the period immediately following reinforcement, are excessive, stereotyped in appearance, unrelated to the demands of the situation and often highly persistent over time (Staddon, 1977). The majority of studies of schedule induced behaviour have taken place in the animal laboratory, focusing upon polydipsia (over-drinking) in rats and aggression in pigeons. Studies with people, however, have been undertaken and have led to reports of schedule induced eating, drinking, aggression, cigarette smoking, grooming, pacing and fidgeting (Emerson & Howard, 1992; although see also Overskeid, 1992).

The potential importance of this phenomenon to the understanding of challenging behaviour shown by people with severe learning disabilities has not gone unnoticed (e.g. Epling & Pierce, 1983; Lewis & Baumeister, 1982). It has, however, generated remarkably few studies.

Emerson and Howard (1992) investigated the possibility of schedule induction in an experimental study involving five children and three adults with severe learning disabilities. The results indicated that seven of the eight participants demonstrated evidence of schedule induction for at least one stereotypic behaviour. In addition, for five of the eight individuals, these behaviours occurred at a significantly greater rate in the period immediately following reinforcer presentation. Subsequent analysis of observational data collected at a special school attended by the five children indicated that: (1) none of the behaviours, which appeared to be socially mediated in the classroom, was evident as induced behaviours under experimental conditions; (2) none of the behaviours which was experimentally induced appeared to be socially mediated in the classroom; and (3) for the one participant for whom sufficient examples of teacher-mediated reinforcement were observed in the classroom, his stereotypic arm-flapping behaviour, which had been experimentally induced, also occurred at significantly higher rates following reinforcement in the classroom (Emerson, 1993). More recently, Emerson *et al.* (in press*c*) have reported evidence to suggest that some examples of self-injurious and disruptive behaviours may be induced under appropriate conditions.

At present, the function of schedule-induced behaviours and their importance in understanding challenging behaviour is very unclear. One possibility is that they may serve to dampen levels of (over) arousal (Mittleman, Blaha & Phillips, 1992). This notion is consistent with evidence concerning the neurobiological function of some forms of stereotypy (see above and Isaacson & Gispin, 1990).

NEUROBIOLOGICAL MODELS

Over the last decade, significant gains have been made in identifying some of the potential neurobiological mechanisms which may underlie challenging behaviour. As was indicated in the first chapter, the primary concern of this book is to present and evaluate approaches to the understanding, assessment and treatment of challenging behaviour which arise from behavioural psychology. However, to attempt to do this in isolation from a consideration of the biological bases of our behaviour would be counter-productive.

Most recent neurobiological theories have focused on the role of various classes of endogenous neurotransmitters in modulating behaviour. These are the chemical messengers of our central nervous system (CNS) which produce an effect by binding to the receptor sites on the cell surfaces of neurones. Different types of neurones are activated by different types of neurotransmitters. Recent research has focused on three different classes of neurotransmitters: dopamine, serotonin (5-hydroxytryptamine) and the opioid peptides (in particular β-endorphin). A number of excellent detailed (and often highly technical) reviews are available of this area and its relation to drug treatments of challenging behaviour (e.g. Aman, 1991; Baumeister & Sevin, 1990; Harris, 1992; Sandman, 1990/1991; Schroeder *et al.*, 1986; Schroeder & Tessel, 1994; Singh *et al.*, 1993*b*; Thompson *et al.*, 1994*a*). Below, is a summary of some of the main points in this complex field.

Dopamine

The dopaminergic system is closely involved in the regulation of motor activity. There are two main groups of dopamine receptors (D1 and D2), each of which contains further subtypes (Cross & Owen, 1989). Evidence is beginning to suggest that abnormalities in the D1 receptor subsystem may be implicated in the development and maintenance of at least some forms of self-injurious behaviour.

☐ People with Lesch–Nyhan syndrome, *all* of whom display injurious self-biting, show a significant deficiency in dopamine pathways in certain areas of the brain, and decreased levels of dopamine and its metabolites in the CNS (see Nyhan, 1994).

☐ Animal studies have shown that, if dopamine pathways are destroyed in unborn rat pups, the administration of dopamine *agonists* (substances which bind to the receptor site and reproduce the effect of dopamine) produces severe self-biting. This can be blocked by the administration of dopamine *antagonists* (substances which displace agonist compounds from the receptor sites and hence stop them producing their biological effect). (For a recent review see Schroeder & Tessel, 1994.)

☐ Rearing rhesus monkeys in isolation almost inevitably produces self-injurious behaviour. This behaviour emerges at 3–4 months, persists into adulthood, involves multiple topographies, some of which lead to severe injury, and is most likely to occur in response to environmental stressors (Kraemer & Clarke, 1990). It is associated with long-term alterations in dopamine receptor sensitivity and destruction of dopaminergic pathways (Lewis, 1992).

☐ Preliminary reports suggest that low dosage of fluphenazine (a D1 and D2 antagonist) may produce significant reductions in self-injury for some people (Gualtieri & Schroeder, 1989).

The accumulated evidence points to destruction of some D1 pathways and supersensitivity (or reduced thresholds for activation) in the remaining D1 receptors being implicated in the genesis of self-biting and, perhaps, other forms of self-injury. This effect appears to be tied to crucial developmental stages since later damage to the dopaminergic system (as occurs in Parkinson's disease and Huntington's chorea) does not lead to self-injury. It is also possible that the effect results not from dysregulation of the dopaminergic system as such but from an imbalance between dopamine and serotonin activity (Schroeder & Tessel, 1994). Similar evidence has accumulated to suggest that abnormalities in the D2 receptor system may underlie the development of stereotyped behaviour (Cooper & Dourish, 1990).

The observation that rearing non-human primates in isolation can produce permanent destruction of dopaminergic pathways, long-lasting supersensitivity to dopamine agonists and very high rates of self-injury may have implications for preventative interventions. If severe social and sensory deprivation were to have similar irreversible effects in humans, there would exist a clear case for the provision of intensive social and sensory stimulation to 'at risk' infants. This may be particularly relevant to people with more severe and complex disabilities, who, because of the severity of their impairments, may have some difficulty in bonding with their parents and may have restricted repertoires for exploring the world around them.

Serotonin (5-HT)

The serotoninergic system is closely linked with a number of processes including arousal, appetite control, anxiety and depression (Dickenson, 1989). Disturbances in the system have been linked with insomnia, depression, disorders of appetite control and obsessive compulsive disorders (Bodfish & Madison, 1993; Gedye, 1993). There are at least 11 different types of serotonin receptors, some of which are inhibitory (class 1), and others excitatory (class 2 and 3) (Gedye, 1993). Accumulating evidence points to a relationship between serotonin and aggression, although links have also been made between serotonin and self-injurious behaviour (Baumeister & Sevin, 1990).

☐ In non-humans, lesions in areas which contain serotoninergic neurones or inhibit serotonin synthesis can lead to an increase in aggression. Similarly, interventions which increase serotonin synthesis or administration of serotonin agonists lead to a reduction in aggression (see Baumeister & Sevin, 1990).

☐ In non-disabled humans, there is some evidence of a negative correlation between levels of serotonin or its metabolites in the cerebral spinal fluid or blood plasma and aggression (Baumeister & Sevin, 1990; Thompson *et al.*, 1994*a*).

☐ Evidence also suggests that serotoninergic agonists or reuptake inhibitors (e.g. fluoxetine) can reduce obsessional compulsive disorders, self-injurious behaviour and aggression (Bodfish & Madison, 1993; Schroeder & Tessel, 1994; Sovner *et al.*, 1993).

☐ Dietary increases in serotonin have been implicated in the reduction of self-injurious behaviour (Gedye, 1990, 1991).

Opioid peptides (β-Endorphin)

Opioid peptides are structurally and functionally related to the opioid alkaloids morphine and heroin and play an important role in pain control systems. There are three general groups of opioid peptides (enkephalins, dynorphins and endorphins) and four types of receptor (mu, kappa, sigma and delta). β-endorphin, which binds to mu receptors, has the greatest analgesic and antinocicoptive (blocking of pain receptors) properties, and may produce a euphoric mood state (Singh *et al.*, 1993*b*). Sandman and his colleagues (e.g. Sandman, 1990/1991) have proposed two models in which β-endorphin activity may be related to self-injurious behaviour. In the *congenital opioid excess* model, it is proposed that excess opioid activity leads to permanently raised pain thresholds. In the *addiction* hypothesis, it is proposed that self-injurious behaviour leads to the release of β-endorphin which, through its analgesic, antinocicoptive and euphoria-inducing properties, acts as an automatic reinforcer for the self-injury. Over time, it is suggested that physical dependence (with associated withdrawal symptoms) may develop.

Evidence in support of a link between β-endorphin and self-injurious behaviour includes:

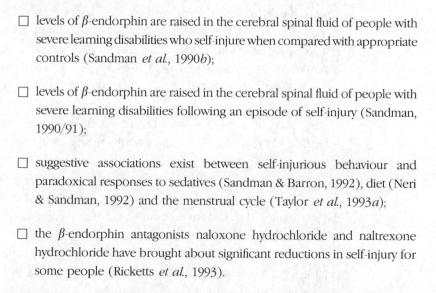

□ levels of β-endorphin are raised in the cerebral spinal fluid of people with severe learning disabilities who self-injure when compared with appropriate controls (Sandman *et al.*, 1990*b*);

□ levels of β-endorphin are raised in the cerebral spinal fluid of people with severe learning disabilities following an episode of self-injury (Sandman, 1990/91);

□ suggestive associations exist between self-injurious behaviour and paradoxical responses to sedatives (Sandman & Barron, 1992), diet (Neri & Sandman, 1992) and the menstrual cycle (Taylor *et al.*, 1993*a*);

□ the β-endorphin antagonists naloxone hydrochloride and naltrexone hydrochloride have brought about significant reductions in self-injury for some people (Ricketts *et al.*, 1993).

As noted above, neurobiological models also need to take account of the interaction between neurotransmitter systems. So, for example, Corbett and Campbell (1980) point out a possible link between serotonin and opioid peptides, in that tryptophan (a precursor of serotonin) enhances the tolerance for, and the development of dependence on, morphine. Oliver (1993) draws links between chronic β-endorphin release and increased sensitivity in dopamine receptors. In this context, and given the probable importance of the timing of damage to dopaminergic systems, it is interesting to note that there is a reported association between fetal distress and increased β-endorphin levels in amniotic fluid (Cataldo & Harris, 1982).

SUMMARY: INTEGRATED BIOBEHAVIOURAL MODELS

The studies which have been reviewed in this chapter provide strong evidence that many examples of challenging behaviours shown by people with severe learning disabilities are maintained by underlying behavioural processes. In particular, evidence suggests that challenging behaviours may be members of discriminated operant response classes. The operant model also provides a coherent account of the types of reciprocal influences between user and carer behaviour which may lead to the development of challenging behaviour (Guess & Carr, 1991; Oliver, 1993) and its maintenance through the process of 'benevolent enslavement' (Taylor & Carr, 1993, 1994; Lovaas, 1982).

Romanczyk and his colleagues, however, warn us that to label challenging behaviour as functional and purposeful

provides a perspective superior to viewing it simply as a psychotic behavior but also lends itself to a simplistic and naïve understanding as well. That is, self-injurious behavior represents a classification of behavior, and therefore, one cannot assume that the causal and maintaining factors are (1) similar across individuals, (2) consistent for the same individual at different points in time, and (3) similar for different topographies of self-injurious behavior both within and across individuals (Romanczyk et al., 1992, p.93).

To this, it could usefully be added that we cannot assume that causal and maintaining factors are (4) consistent for the same individual across different contexts and (5) not complex and diverse within specific topographies. Indeed, the variety of possible behavioural functions and aetiological processes, the frequent co-occurrence of different forms of challenging behaviours and the importance of the contextual control of behavioural *relationships* should all serve to guard us against such naïveté.

In the sections below, the studies which highlight the need for such cautions will be reviewed. In addition, evidence relating to the possible interface between behavioural and neurobiological models will be discussed.

Causal and maintaining factors may be dissimilar across individuals

The evidence which was reviewed earlier in this chapter suggests that challenging behaviours may be maintained by:

☐ positive reinforcement involving the presentation of attention from carers (e.g. Derby et al., 1992; Iwata et al., 1982; Iwata et al., 1994b; Lovaas & Simmons, 1969; Mace et al., 1986; Paisey et al., 1991) or material reinforcers such as food (e.g. Durand & Crimmins, 1988);

☐ negative reinforcement involving escape from the attention or presence of carers (Emerson, 1990), the demands of carers (Carr *et al.*, 1976; Carr, Newsom & Binkoff, 1980; Derby *et al.*, 1992; Iwata *et al.*, 1982; Iwata *et al.*, 1994*a, b*; Mace *et al.*, 1986; Paisey *et al.*, 1991), ambient noise (Iwata *et al.*, 1994*b*) and medical examinations (Iwata *et al.*, 1990*a*);

☐ automatic positive reinforcement resulting from perceptual feedback from the behaviour itself (Lovaas *et al.*, 1987; Vollmer, 1994) or the mood altering effects of β-endorphin release (Sandman, 1990/1991);

☐ automatic negative reinforcement involving the attenuation of states of overarousal (e.g. Duker & Rasing, 1989; Emerson *et al.*, in press*c*) or pain reduction (e.g. Carr & McDowell, 1980; Romanczyk *et al.*, 1992).

In addition, the challenging behaviour shown by some individuals may result primarily from disturbances in neurotransmitter systems (e.g. Nyhan, 1994).

Maintaining factors may vary over time

It is important when considering the development of challenging behaviour to distinguish between causal and maintaining factors. Those factors which lead to the initial emergence of challenging behaviour may be very different from those which, at later points in time, are responsible for its maintenance. While the behavioural model may provide a convincing account of the processes shaping and maintaining challenging behaviour, it is less convincing when attempting to account for how it initially emerges.

Indeed, very little is known regarding the early development of challenging behaviour in people with severe learning disabilities. The following accounts are, therefore, primarily speculative. To understand the emergence of challenging behaviour it is probably important to address the natural occurrence during development of repetitive, potentially injurious or minor aggressive/tantrum behaviours in the specific developmental context provided by learning disabilities (Guess & Carr, 1991; MacLean, Stone & Brown, 1994; Tröster, 1994).

In both non-disabled children and children with learning disabilities, repetitive movements commonly occur at transition points in motor development. Thus, for example, rocking on hands and knees occurs prior to the onset of crawling. A number of studies have also indicated that head banging occurs in up to 20% of non-disabled children between the age of 5 and 17 months (e.g. de Lissovoy, 1962; Werry, Carlielle & Fitzpatrick, 1983), possibly in response to ear infections or teething (de Lissovoy, 1963).

As most parents will know, tantrums, aggression and property destruction are extremely common in non-disabled children, reaching a peak at two to three years of age. They then gradually diminish in both severity and frequency, probably as a combined result of the punishment of these behaviours, the development of verbal self-regulation and because the child learns alternative ways of solving life's problems.

The specific developmental context provided by having a learning disability may be important in a number of ways.

☐ Children with severe learning disabilities may, as a result of their slower pace of development, exhibit behaviour which is developmentally appropriate, but inappropriate to their chronological age. They may also exhibit such behaviours for a longer period of time (MacLean *et al.*, 1994).

☐ Specific impairments associated with the child's severe learning disability (e.g. specific sensory impairments, language delay, physical disabilities) may result in the child having an additionally restricted behavioural repertoire. As such, they may have greater difficulty in developing alternative ways of responding to challenging situations.

☐ Specific neurological abnormalities associated with learning disabilities (e.g. destruction of dopamine pathways in Lesch–Nyhan syndrome) increase an individual's vulnerability to developing particular behaviours (e.g. self-biting). Similarly, specific disorders which are more common among people with learning disabilities (e.g. feeding difficulties, autism) may be associated with difficulties in establishing bonding with carers and an increased risk of experiencing common events (e.g. eating, interactions with carers) as stressful and/or aversive.

☐ The social consequences of having a learning disability may result in reduced opportunities for learning appropriate adaptive behaviours and may put the child at greater risk of experiencing some adverse life events. These may, again, help establish common events as stressful or aversive.

The above discussion illustrates the potential for minor challenging behaviours, whose expression is part of the normal process of development, to occur more commonly, with a greater severity and for a longer period of time, among children with learning disabilities. This, in itself, provides greater opportunity for alternative maintaining mechanisms to come into play. Thus, for example, the 'comforting' reaction of carers to stress-induced tantrums may, over time, come to play an important role in maintaining the behaviour. That is, behaviours which emerge as part of a normal developmental process may, at a later stage, come to be maintained by operant processes (Guess & Carr, 1991). The reciprocal nature of these processes (Hastings & Remington, 1994*b*; Oliver, 1993; Taylor & Carr, 1993, 1994) may then, through a process of shaping, act to select more extreme, abnormal and severe variants of the initial behaviour.

It is also possible that the nature of the maintaining operant processes may vary over time. Carr and McDowell (1980), for example, describe the treatment of self-injurious scratching shown by a non-disabled 10 year-old boy. While first arising in response to contact dermatitis, the scratching was apparently maintained by positive social attention at the time of referral. More recently, Lerman and her colleagues examined the possibility that transfer of behavioural function may have been responsible for treatment relapse in four people with self-injurious behaviour (Lerman et al., 1994). Re-analysis of behavioural function following relapse was rather inconclusive but suggested that, for two people, self-injury had acquired an additional function (positive reinforcement in addition to negative reinforcement; automatic reinforcement in addition to negative reinforcement), while for another it had acquired an alternative function (automatic reinforcement rather than positive social reinforcement).

For self-injurious behaviour, the importance of this operant process may, at a later point in time, be replaced in whole or in part by automatic reinforcement through the contingent release of β-endorphin. That is, as the self-injury becomes more severe it is more likely to lead to the release of β-endorphin which, over time, may result in physical dependency. Thus, during the course of a person's self-injury that 'same' behaviour may be maintained by a variety of different process, all of which may be functionally unrelated to the original cause(s) of the behaviour.

Causal and maintaining factors may vary across different forms of challenging behaviour shown by the same individual

As has been discussed, the behavioural approach is interested primarily in the relationship between response classes and environmental events rather than in the topographical form of the behaviour itself. It does not assume that similar topographies serve similar functions. This is an important point given the common co-occurrence of different forms of challenging behaviour (see Chapter 3). Unfortunately, much applied research has implicitly made the assumption that similar forms of behaviour are likely to serve similar functions. Thus, for example, many studies have investigated the relationship between environmental events and broad classes of self-injurious, aggressive or disruptive behaviour. A few studies, however, have examined the relationships between different forms of challenging behaviour shown by individuals.

Emerson, Thompson, Reeves et al. (in pressb) and Emerson, Reeves et al. (in pressa), for example, provided descriptive and experimental analysis of multiple forms of challenging behaviour shown by five children and one young adult with severe learning disabilities. Their results indicated the existence of distinct response classes *within* the various forms of challenging behaviour shown by some of the participants. Thus, Susan (Figs. 4.3 and 4.4) showed three forms of self-injurious behaviour (hair pulling, back poking and ear poking) which appeared to be maintained by a process of negative reinforcement involving escape from teacher demands, and two forms of self-injury (fist-to-cheek hitting and body digging) which appeared to be maintained by a process of automatic reinforcement. As can be seen in Fig. 4.7, during the presentation of demands, fist-to-cheek hitting and body digging were suppressed while hair pulling, back poking and ear poking exhibited similar patterns of response acceleration as the duration of the episode of demands increased.

Derby *et al.* (1994) used extended and brief experimental analyses to identify aspects of the contextual control of multiple forms of challenging behaviour shown by four people with learning disabilities. They presented results which indicated that apparently random responding across experimental conditions was attributable to adding together the results relating to different behaviours shown by the person which served different behavioural functions (see also Day *et al.*, 1988; Mace *et al.*, 1986; Slifer *et al.*, 1986; Sprague & Horner, 1992; Sturmey *et al.*, 1988).

Maintaining factors may vary across contexts

If maintaining factors can vary over time, it is also likely that they can vary across contexts. That is, not only may the presence or absence of a functional relationship be contextually controlled (cf. Carr *et al.*, 1976; Kennedy & Itkonen, 1993), the form of the functional relationship may be sensitive to environmental establishing operations (Michael, 1982) or conditional stimuli (Sidman, 1986).

This is illustrated by the self-injurious body digging shown by Susan (Fig. 4.7). More detailed analysis indicated that the function of this particular form of self-injury was dependent on context (Emerson *et al.*, in press*a*). Figure 4.8 presents an analysis of the relationship between episodes of demand and her body digging in the classroom and the residential area. As can be seen, while in the classroom, demands suppressed her body digging (which occurred at its highest rate while alone), in the residential area demands appeared to elicit her back poking (which occurred at chance levels whilst alone). Thus, it would appear that, for Susan's body digging, membership of a response class was contextually determined; in the classroom body digging being one topographical variant of the cluster of automatically reinforced self-injurious behaviours, while in the residential area it formed one topographical variant of the cluster of her negatively reinforced self-injurious behaviours.

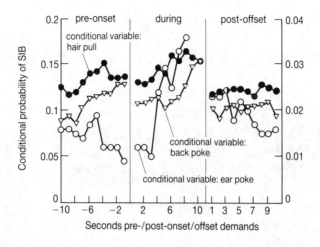

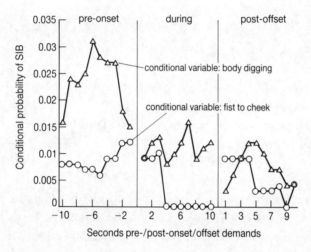

Fig. 4.7. The conditional probability of Susan's self-injurious ear poking, back poking, hair pulling, fist-to-cheek hitting and body digging prior to, during and following, teacher demands.

Similarly, Romanczyk *et al.* (1992) described a case in which severe self-injury appeared to either increase or decrease levels of arousal dependent on the context in which the behaviour occurred. The importance of evaluating the clustering or organisation of behaviours is provided by Bodfish (1990). He employed a 30-second partial interval system to record the behaviours of 15 institutionalised residents with severe learning disabilities and a series of ecological variables in two settings: a special education classroom during group teaching and the unit's day room during a free-time period. The resulting data suggested that, for a subgroup of five residents who showed high rates of stereotypy, negative covariation between stereotypy

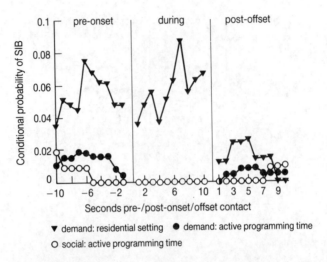

Fig. 4.8. The conditional probability of Susan's self-injurious body digging prior to, during and following, teacher demands in the classroom and residential area.

and the variables of task engagement, social interaction and eye-contact were *only* apparent in the classroom context. For another subgroup of five residents, who showed high rates of self-injury, no evidence of response covariation was apparent in the classroom but self-injury was significantly negatively correlated with engagement and positively correlated with social interaction in the day-room.

Finally, Haring and Kennedy (1990) demonstrated that the effectiveness of two approaches to intervention (differential reinforcement of other behaviours and time-out) varied across contexts. They demonstrated that the differential reinforcement procedure was effective in reducing stereotypy for two students in the context of academic instruction but ineffective in a leisure context. Conversely, they demonstrated that, while a time-out procedure was ineffective during academic instruction, it was effective in a leisure context. While clearly demonstrating the contextual control of intervention efficacy, these results also suggest that the differential efficacy may be related to the stereotypy serving different functions across settings (see also Carr & Durand, 1985*a*).

Causal and maintaining factors may be complex

Finally, it is possible that operant behaviours may be under multiple control (Skinner, 1953). That is, they may be controlled by more than one reinforcement contingency. Day *et al.* (1994), for example, demonstrated that the challenging behaviours (aggression or self-injury) of three people with severe learning disabilities were maintained by contingencies of negative reinforcement (escape from difficult tasks) *and* positive reinforcement (access to preferred materials, e.g. food, coffee, a necklace). Similarly, Smith *et al.* (1993*a*) identified the multiple control of self-injurious behaviour shown by two people with severe learning disabilities. Automatic reinforcement and positive social reinforcement were shown to be maintaining the self-injurious behaviour shown by a 19 year-old non-ambulatory man, while automatic reinforcement and negative reinforcement (involving escape from social demands), were shown to underlie the self-injury shown by a 37 year-old woman with Down's syndrome.

As we have suggested above, it is also possible that self-injurious behaviour may be multiply controlled by external (operant) processes and automatic reinforcement involving the release of β-endorphin (Oliver, 1993). This, in itself, may involve components of both positive (automatic) reinforcement arising from the euphoric mood state induced by opioid release and negative (automatic) reinforcement arising from the analgesic and antinociceptive properties of β-endorphin. Indeed, the face validity of such a suggestion is quite strong in that it would possibly lower the response cost of self-injury (i.e. pain) to the extent that it could be more easily selected as an operant behaviour. The possibility of multiple control by operant and neurobiological processes is also indicated by evidence of the effectiveness of behavioural approaches in partially reducing the self-injurious biting in people with Lesch- Nyhan syndrome (Grace, Cowart & Matson, 1988; Hile & Vatterott, 1991).

Summary

In this chapter some of the behavioural and neurobiological evidence which is currently available regarding the aetiology and maintenance of challenging behaviours shown by people with severe learning disabilities has been reviewed. There can be no doubt that behavioural (operant) processes are important in the maintenance of many examples of such behaviours. It is also clear, however, that this is not the sole explanation. Challenging behaviour is a complex phenomenon. Neurobiological factors are clearly implicated in some examples of challenging behaviour and it seems plausible to suggest that a fuller understanding of challenging behaviour will be provided by more comprehensive bio-behavioural models which address the interface between developmental, operant, neurobiological and ecological processes (e.g. Guess & Carr, 1991; Murphy, 1994; Oliver, 1993).

The complexity of the issues is also apparent within behavioural and neurobiological models. Behavioural accounts need to attend to issues arising from the multiple and contextual control of different forms of challenging behaviour, and the interaction of these behaviours with other components of the person's behavioural repertoire. They also need to consider the role played by respondent and induced behaviours (Emerson & Howard, 1992; Romanczyk *et al.*, 1992). Similarly, neurobiological models may also need to take into account complex interactions *between* neurotransmitter systems.

5 THE BASES OF INTERVENTION

In this chapter some of the characteristics of approaches to intervention will be discussed. It will be argued that, wherever possible, interventions, whether behavioural, psychopharmacological or based on alternative approaches, should be constructional, functionally based and socially valid.

THE CONSTRUCTIONAL APPROACH

Israel Goldiamond, in one of the classic contributions to the development of applied behaviour analysis, identified two broad orientations which characterise most approaches to intervention (Goldiamond, 1974; see also Cullen, Hattersley & Tennant, 1981). First, he identified a *pathological* approach which focuses on the elimination of behaviours (e.g. self-injury) or states (e.g. anxiety, distress). As Goldiamond points out

such approaches often consider the problem in terms of a pathology which, regardless of how it was established, or developed, or is maintained, is to be eliminated (Goldiamond, 1974, p.14).

He contrasted this with what he termed a *constructional* approach,

an orientation 'whose solution to problems is the construction of repertoires (or their reinstatement or transfer to new situations) rather than the elimination of repertoires' (Goldiamond, 1974, p.14)

To give a practical example, a pathological approach to the aggressive behaviour shown by a young man with severe learning disabilities under conditions of stress would pose the question: how can we stop him being aggressive? A constructional approach would formulate the problem in terms of: what do we want him to do in such situations in the future? As can be seen, while the pathological approach is concerned with the *elimination* of aggression, the constructional approach is concerned with the *establishment* of more appropriate ways of acting in the situations which evoke aggression.

There may, of course, be situations in which it is easier and simpler to adopt a pathological rather than a constructional approach. Consider, for example, the case in which challenging behaviour only occurs in response to a particular easily identifiable situation which is not itself particularly important for the person's health, development or quality of life (e.g. travelling to school by a particular route, Kennedy & Itkonen, 1993). One approach to such a situation would be simply to avoid the eliciting stimuli. While not constructional, this may be the least intrusive and most effective option. It is likely, however, that such situations are relatively rare and that pathological approaches as defined by Goldiamond should be considered the exception rather than the rule.

Cullen *et al.* (1981) identify three reasons for adopting a constructional approach. First, and as Goldiamond (1974) argued at length, constructional interventions may be more consistent with notions of basic human rights. This is perhaps best illustrated by the tendency for criticisms of behavioural approaches to focus on the questionable ethical value of eliminative procedures (e.g. Repp & Singh, 1990; Winnet & Winkler, 1972; Zangwill, 1980). It would certainly appear to offer some kind of safeguard against the more excessive examples of the abuse of therapeutic power which can occur when such procedures are applied to very vulnerable populations.

Secondly, the majority of basic and applied behavioural research concerns the establishment of new behaviours or repertoires (cf. Bailey *et al.*, 1987; Iversen & Lattal, 1991*a*, 1991*b*; Remington, 1991*b*). Indeed, the particular strength of the behavioural approach – and its greatest contribution to the field of learning disabilities – is its store of knowledge concerning the establishment, maintenance and generalisation of behaviour. This, in effect, provides a very strong foundation for constructionally based interventions.

Finally, a successful pathological intervention *must* involve a constructional component. If a particular behaviour is eliminated, new behaviour(s) will take their place. Behaviour is a dynamic process and (like nature) abhors a vacuum. On the face of it, a pathological orientation leaves this aspect of the intervention process to chance. A constructional intervention addresses it directly. Some of the potential benefits of doing so are demonstrated by Sprague and Horner (1992). They examined the effects of a pathological intervention and a constructional intervention on the aggression and tantrums shown by Alan, a 15 year-old boy with learning disabilities. Assessment had indicated that his aggression and tantrums were maintained by a process of negative reinforcement, in that they elicited teacher help when presented with a difficult task. Each intervention was applied in sequence to only one of Alan's challenging behaviours, his hitting out. While the pathological intervention (verbal reprimands and response blocking) markedly reduced his hitting out, other problem behaviours (head and body shaking, screaming, hitting objects and putting his hands to his face) all increased so that, overall, there was no change in the total rate of challenging behaviours. The constructional intervention (prompting Alan to ask for help in response to difficult tasks) eliminated all problem behaviours, a result which was maintained after two months. Given the very real risks of response covariation or 'symptom substitution' in response to intervention (Schroeder & MacLean, 1987), an approach which centres upon the introduction of alternative behaviours would appear to have much to offer.

THE FUNCTIONAL PERSPECTIVE

Perhaps the single most significant development in behavioural practice in relation to learning disabilities during the 1980s was the widespread application of a *functional perspective* to analysis and intervention (Axelrod, 1987*a*, *b*; Carr, Robinson & Palumbo, 1990*a*; Mace & Roberts, 1993; Mace, Lalli & Lalli, 1991; Mace *et al.*, 1992). This perspective is based on a belief that *the selection or design of approaches to intervention should reflect knowledge of the causal and maintaining factors underlying the person's challenging behaviour.*

Such a belief is, of course, axiomatic to medical practice. If we are interested in moving beyond symptomatic relief, diagnosis must precede treatment. Indeed, a similar concern with analysis providing the foundation for intervention was evident in the earlier days of applied behaviour analysis. In the intervening period, however, 'behaviour modification' took precedence. As Mace and Roberts point out, this approach

> *relied largely on [the use of] potent reinforcers or punishers to override the reinforcement contingencies or biologic (sic) processes that maintained problem behavior. The treatments were effective, but they were often artificial, conspicuous, difficult to implement for long periods of time, and deemed unacceptable by some caregivers.* (Mace & Roberts, 1993, p. 113).

They were also primarily pathological in orientation.

The significance of adopting a functional approach can be illustrated simply by considering the use of time-out procedures. The logic of such procedures is that, by arranging the person's environment to ensure that occurrence of challenging behaviour reliably results in reduced *opportunity* for reinforcement, the challenging behaviour should become less frequent over time and eventually disappear. Indeed, this is the most likely outcome if time-out were applied to a challenging behaviour maintained by positive reinforcement, for example contingent adult attention. In such a case, the time-out procedure would effectively combine extinction (preventing access to adult attention) with a temporary reduction in the background rate of reinforcement; but what would happen if the person's challenging behaviour was maintained by negative reinforcement, e.g. escape from aversive tasks or unwanted attention? In this case, application of a typical 'time-out' procedure would *guarantee* that each episode of the challenging behaviour was (negatively) reinforced by the contingent removal of aversive materials and/or attention (e.g. teacher demands). At best such an intervention would be ineffective, at worst it could lead to a significant strengthening of the behaviour (cf. Durand *et al.*, 1989; Solnick, Rincover & Peterson, 1977).

Certain approaches to intervention, including much of the emerging 'non-aversive' technology of behavioural support, are dependent for their success on an accurate knowledge of maintaining factors. Such approaches include extinction, time out and functional communication training. Those approaches, which can be applied in the absence of knowledge of underlying processes, tend to be either relatively ineffective (e.g. many differential reinforcement procedures: Lancioni & Hoogeveen, 1990; O'Brien & Repp, 1990), or procedurally unacceptable in many situations (e.g. punishment). Indeed, one of the potential benefits of adopting a functional approach is that it may lead to a reduced reliance on such intrusive methods (Axelrod, 1987*a*, *b*; Carr, Robinson & Palumbo, 1990*a*).

The discussion in the last chapter regarding the potential complexity of underlying mechanisms indicates that the adoption of a functional approach may be demanding in that:

☐ there is no clear link between the topography and function of challenging behaviour. Indeed, very similar topographies shown by the same person may serve different behavioural functions (Emerson *et al.*, in press*a*);

☐ the maintaining factors underlying a person's challenging behaviour may vary over time (Lerman *et al.*, 1994) and across contexts (Emerson *et al.*, in press*a*; Haring & Kennedy, 1990);

☐ challenging behaviours may be multiply controlled by different contingencies of reinforcement (Day *et al.*, 1994; Smith *et al.*, 1993*a*) and may reflect a combination of biological and behavioural processes (cf. Oliver, 1993).

The viability of this approach, therefore, lies in the availability of reliable, valid and user-friendly approaches to assessment. This issue will be discussed again in the next chapter. As Romanczyk and his colleagues point out, however, a

focus upon the individual's characteristics that set the person apart with respect to unique abilities, learning history, biological status, physiological response patterns, reaction to stimuli and events, and speed and capacity for change must take precedence over focus upon specific treatment approaches, techniques or ideologies (Romanczyk *et al.*, 1992, p.117).

SOCIAL VALIDITY

In Chapter 2 the notion of social validity was introduced. An intervention which is socially valid should (a) address a socially significant problem, (b) be undertaken in a manner which is acceptable to the main constituencies involved and (c) result in socially important outcomes or effects. In that chapter some time was spent discussing the social significance of challenging behaviours and approaches to measuring 'meaningful outcomes' of intervention (Evans & Meyer, 1985; Meyer & Evans, 1993*a*; Meyer & Janney, 1989). We will return to the latter topic in the next chapter.

The remaining component of social validity – the acceptability of behavioural procedures – has generated much controversy over recent years. Indeed, many thousands of words have been written on the acceptability (or not) of using 'aversive' or 'intrusive' procedures to reduce challenging behaviour (e.g. G. Allen Roeher Institute, 1988; Griffith, 1989; Guess *et al.*, 1987; Horner *et al.*, 1990*a, b*; LaVigna & Donnellan, 1986; McGee *et al.*, 1987; Mulick, 1990; O'Brien, 1991; Repp & Singh, 1990; Schroeder & Schroeder, 1989; Van Houten *et al.*, 1988).

In a highly influential position statement made by The Association for Persons with Severe Handicaps in 1982, intrusive interventions were defined as:

any treatment option which exhibits some or all of the following characteristics: (1) obvious signs of physical pain experienced by the individual; (2) potential or actual side effects such as tissue damage, physical illness, severe physical or emotional stress, and/or death that would properly require the involvement of medical personnel; (3) dehumanization of persons with severe handicaps because the procedures are normally unacceptable for persons who do not have handicaps in community environments; (4) extreme ambivalence and discomfort by family, staff, and/or caregivers regarding the necessity of such extreme strategies or their own involvement in such interventions; and (5) obvious repulsion and/or stress felt by peers who do not have handicaps and community members who cannot reconcile extreme procedures with acceptable standard practice' (Resolution on the Cessation of Intrusive Interventions, The Association for Persons with Severe Handicaps, 1982).

Opinions expressed concerning this issue have ranged from suggestions that the use of such procedures may be the most ethically appropriate course of action in certain situations (Van Houten *et al.*, 1988), to calls for a blanket condemnation of the use of intrusive interventions (G. Allen Roeher Institute, 1988). This debate has recently culminated in a number of organisations sponsoring a 'call to action' to Amnesty International to investigate the use of such procedures as a form of torture (Weiss, 1992).

Given such an extensive coverage elsewhere, the next section will focus upon summarising some of the main points of this contentious issue with regard to the use of intrusive procedures within applied behaviour analysis, and the ethics of intervention.

The use of intrusive procedures in applied behaviour analysis

One unfortunate outcome of the controversy over the use of intrusive procedures has been the implicit (or at times explicit) assumption that the use of intrusive procedures is in some way inherent to behavioural theory and practice. Evans and Meyer (1990), for example, suggest that the 'narrow' and 'rigid' approach of applied behaviour analysis is characterised by 'the use, refinement, and fascination with procedures for delivering aversives to people with disabilities' (p. 135). On the face of it, such a statement clearly fails to reflect the diverse activities of applied behaviour analysis as they have been applied to supporting people with learning disabilities (cf. Bailey *et al.*, 1987; Matson, 1990; Remington, 1991b).

In other ways, however, it is easy to see how such an apparent association may have come about. As was noted in Chapter 2, a number of accounts have been published of what can only be considered as unnecessarily degrading behavioural practice (e.g. Altmeyer *et al.*, 1985; Conway & Butcher, 1974; Freagon, 1990; G. Allan Roeher Institute, 1988). Less sensationally, perhaps, the behavioural community has taken a lead in supporting the individual's right to effective treatment in sometimes contentious situations (Etzel *et al.*, 1987). Some leading behaviour analysts have also played a very visible role in contributing to the continued development of punitive procedures or 'default technologies' (e.g. Iwata, 1988; Linscheid *et al.*, 1990). Finally, reviews of the behavioural literature do indicate a major reliance in research upon punitive procedures focusing upon the reduction of challenging behaviour (cf. Gorman-Smith & Matson, 1985; LaGrow & Repp, 1984; Lennox *et al.*, 1988; Lundervold & Bourland, 1988; Matson & Taras, 1989; Schlosser & Goetze, 1992; Scotti *et al.*, 1991a). These factors have undoubtedly contributed to the public perception of applied behaviour analysis as an essentially repressive, if not abusive, approach.

However, the actual prevalence of the use of intrusive behavioural procedures is unclear. The available evidence suggests that, in both North America and the UK, the majority of individuals with challenging behaviours fail to receive any formal behavioural treatment (Altmeyer *et al.*, 1987; Griffin *et* al., 1986b, 1987; Oliver et al., 1987; Qureshi, 1994; although see also Jacobsen, 1992). The few studies which have investigated the types of behavioural programmes implemented within services have, however, indicated that approximately two thirds of programmes include restrictive or aversive components (Altmeyer et al., 1987; Griffin et al., 1987). Furthermore, 36% of the 91 behaviourally orientated services for people with autism sampled in the USA by Harris et al. (1991) reported the use of 'strong' aversives including 'slap, pinch, electric shock, noxious odour, noxious liquid and hair pull' (p.19).

The reliance of behaviour analysts on intrusive procedures needs to be understood in terms of the dominance in the 1970s of 'behaviour modification' as well as the social situation of people with severe learning disabilities.

As we have seen, the discipline of behaviour modification paid little attention to analysis of the factors underlying challenging behaviour. Instead, it developed a set of procedures based upon overriding the behaviour maintaining contingencies with powerful new 'bolt-on' contingencies. In general, the use of positive reinforcement to encourage competing behaviours proved insufficient to bring about socially significant changes in severe challenging behaviour (cf. Lancioni & Hoogeveen, 1990; O'Brien & Repp, 1990). Not surprisingly, therefore, given the strength of the contingencies responsible for the persistence of challenging behaviour, many of these 'bolt-on' contingencies were punitive in nature, their use being justified in terms of their apparent necessity.

The use of punishment procedures also needs to be understood in the context of the social status of people with severe learning disabilities. As we have seen in Chapter 2, people who show challenging behaviour are at risk of socially sanctioned exclusion, neglect and systematic abuse. It is not perhaps surprising then, that technologies for the control of challenging behaviour, including applied behaviour analysis and psychopharmacological interventions, have been misapplied in ways which reflect the extremely low social status of their recipients (cf. Emerson & McGill, 1989; McGill & Emerson, 1992).

The association between behavioural techniques and intrusive procedures is in some ways rather ironic since behavioural theorists have, in general, been forceful advocates of the use of procedures based upon positive reinforcement rather than punishment in many areas of human affairs (e.g. Sidman, 1989; Skinner, 1971). As Skinner himself pointed out:

to remain satisfied with punishment without exploring nonpunitive alternatives is the real mistake ... I have been proud of the success we have had in finding many alternatives to punishment and I regret that this controversy is likely to renew the view that behaviorism means punishment. It is, I believe, the only hope for the eventual elimination of punitive control in all fields (Griffin et al., 1988, p.105).

As was noted above, the adoption of constructional and functionally based approaches may significantly reduce the historical reliance of behavioural procedures on more intrusive interventions.

Intrusive procedures and the ethics of intervention

A number of stances have been taken by contributors to the 'aversives' debate with regard to the moral or ethical acceptability of intrusive procedures.

These have ranged from what appears to be the blanket condemnation of the use of any such procedure (e.g. Endicott, 1988; Ewen, 1988; Freagon, 1990; O'Brien, 1991) to arguments that, under certain circumstances, the costs to the person and others in terms of distress experienced may be justified, given the likely benefits of intervention when compared with either no intervention or currently available alternatives (e.g. Van Houten *et al.*, 1988).

It is important to note that in all cases the conclusions reached reflect a set of beliefs regarding the actual or likely effects of intrusive procedures. Thus, for example, Endicott (1988), states that the use of any form of aversive procedure 'is unacceptable because it undercuts the factor that is most likely to lead to permanent freedom from serious destructive behaviour, namely bonding based on affection and trust between one human being and another' (p. 100). The central issue of the debate, therefore, is one of defining the conditions under which a set of procedures, of a given level of intrusiveness and with certain predictable outcomes, may be justified.

This is of central importance to the issue of social validity, since concerns about procedural acceptability may, at times, need to be balanced against the social significance of the outcomes of intervention. This is more than an academic argument as meta-analyses of the behavioural literature in the area do suggest that intrusive interventions are more effective in suppressing challenging behaviour both initially and at follow-up (Scotti *et al.*, 1991*b*).

Meinhold and Mulick (1990) have made a useful contribution to the debate by drawing on the literature of 'comparative risk assessment' in decision-making with regard to such potentially dangerous technologies as nuclear power. This approach involves careful consideration of the risks, costs and benefits of the alternative courses of action which are open to us when confronted by a difficult social problem. The stages involved in this process are:

☐ identifying the problem;

☐ conducting a feasibility assessment of potential solutions;

☐ assessing the risks, costs and benefits of potential solutions and of inaction;

☐ making a decision.

Some of the issues involved in these four stages will be briefly discussed below.

Identifying the problem

As was indicated in Chapter 2, the problem or social significance of challenging behaviour needs to be conceptualised broadly. It involves significant social costs and financial costs to the persons themselves, to carers and to other family members, co-residents and co-workers, care staff and agencies responsible for the purchase and provision of health and welfare services.

Feasibility assessment of potential solutions

Potential solutions to the problem must satisfy two criteria. First, they must be technically feasible. That is, it must be possible to design a solution using a particular approach based on knowledge concerning the causes of the problem. Thus, for example, it is not technically feasible to replace self-injurious behaviour maintained by β-endorphin release with an alternative communicative response (communicative responses do not lead to β-endorphin release). Similarly, visual screening would not be feasible for someone who had no vision.

Secondly, potential solutions must be practically feasible. That is, the human and other resources necessary for the successful implementation of the approach need to be identified and compared with what is actually available. Advocating solutions which are not feasible in a given context is equivalent to advocating inaction.

Assessing risks, costs and benefits

Identifying the nature of the problem indicates the areas in which the risks, costs and benefits of potential solutions need to be evaluated. Figure 5.1 (adapted from Meinhold & Mulick, 1990) illustrates the application of this approach to the selection of interventions to reduce challenging behaviour.

Unfortunately, much of the information which is required in such an analysis is not available. Thus, while much is known about the short-term effects of intervention on the targeted behaviour, little is known regarding such issues as:

☐ the generalisation and long-term maintenance of reductions in challenging behaviour achieved through *either* aversive, mixed or non-aversive procedures (cf. Carr *et al.*, 1990*b*; Cataldo, 1991; Scotti *et al.*, 1991*b*);

☐ positive or negative changes in collateral behaviours in response to either aversive *or* non-aversive interventions. Existing data do indicate, however, that both aversive *and* non-aversive procedures can result in undesirable side-effects (e.g. Balsam & Bondy, 1983; Emerson & Howard, 1992), but that for *both approaches* these tend to be outweighed by desirable side-effects (Carr & Lovaas, 1983; Linscheid, 1992; Matson & Taras, 1989; Newsom *et al.*, 1983);

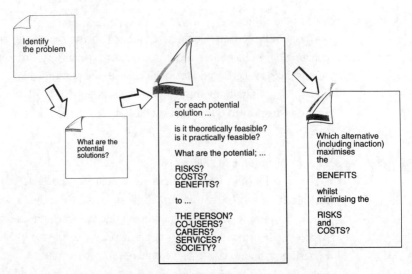

Identify
the problem

What are the
potential
solutions?

For each potential
solution ...

is it theoretically feasible?
is it practically feasible?

What are the potential; ...

RISKS?
COSTS?
BENEFITS?

to ...

THE PERSON?
CO-USERS?
CARERS?
SERVICES?
SOCIETY?

Which alternative
(including inaction)
maximises
the

BENEFITS

whilst
minimising the

RISKS
and
COSTS?

Fig. 5.1. Evaluating the risks, costs and benefits of intervention.

☐ the impact of either aversive or non-aversive strategies upon the social
ecology of service settings. The available evidence suggests a far from
clear-cut picture. For example, the reported associations between the use
of non-aversive programming and increased use of mechanical restraint
(Altmeyer *et al.*, 1987), and increased staff stress (Harris *et al.*, 1991)
clearly warrant further investigation;

☐ the impact of the use of aversive procedures upon the social status of
members of such a disadvantaged group. There are, however, strong
conceptual reasons (e.g. Wolfensberger & Thomas, 1983) for suggesting
that such issues need to be taken considerably more seriously than at
present (Emerson & McGill, 1989; McGill & Emerson, 1992).

Not surprisingly, given the emotive nature of the debate, considerable
differences have emerged between participants in the interpretation of the
evidence which does exist (e.g. Axelrod, 1990; Donnellan & LaVigna, 1990;
LaVigna & Donnellan, 1986; Mulick, 1990). To characterise intervention
procedures in terms of their aversiveness is, of course, highly problematic,
especially since such attempts have been confounded by confusion between
the concept of aversiveness and technical and lay definitions of punishment
(Mulick, 1990).

From a behavioural perspective, of course, stimuli are neither intrinsically
reinforcing nor aversive. Stimuli act as punishers or reinforcers dependent
upon such factors as prior experience, current levels of deprivation or
satiation or the nature of the individual's access to an activity in relation to free
operant baselines (Konarski *et al.*, 1981). Indeed, procedures reliant upon

positive reinforcement are only effective in so far as the individual is concurrently deprived of free access to the reinforcing stimuli. The planned or unplanned establishment of deprivational conditions could, of course, be considered an aversive procedure in its own right (Remington, 1991a).

Thus, stimuli which common consensus may regard as aversive, e.g. being mechanically restrained, do, for some individuals, act as powerful reinforcers (e.g. Favell et al., 1981). This is of some importance given the tendency to categorise *procedures* as intrusive or aversive, independently of the context in which they are applied. For example, some nominally non-aversive procedures may involve components which some individuals with challenging behaviours may find distressing. Procedures involving sustained social interaction, such as Gentle Teaching (eg. McGee et al., 1987, McGee & Gonzalez, 1990), may be aversive to people with autism. Paisey, Whitney and Moore (1989), for example, in a comparison of Gentle Teaching (McGee et al., 1987), Graduated Guidance (Foxx & Azrin, 1972) and differential reinforcement of incompatible behaviour (DRI) plus Response Interruption (Azrin et al., 1988) reported higher levels of both self-injury and collateral 'distress' behaviours for one of their two clients during Gentle Teaching than in other sessions. Indeed, it is plausible to suggest that, for individuals who find social interaction aversive, procedures such as Gentle Teaching may primarily involve the use of negative reinforcement to increase compliance and reduce challenging behaviours. That is, task compliance and the absence of challenging behaviour may be reinforced by the avoidance of aversive stimulation (trainer contact). That pro-social behaviours, or 'bonding', directed toward the trainer should occur under such conditions would not be surprising given the evidence that such behaviours do occur in response to punitive procedures (Carr & Lovaas, 1983; Newsom et al., 1983). For some, 'Gentle' Teaching may not be very gentle at all (cf. Mudford, 1985).

These observations suggest that the aversiveness of procedures, including more 'humanistic' procedures such as psychotherapy or the 'creative therapies', can only be considered in the context of their actual implementation. That is, the aversiveness of a procedure is a product of the interaction between the individual, the context of intervention, and the intervention process.

Decision making

The final stage in the process of comparative risk assessment involves the weighing up of the risks, costs and benefits of the potential courses of action and the 'default' option of inaction. Obviously, this will be a complex process with different stakeholders in the intervention process placing different weights on the importance of the various possible outcomes. Normally, of course, the persons themselves would play a major role in this process by

giving consent to a treatment selected out of a range of proffered options. Situations in which the user of services is defined as legally incompetent raise some complex problems regarding issues of consent. Interestingly, these have been infrequently discussed in the context of the aversives debate (Kiernan, 1991; Murphy, 1993).

6 APPROACHES TO ASSESSMENT

In this chapter a number of issues will be discussed which concern the assessment of challenging behaviours shown by people with severe learning disabilities. In the light of the discussions in the previous chapter, it is clear that a comprehensive approach to assessment will need to address a number of factors.

First, the adoption of a *functional perspective* indicates that a key task of assessment will be to identify the behavioural (and other) processes responsible for maintaining the person's challenging behaviours; this general process will be referred to as *functional assessment.* Secondly, the adoption of a *constructional approach* indicates that attention will need to be paid to assessing aspects of the individual's existing behavioural repertoire and to identifying potential reinforcers which may be employed in establishing new behaviours. Finally, the requirement that interventions be *socially valid* indicates the need to evaluate aspects of the risks, costs and benefits of the intervention process.

FUNCTIONAL ASSESSMENT

Table 6.1 summarises the main aims of a functionally based approach to assessment. Following Lalli and Goh (1993), a distinction has been made between primary and secondary objectives. In the sections below, attention will be focused on the extent to which various techniques can meet the primary objectives of a functional assessment. In particular, discussion will address the extent to which different approaches themselves can be thought of as providing a 'believable demonstration' of either the operation of underlying processes or the stimulus or contextual control of challenging behaviour.

The process of conducting a functional assessment may be conceptualised as comprising four interlinked processes.

☐ The selection and definition of challenging behaviours as potential targets for intervention.

Table 6.1. *Primary and secondary objectives of functional assessment*

Primary objective: to determine the processes underlying the individual's challenging behaviour

Identify the contingencies maintaining the challenging behaviour

Identify the reinforcers involved in the maintenance of the challenging behaviour

Identify the discriminative stimuli and establishing operations or setting events which set the occasion for the challenging behaviour to occur

Identify common membership of response classes across challenging behaviours

Secondary objective: to provide additional information relevant to intervention

Identify appropriate functionally equivalent or alternative behaviours

Identify the schedules of reinforcement (type, rate, quality and immediacy) operating on the challenging and alternative behaviours

Identify the topographical components of the functional operant (e.g. rate, duration, co-occurrence of challenging behaviour)

Identify resources available within the setting

Identify staff beliefs regarding the causes and/or functions of challenging behaviours

Identify the pattern of staff responses to challenging behaviour

---

☐ The description of relationships between the occurrence of challenging behaviour, environmental events and biobehavioural states.

☐ The generation of hypotheses concerning the nature of the contingencies maintaining the person's challenging behaviours, the setting events or establishing operations which set the occasion for challenging behaviour to occur, and aspects of the organisation of behaviour.

☐ The further evaluation of these hypotheses prior to intervention.

In general, the second stage involves the descriptive (or structural) analysis of challenging behaviour, the fourth stage involves the functional analysis of challenging behaviour (Axelrod, 1987*a*). Descriptive or structural analyses focus upon the description of relationships between the rate and form of a behaviour and aspects of the context within which it occurs. A functional analysis extends this descriptive process by providing an experimental analysis (i.e. 'believable demonstration') of the contextual control of behaviour.

It is important to see these aims as interlinked processes, rather than as distinct stages. The relationship between hypothesis formulation and data collection is not linear. Descriptive analyses themselves are based upon hypotheses regarding the kinds of processes which may underlie challenging behaviours. One cannot just 'observe'. The results of descriptive and experimental analyses are likely to feed back into refining the definition of response classes. Nevertheless, for the sake of simplicity these four areas will be addressed separately in the sections below.

In recent years a number of reviews and practical guides have focused on the procedures and techniques which may be involved in a functional behavioural assessment (e.g. Bailey & Pyles, 1989; Berg & Wacker, 1991; Donnellan *et al.*, 1988; Donnellan *et al.*, 1984; Durand, 1990; Durand & Crimmins, 1991; Emerson, Barrett & Cummings, 1990; Gardner & Cole, 1990; Halle & Spradlin 1993; Iwata, Vollmer & Zarcone, 1990; Lalli & Goh, 1993; Lennox & Miltenberger, 1989; McBrien & Felce, 1994; Meyer & Evans, 1989; Murphy, 1986; Murphy & Oliver, 1987; Oliver, 1991; O'Neill *et al.*, 1990; Pyles & Bailey, 1990; Zarkowska & Clements, 1994). In the following sections, some of the key issues and important trends in this burgeoning area will be discussed.

The identification and definition of behaviours

Four issues need to be considered in relation to the identification and definition of behaviours:

- ☐ the selection of targets for intervention on the basis of their personal and social impact;

- ☐ the importance of assessing the function of separate forms of challenging behaviour;

- ☐ the inclusion within the assessment process of functionally equivalent behaviours and

- ☐ choice of the unit of assessment.

Selecting socially valid targets for intervention

If interventions are to be socially valid, then the selection of target behaviours should reflect their personal and social significance. That is, they should include those behaviours which, if reduced, would result in the most socially significant (or 'meaningful') outcomes. This will require an assessment of the extent to which the challenging behaviour(s) shown by the person have, or are likely to have, a direct impact upon such factors as:

- ☐ the short- and medium-term physical risk to the person and others;

- ☐ the restriction of access to functional age-appropriate community-based activities;

- ☐ exclusion from their family or community-based services;

- ☐ stress and strain experienced by carers and care staff;

- ☐ the quality of relationships between the service user and carers;

- ☐ the need for more restrictive management practices (e.g. restraint, sedation, seclusion).

Unfortunately, this area has received scant attention. While attention has been drawn to the importance of these issues and some general measurement strategies outlined (e.g. Evans & Meyer, 1985; Meyer & Evans, 1989, 1993*a*; Meyer & Janney, 1989), no structured approaches are currently available which seek to identify the broader impact of the person's challenging behaviour in their particular context.

Approaches to assessing change in these broader outcomes were introduced in Chapters 2 and 5, and will be discussed in more detail in the final section of this chapter.

The form and function of behaviour

The selection and definition of intervention targets should also be guided by knowledge about the potential types of relationship which may exist between behaviour and maintaining processes. As discussed in Chapter 4, the relationship between the form and function of challenging behaviours is far from straightforward. Maintaining factors may be complex, are likely to vary significantly across individuals, and may vary within individuals over contexts and time. It is also possible that different forms or topographies of the person's challenging behaviour may be maintained by different processes (e.g. Day *et al.*, 1988; Derby *et al.*, 1994; Emerson *et al.*, in press*a*, *b*; Slifer *et al.*, 1986; Sprague & Horner, 1992).

This has considerable implications for the selection and definition of target behaviours. It strongly suggests that the assessment process should aim to identify the function of each topographically distinct form of challenging behaviour shown by the individual, rather than aggregate challenging behaviours together under such general terms as 'self-injury' or 'disruption'. The latter option runs the risk that the results of the assessment process may be contaminated by summing together behaviours which are maintained by different processes. This may result in apparently undiscriminated patterns of responding in the results of assessment (e.g. Derby *et al.*, 1994). Alternatively, it may overlook the functions of behaviours which occur at a relatively lower rate within the person's repertoire. This latter risk is illustrated in Figs. 6.1 and 6.2.

Figure 6.1 displays the rate of 'self-injurious behaviour' shown by Susan (the 13 year-old girl introduced in Chapter 4). This was examined under brief conditions of 'academic demand', 'social disapproval', 'alone' and 'continuous social attention' (see Chapter 4 for a description of the conditions, also Halle & Spradlin, 1993; Iwata *et al.*, 1982; Iwata *et al.*, 1990*c*; Iwata *et al.*, 1994*b*; Oliver, 1991). The data suggest that her self-injury is maintained by a process of automatic reinforcement, in that it occurs relatively consistently at higher rates in the 'alone' condition. As was indicated previously, however, Susan exhibited a range of self-injurious behaviours which descriptive analyses had

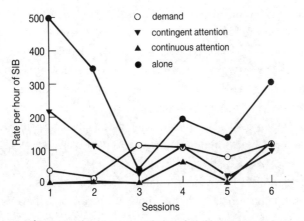

Fig. 6.1. Rate of occurrence of Susan's self-injurious behaviours across experimental conditions.

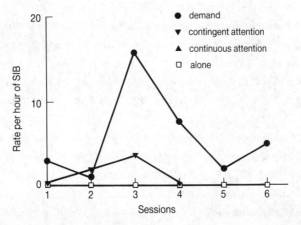

Fig. 6.2. Rate of occurrence of Susan's self-injurious behaviour, back poking, across experimental conditions.

suggested were maintained by either automatic reinforcement or negative (social) reinforcement. Figure 6.2 shows the rate of one of her less frequent forms of self-injury (back poking) when it is disaggregated from the overall results.

As can be seen, this particular behaviour appears to be maintained by a process of negative (social) reinforcement, in that it occurs relatively consistently at a higher rate under conditions of teacher demand. In this case, relying on aggregated data, or only recording 'self-injury' in the first place, would have resulted in overlooking the process maintaining at least one of Susan's forms of self-injury. This could have been problematic since a logical approach to intervention for behaviours maintained by (positive) automatic reinforcement would be to provide alternative external stimulation (Vollmer, 1994). While this may have reduced the rate of those forms of self-injury maintained by automatic reinforcement (Favell *et al.*, 1982), it may well have *increased* the rate of those behaviours maintained by negative reinforcement.

One of the major tasks of assessment is to identify relationships *between* behaviours in terms of which particular behaviours belong to which particular response classes. This can only be achieved, of course, if we begin by defining the separate and topographically distinct forms of challenging behaviour shown by the person. Whether to aggregate behaviours together into larger units should be determined by the assessment data.

Including functionally equivalent behaviours in the assessment process

A focus on the function, rather than the form, of behaviour also draws attention to the potential value of including behaviours which may be functionally equivalent to the targeted challenging behaviour within the assessment process. This has two possible advantages. First, if it is possible to identify existing socially appropriate functionally equivalent behaviours, these may be used during intervention to substitute for and displace the target behaviour (Carr, 1988).

Secondly, it may increase the opportunity for examining aspects of the contextual control of low frequency challenging behaviours. Functional assessment (and, in particular, functional analysis) is often problematic when applied to behaviours which occur at a very low rate. In such instances, it may be possible to identify other members of the same response class as the challenging behaviours which occur at a higher rate. This would then allow us to examine the contextual control of the more frequent behaviours as 'proxy' behaviours for the main intervention target. For example, a preliminary descriptive analysis may suggest that screaming (which occurs relatively frequently) and aggression (which occurs much more rarely) are members of the same response class. That is, they both appear to be controlled by the same contingencies. Assessment could then proceed by gathering more detailed information on the contextual control of the person's screaming as a 'proxy' behaviour for the low rate aggression. At the end of the day, of course, it would be necessary to demonstrate, rather than simply assume, the applicability of hypotheses generated from descriptive and functional analyses of such proxy behaviours to the target behaviour of interest.

Behavioural units

The functional classification of behaviours also has implications for the size of the behavioural 'units' selected for analysis. As Scotti *et al.* (1991*a*, *b*) point out, there is probably no greater truism in psychology than 'behaviour consists of a complex stream within which elements are defined and abstracted by the human observer' (p.140). Obviously, the way in which we abstract units or chunks of behaviour for the purpose of assessment will have significant implications.

A functional approach will attempt to abstract units on the basis of their functional integrity. That is, it will aim to identify chunks of behaviour which are controlled by their end-point maintaining consequences. So, for example, the sequence of behaviours involved in making a cup of coffee, including all behaviours from getting up to go to the kitchen to sitting down with a freshly brewed cup of coffee, is probably, for most of us, a single functional unit controlled by the reinforcing consequences of coffee drinking. This is only the case, however, when the chain of behaviours is under the control of a specific end-point contingency. In a teaching programme to make coffee, of course, this may not be the case. In such instances, this larger sequence may be composed of any number of separate functional units each controlled by, for example, instructor praise or, alternatively, escape from instructor prompts.

Applying this approach to the identification of challenging behaviours does mean that we need to be constantly aware of the possibility that the composition of functional units containing challenging behaviours may vary across individuals and settings. While, for one person, a blow to the face may consist of a functional unit maintained by social attention, for another person the functional unit may consist of a complete 'tantrum' of which self-injury is but one part. Hall and Oliver (1992) illustrated this point with regards to the self-injurious behaviour shown by a 28 year-old man with severe learning disabilities. They presented elegant descriptive data which indicated that high-rate bursts of self-injury were maintained by positive social reinforcement. No such relationship was apparent, however, when they examined the relationship between low-rate bursts or single occurrences of self-injury and carer attention. There are, of course, plausible reasons to suggest that issues such as behavioural rate, intensity and the presence of concurrent behaviours may be important in defining functional units or operants.

In summary, then, it has been suggested that:

☐ the targets for intervention (of which assessment is the first stage) should be primarily guided by the current personal and social impact of the behaviours and the possibility of bringing about more widespread change as a result of successful intervention;

☐ a key aim of assessment is to identify which of the challenging behaviours shown by the person belong to which response classes. As such, it is important that assessment begins by identifying the behavioural function associated with individual behaviours;

☐ there may be practical value in including in the assessment process behaviours which may be functionally equivalent to the primary targets of intervention;

☐ the definition of the target behaviours should aim to capture a functionally integrated unit of behaviour, the nature of which is likely to vary between people and, possibly, across contexts.

Descriptive analyses

In this section some of the main approaches to the descriptive analyses of challenging behaviour will be examined. The primary objective of these techniques is the identification of the processes responsible for maintaining the person's challenging behaviour. That is, they are approaches to 'behavioural diagnosis' (Bailey & Pyles, 1989; Pyles & Bailey, 1990). They differ from techniques of functional analysis in that they do not involve the systematic manipulation of environmental variables in order to demonstrate experimental control over the person's challenging behaviour.

The value of informant-based approaches will be considered first, followed by an examination of the use of more complex observational methods. It will be shown that, while informant-based approaches are simple to administer and provide comprehensive preliminary information, concerns regarding the accuracy of informant reports suggest that they need to be combined with more detailed observational or experimental methods in order to provide a reliable and valid set of information.

Informant-based approaches

Structured and semi-structured interviews with key informants are the most widely used approach to the descriptive analysis of challenging behaviour. They are easy to conduct and can provide a wealth of information on a broad range of topics of direct relevance to both the primary and secondary objectives of a functional assessment. Indeed, their use should be considered a logical prerequisite to more complex observational and experimental approaches. A number of structured approaches to collecting information from third parties are now available (e.g. Bailey & Pyles, 1989; Donnellan *et al.*, 1988; Evans & Meyer, 1985; McBrien & Felce, 1994; Meyer & Evans, 1989; O'Neill *et al.*, 1990; Pyles & Bailey, 1990; Wieseler *et al.*, 1985; Zarkowska & Clements, 1994).

O'Neill *et al.* (1990), for example, describe the use of a 'Functional Analysis Interview Form' for collecting information from key informants in relation to:

☐ the topography, frequency, duration, intensity, impact and covariation of the person's challenging behaviours;

☐ potential setting events (e.g. medications, medical complaints, sleep cycles, eating routines and diet, daily schedule of activities, predictability, control and variety of activities, crowding, staffing patterns) which may be correlated with general variations in the probability of occurrence of the challenging behaviours;

☐ specific events or situations (e.g. time of day, setting, activity, identity of carer) which are predictive of either high or low rates of occurrence of the challenging behaviours;

☐ the environmental consequences of the challenging behaviours;

☐ the efficiency of the challenging behaviours in relation to physical effort, rate and delay of reinforcement;

☐ alternative communicative strategies used by the person in the context of everyday activities;

☐ potential reinforcers;

☐ existing functionally equivalent behaviours;

☐ the history of previous approaches to intervention.

In addition to these topics, it may be desirable for the clinical interview to cover such issues as:

☐ the resources (human and material) available in the settings in which challenging behaviours occur;

☐ staff beliefs about the causes and/or functions of the person's challenging behaviour;

☐ the pattern (including its consistency) of the physical and emotional responses of staff to episodes of challenging behaviour;

☐ informal strategies adopted by staff to prevent the occurrence of challenging behaviour.

Structured interview formats are of considerable value in providing a series of prompts to guide the process of behavioural interviewing and, as noted above, they are undemanding of resources and capable of addressing a broad range of issues. Unfortunately, however, the reliability or validity of information collected with such schedules are unknown. Research evidence, however, suggests that such information should be treated with extreme caution.

Green *et al.* (1988) and Green *et al.* (1991), for example, report a series of studies examining the correspondence between: (1) staff rating of the preference of students with profound multiple handicaps for specific stimuli; (2) actual student approach to, and use of, these stimuli; and (3) the extent to which they functioned as positive reinforcers in a teaching task. They reported that, while student approach predicted the reinforcing potential of stimuli, the considerable majority of care staff were unable to predict either student approach or the reinforcing potential of stimuli at greater than chance levels (although see also Newton, Ard & Horner, 1993). Similarly, Durand and Crimmins (1988) found a non-significant correlation between teachers' opinions regarding the motivational basis of self-injury shown by their pupils and the results of the Motivation Assessment Scale, which, in their study, predicted the results of more detailed experimental analyses of the children's self-injury.

These few studies, limited in scope as they are, do suggest that the global opinions of informants on such varied topics as student preference for specific stimuli and the function of challenging behaviour may be of highly questionable validity. Durand (1990) suggests that consistency of responding across informants may increase the confidence with which the resulting data are viewed. That is, increased levels of inter-informant agreement may be taken as an indicator of validity. While such a suggestion has a certain intuitive appeal, it does presuppose that the development of an *inaccurate* consensus of opinion among informants is a rare event. At present we simply do not know whether or not this is likely to be the case.

Durand and Crimmins (1988) described the development of the Motivation Assessment Scale (MAS: see also Durand, 1990; Durand & Crimmins, 1992). This is a 16-item questionnaire in which informants rate each item on a 7-point scale. Each item is designed to ascertain the extent to which challenging behaviour occurs under stimulus conditions associated with behaviours maintained by:

☐ *sensory consequences* (e.g. 'When the behaviour is occurring, does the person seem calm and unaware of anything else going on around them?');

☐ *positive social reinforcement* (e.g. 'Does the behaviour seem to occur in response to you talking to other persons in the room?');

☐ *positive tangible reinforcement* (e.g. 'Does the behaviour stop occurring shortly after you give this person the toy, food or activity he or she has requested?'); or

☐ *negative social reinforcement* (e.g. 'Does the behaviour occur following a request to perform a difficult task?').

They reported acceptable levels of inter-informant agreement for individual items ($r = 0.66–0.92$), and acceptable test–retest reliability over a 30-day period ($r = 0.89–0.98$). They also reported 100% correspondence between the results of the MAS and more detailed functional analyses of the self-injury shown by eight randomly selected pupils (see also Durand & Carr, 1992).

More recently, however, conflicting evidence has accumulated concerning the utility of the MAS as a clinical tool. While two studies have shown the MAS to possess a coherent factor structure (Bihm *et al.*, 1991; Singh *et al.*, 1993*a*), six studies have reported low levels of inter-informant agreement (Kearney, 1994; Lawrenson, 1993; Newton & Sturmey, 1991; Sigafoos, Kerr & Roberts, 1994; Thompson & Emerson, in press; Zarcone *et al.*, 1991). In addition, Emerson *et al.* (in press*b*) have reported unacceptably low levels of correspondence between the results of the MAS and the results of more detailed descriptive and experimental analyses carried out on 21 forms of challenging behaviours shown by five young people with severe learning disabilities.

These concerns regarding the reliability and validity of data derived from informant-based approaches do suggest that the behavioural interview should *only* be considered as an initial stage in functional assessment and should *always* be followed by the use of more detailed observational and/or experimental analyses.

However, while information collected from carers and staff may not provide accurate data concerning the processes underlying a person's challenging behaviour, it may still provide useful information regarding staff or carer beliefs about the behaviour's cause or function. Marked discrepancies between the demonstrated function of a behaviour and staff or carer beliefs about its function will need to be taken into account when planning interventions (Hastings & Remington, 1994*a*, *b*).

Observational methods

The use of non-participant observation in functional assessments raises a number of important methodological issues. These include: the selection and definition of target behaviours, concurrent behaviours and environmental events; the selection of recording methods and sampling strategies; the reliability and validity of observational methods; observer training; the assessment of inter-observer agreement; subject reactivity; observer drift; and the use of graphical and statistical methods of data analysis. To review these issues is beyond the scope of the present book. It would also unnecessarily

Name:				Dates:	
For each episode of challenging behaviour please note the time and date and describe in detail: what happened **before** the episode, what **specific challenging behaviours** occurred and what happened **after** the episode. Please be as specific as possible.					
Date	Time	What happened before?		What did he/she do?	What happened afterwards?

Fig. 6.3. A narrative ABC chart.

duplicate a number of excellent texts which address these matters in some detail (Bakeman & Gottman, 1986; Hartmann, 1984; Kratochwill & Levin, 1992; Poling & Fuqua, 1986; Sackett, 1978; Suen & Ary, 1989). Discussion will, therefore, be restricted to an examination of some of the observational methods which have been used in descriptive analyses of challenging behaviours in applied settings.

Identifying maintaining contingencies: ABC charts and sequential analyses Probably the most frequently used observational approach to descriptive analysis in clinical practice involves the recording by carers of narrative descriptions of a sample of occurrences of:

☐ antecedent (A) events;

☐ the target challenging behaviour (B);

☐ and consequent (C) events.

This approach attempts to identify components of the *three-term contingency* in relation to the maintenance of challenging behaviour (Bailey & Pyles, 1989; Evans & Meyer, 1985; Gardner, Karan & Cole, 1984; Groden, 1989; Meyer & Evans, 1989; Murphy, 1986; Murphy & Oliver, 1987; Pyles & Bailey, 1990). Figure 6.3 illustrates a typical narrative ABC chart. Figure 6.4 illustrates the Inappropriate Behavior Record developed by Pyles and Bailey (1990). As can

Inappropriate Behavior Record

Instructions: Each time Tony engages in inappropriate behavior, check ALL boxes that apply describing the events occuring before, during and after the behavior.

Definitions:
- Physical Aggression: any occurrence of hitting, scratching, kicking, etc. directed at staff or clients.
- Verbal Aggression: any occurrence of cursing, yelling, or threatening others.
- Noncompliance: refusing to follow requests made of him by staff, not following directions within 30 seconds of request.
- Stealing: taking or having possession of any item not belonging to him without owner's permission.
- Public Masturbation: masturbating or fondling genitals any place other than in his bedroom

---

Date:_____ Time:_____a.m./p.m. Staff:_____

What Happened BEFORE Episode?
- ☐ Nothing--happened "out of the blue"
- ☐ Asked to do something (not training)
- ☐ Asked to do something (training)
- ☐ Asked to go somewhere
- ☐ Asked to move out of the way
- ☐ Stopped from doing something
- ☐ Had toileting accident
- ☐ Had a seizure
- ☐ Other (specify)_____
  _____

Inappropriate Behavior
- ☐ Physical aggression
- ☐ Verbal aggression
- ☐ Noncompliance
- ☐ Stealing
- ☐ Public masturbation
  Location:_____
- ☐ Other problematic behavior
  (Specify)_____
  _____

What Happened AFTER Episode?
- ☐ Separated within environment
- ☐ Taken to room
- ☐ He calmed down on his own
- ☐ Had to make restitution (pay back something stolen, clean mess, etc.)
- ☐ Staff ignored his behavior
- ☐ Staff lectured/got in argument with him.
- ☐ Other (Specify)_____
  _____

Date:_____ Time:_____a.m./p.m. Staff:_____

What Happened BEFORE Episode?
- ☐ Nothing--happened "out of the blue"
- ☐ Asked to do something (not training)
- ☐ Asked to do something (training)
- ☐ Asked to go somewhere
- ☐ Asked to move out of the way
- ☐ Stopped from doing something
- ☐ Had toileting accident
- ☐ Had a seizure
- ☐ Other (specify)_____
  _____

Inappropriate Behavior
- ☐ Physical aggression
- ☐ Verbal aggression
- ☐ Noncompliance
- ☐ Stealing
- ☐ Public masturbation
  Location:_____
- ☐ Other problematic behavior
  (Specify)_____
  _____

What Happened AFTER Episode?
- ☐ Separated within environment
- ☐ Taken to room
- ☐ He calmed down on his own
- ☐ Had to make restitution (pay back something stolen, clean mess, etc.)
- ☐ Staff ignored his behavior
- ☐ Staff lectured/got in argument with him.
- ☐ Other (Specify)_____
  _____

Date:_____ Time:_____a.m./p.m. Staff:_____

What Happened BEFORE Episode?
- ☐ Nothing--happened "out of the blue"
- ☐ Asked to do something (not training)
- ☐ Asked to do something (training)
- ☐ Asked to go somewhere
- ☐ Asked to move out of the way
- ☐ Stopped from doing something
- ☐ Had toileting accident
- ☐ Had a seizure
- ☐ Other (specify)_____
  _____

Inappropriate Behavior
- ☐ Physical aggression
- ☐ Verbal aggression
- ☐ Noncompliance
- ☐ Stealing
- ☐ Public masturbation
  Location:_____
- ☐ Other problematic behavior
  (Specify)_____
  _____

What Happened AFTER Episode?
- ☐ Separated within environment
- ☐ Taken to room
- ☐ He calmed down on his own
- ☐ Had to make restitution (pay back something stolen, clean mess, etc.)
- ☐ Staff ignored his behavior
- ☐ Staff lectured/got in argument with him.
- ☐ Other (Specify)_____
  _____

Fig. 6.4. Inappropriate Behavior Record. (From Pyles & Bailey, 1990).

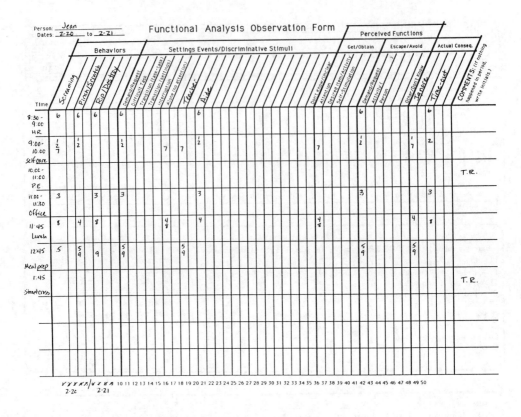

Fig. 6.5. Functional analysis observation form. (From O'Neill *et al.*, 1990).

be seen, this more precise approach involves the prior specification of categories of antecedent and consequent events.

A slightly different approach is taken by O'Neill *et al.* (1990). They describe the 'Functional Analysis Observation Form' (Fig. 6.5) which is used to record the antecedent events and *perceived function* of multiple challenging behaviours over several days.

As with all observational measures, adequate observer training as well as regular monitoring of levels of inter-observer agreement are essential if the resulting data are to have any clinical value (Murphy, 1986; Pyles & Bailey, 1990). The data collected may be summarised to provide, depending upon the sampling strategy employed, estimates of the rate or probability of occurrence of events within specified periods of time or contexts. As Iwata *et al.* (1990c) point out, however, the main aim of such an approach is to provide information regarding *behavioural sequences*, e.g. the probability that a particular event (e.g. a child's aggression) will be preceded or followed by another event (e.g. teacher demands, teacher attention).

Reliance on simple narrative descriptions, however, means that the resulting information is rarely provided in a manner which is readily interpretable. To do so would require that:

1. specific time periods are defined in which antecedent and consequent events are recorded;

2. the same classes of environmental events are recorded as both antecedents and consequences; and

3. the unconditional probability* of the events of interest occurring in the defined time period is also known.

To illustrate these points, let us assume that the data we have collected indicate that episodes of an individual's aggression are followed within five seconds by teacher attention in 30 out of 50 recorded instances. Thus, the conditional probability of teacher attention following self-injury is 0.6 (30/50). This observation would have radically different implications depending on the value of (1) the *unconditional or chance probability* of teacher attention occurring within a five second interval and (2) the *conditional probability* of teacher attention occurring in the periods leading up to aggression.

If the unconditional (chance) probability of teacher attention was lower than 0.6, then episodes of aggression would be followed by greater than expected rates of teacher attention. This is consistent with aggression being maintained by positive (teacher mediated) reinforcement. If the unconditional probability of teacher attention were higher than 0.6, however, episodes of aggression would be followed by lower than expected rates of teacher attention. This is consistent with aggression maintained by negative social reinforcement involving escape from teacher attention.

These interpretations are further complicated, however, when we consider the effects of *shifts* in the conditional probability of teacher attention. In the examples above, we have implicitly assumed that teacher attention was being delivered at chance levels prior to aggression. This is not, of course, a safe assumption to make.

Thus, our interpretation of the observation that the individual's aggression is followed by greater than chance levels of teacher attention would vary depending upon the conditional probability with which teacher attention *preceded* aggression. If, for example, teacher attention preceding aggression occurred at levels at, or lower than, those that would be expected by chance, then our original interpretation would stand. On the other hand, teacher

* The unconditional probability of a behaviour occurring is equivalent to its chance level of occurrence within a defined period. Thus, for example, a behaviour which occurs overall for 25% of the time has an unconditional probability of occurring at any given second of 0.25. Similarly, a behaviour which occurs in 30% of all observed 5-second intervals has an unconditional probability of occurring within any single 5-second interval of 0.3.

attention may have been occurring at levels greater than would be expected by chance in the periods both preceding *and* following aggression. Such a pattern of results is inconsistent with an explanation based on social reinforcement (there is no *contingent increase* in the probability of attention). It may, however, indicate stimulus control of aggression by teacher attention.

As we can see, the correct interpretation of behavioural sequences from the information provided by ABC charts requires precise data concerning: (1) the unconditional probability of the events of interest (e.g. carer behaviours) and (2) contingent shifts in the conditional probabilities of these events in relation to a second event (e.g. challenging behaviour).

In practice, however, the antecedent and consequent periods involved in narrative ABC records are rarely defined in a sufficiently precise way that either conditional or unconditional probabilities can be determined with any degree of confidence. As a result, the information provided by narrative ABC charts can only have a very general value in determining basic response dimensions (e.g. the rate of occurrence of challenging behaviours) and the relationship between challenging behaviour and general setting variables (e.g. time of day, location) which can be determined independently of the ABC record (e.g. from the student's daily timetable). Thus, while the narrative descriptions of antecedent and consequent events may generate some tentative hypotheses for further investigation (e.g. Lalli *et al.*, 1993), they are far from providing a 'believable demonstration' of underlying behavioural processes.

The interpretative problems associated with narrative ABC charts can be resolved by the use of more complex approaches to recording and analysis (e.g. Bijou, Peterson & Ault, 1968; Emerson *et al.*, in press*a*; Hall & Oliver, 1992; Lalli *et al.*, 1993; Lerman & Iwata, 1993; Maurice & Trudel, 1982; Sasso *et al.*, 1992).

As described in Chapter 4, Edelson *et al.* (1983) used a 10-second partial interval observational procedure* to record the occurrence of self-injurious behaviours and staff demands, denials or punishment for approximately five hours for each of 20 institutionalised young people with learning disabilities. They reported sharp increases in the rates of staff contact prior to episodes of self-injury for 19 of the 20 participants. Similar procedures have been employed more recently by Lalli *et al.* (1993), Lerman and Iwata (1993) and Mace and Lalli (1991).

Lalli *et al.* (1993), for example, used a continuous 10-second partial interval recording procedure to monitor clearly defined environmental events occurring antecedent, and subsequent to, challenging behaviours shown by

---

* In a partial interval procedure a record is made of whether the target behaviour occurred *at all* during a specified interval. Thus, each interval has a possible score of 0 (behaviour not observed) or 1 (behaviour observed) for each target behaviour.

three students with severe learning disabilities. Five hours of observational data were collected for each child. The resulting data suggested that the challenging behaviour of two participants was maintained by positive (social) reinforcement. The challenging behaviour of the third participant appeared to be controlled multiply by both positive and negative (social) reinforcement.

A limited number of studies have examined agreement between these types of descriptive approaches and the results of experimental (functional) analyses. Overall, they have suggested that descriptive approaches tend to identify a greater number of potential functions for a given behaviour than experimental approaches (Lerman & Iwata, 1993; Mace & Lalli, 1991; although see also Crawford *et al.*, 1992). In particular, while descriptive and experimental approaches may both agree that the target behaviour is socially mediated, descriptive approaches may fail to discriminate between processes of positive and negative social reinforcement (Lerman & Iwata, 1993; Mace & Lalli, 1991). A number of factors may account for this apparent insensitivity of descriptive analyses. These include:

☐ the application of descriptive analyses in relatively barren settings in which carer responses to challenging behaviour may be inconsistent (Lerman & Iwata, 1993);

☐ the inherent difficulties of using descriptive analyses to identify relatively 'thin' schedules of reinforcement (Iwata *et al.*, 1990c; Mace *et al.*, 1991);

☐ failure to identify the appropriate functional unit in descriptive analyses (Hall & Oliver, 1992);

☐ failure to identify distinct response classes among topographically similar behaviours (Emerson *et al.*, in press*a*); and

☐ the use of relatively unsophisticated approaches to the identification of behavioural sequences.

This last issue may be addressed by the use of portable computers to undertake more sophisticated observational and statistical analyses (Emerson *et al.*, in press*a*; Hall & Oliver, 1992; Repp & Felce, 1990; Repp & Karsh, 1994*a*; Saunders, Saunders & Saunders, 1994).

Emerson *et al.* (in press*a*), for example, have illustrated the use of time-based lag sequential analysis (Sackett, 1979, 1987) to identify relationships between challenging behaviours and environmental events. This approach involves the calculation of the conditional probability of the onset, occurrence or termination of one event (the conditional variable) at specific points in time in relation to the onset or termination of a second event (the base variable). Let us suppose, for example, that we wished to investigate the possibility that a person's aggression was negatively reinforced by escape from academic demands made by teaching staff. Evidence consistent with a demand–escape hypothesis would include: (1) an increased rate of aggression under conditions of demand; and (2) an increased rate of demands preceding the onset of aggression.

Lag sequential analysis could be used to investigate the first of these relationships by calculating the conditional probability of aggression (the conditional variable) at each second for a defined period of time leading up to the onset, during and following the offset of teacher demands (the base variable). The impact of aggression on demands could be addressed in a parallel fashion by treating demands as the conditional variable and self-injury as the base variable. Calculating the conditional probability of self-injury at a given time lag (e.g. 7 seconds preceding the onset of demands) would involve taking each onset of demands (the base variable) in the observational record and noting whether aggression was present at the point in time defined by the lag (- 7 seconds). The conditional probability of an event is given by dividing the number of times it occurred by the number of times it could have occurred in the observational record (i.e. number of occurrences plus the number of non-occurrences)*.

The unconditional (or chance) probability of aggression occurring at any point in time is given by the number of intervals in the total observational record during which aggression occurred divided by the total number of intervals in the record. Allison and Liker (1982) have demonstrated that the statistical significance, in terms of the conventional z statistic, of the difference between the conditional and unconditional probability of the conditional variable at any point in time is given by

$$z = \frac{Pc - Pu}{\sqrt{\dfrac{Pu(1 - Pu)(1 - Pb)}{N}}}$$

where Pc is the conditional probability of the conditional variable at a given second, N is the number of possible occurrences of the conditional variable for a given lag, Pu is the (overall) unconditional probability of the conditional variable and Pb is the unconditional probability of the base variable.

Emerson et $al.$ (in press$a$) used this method in the analysis of multiple forms of challenging behaviour shown by two girls and one boy with severe learning disabilities. Eight hours of videotape per child was transformed into a

---

* It should be noted that this is not necessarily equivalent to the number of onsets of the base variable as, at some lags, it may not have been possible for the conditional event to be observed owing to overlap with the start or termination of the observational session.

real-time event record* using hand-held computers. The potential value of the approach was indicated by the findings that 11 of the 12 topographies of challenging behaviours shown by the three children demonstrated statistically significant variation under particular environmental conditions. For 10 of these behaviours, the variations were consistent with possible behavioural functions including: socially mediated positive and negative reinforcement; automatic reinforcement and schedule induction.

Emerson *et al.* (in press *c*) compared the results obtained by this approach with the results of experimental (functional) analysis for 21 topographies of challenging behaviour shown by five people with severe learning disabilities. Their results indicated a high degree of agreement (85%) between the results of sequential and experimental analyses in the 13 examples in which both pro-cedures positively identified a function of the behaviour. This level of agreement compares well with previous comparisons between the results of descriptive and experimental analyses (e.g. Lerman & Iwata, 1993). They also noted that the descriptive approach was more likely to positively identify a function for behaviours than the experimental approach (86% compared with 67%).

While the increasing use of portable computers has made the collection of continuous observational data considerably more viable, the use of such procedures does require the use of trained non-participant observers, a requirement which has obvious resource implications. In addition, more complex and intrusive approaches to data collection may involve an increased risk of subject and carer reactivity.

Such techniques do, however, appear to provide a powerful way of investigating naturally occurring sequences of behaviour in intact environments. The high degree of correspondence between the results of this approach and subsequent experimental (functional) analyses does raise the question of whether such approaches may be considered to provide a 'believable demonstration' of the operation of underlying behavioural processes.

In effect, a thoroughly convincing demonstration of the controlling function of a reinforcement contingency can only be provided by direct manipulation of the contingency itself. This is rarely possible in applied studies, since the required operations (e.g. repeated extinction and re-introduction of the maintaining contingency) can be exceedingly lengthy and, in themselves, raise a number of ethical issues. In place of this, applied studies have relied on procedures which demonstrate the stimulus control of challenging behaviour (Halle & Spradlin, 1993; Iwata *et al.*, 1990; Oliver, 1991).

As indicated in Chapter 4, however, the demonstration of stimulus control cannot be taken as proof of the operation of underlying processes.

---

* The onset, occurrence and offset of multiple events were recorded for each second of the videotape.

Thus, for example, increased rates of responding under conditions of academic demand are consistent with a number of hypotheses including negative (social) reinforcement, positive (social) reinforcement in that conditions of demand may be discriminative for the operation of contingencies of positive reinforcement (e.g. Repp & Karsh, 1994*b*), negative (automatic) reinforcement (cf. Isaacson & Gispin, 1990) and elicited responding (cf. Romanczyk *et al.*, 1992).

While descriptive analyses, of course, can only ever provide correlational evidence (Bijou *et al.*, 1968), they do possess a sound statistical basis for decision making and can identify with precision the temporal relationships between variables. Taken together these can provide powerful evidence to support the drawing of causal inferences (Sackett, 1987).

In general, applied behaviour analysis has placed little value on the statistical analysis of observational data. This has, in effect, served to restrict its focus to the relationships between events which can be easily manipulated. One of the significant drawbacks which results from this methodological bias is the failure of applied behaviour analysis to attend to the potentially important role played by setting events or establishing operations in providing the motivational basis for challenging behaviour (Wahler & Fox, 1981). This issue will be considered in the next section.

Setting events and other aspects of contextual control:

scatter plots and related techniques Analysis of aspects of the broader context within which behaviour occurs is one of the hallmarks of ecobehavioural analysis, an emerging discipline which combines the conceptual frameworks of applied behaviour analysis, behavioural ecology (Willems, 1974) and J.R. Kantor's interbehavioural psychology (Kantor, 1959). Central to ecobehavioural psychology is the concept of setting events (Wahler & Fox, 1981).

Setting events (or setting factors in interbehavioural psychology) are those environmental events or conditions which potentiate or suppress established behaviour–environment relationships 'by altering the strengths and characteristics of the particular stimulus and response functions involved in an interaction' (Bijou & Baer, 1978, p.26). They include such phenomena as temperature changes, deprivation/satiation conditions, physiological or bio-behavioural states, drug effects, prior stimulus–response interactions, instructions and the nature and scheduling of preceding activities.

The concept of setting events overlaps with the concepts of establishing operations and establishing stimuli (Michael, 1982, 1993). Michael (1982) defined an establishing operation as 'any change in the environment which alters the effectiveness of some object or event as reinforcement and simultaneously alters the momentary frequency of the behavior that has been followed by that reinforcement' (Michael, 1982, p.150–151)*.

As indicated in Chapter 4, establishing operations are distinct from discriminative stimuli in that establishing operations evoke responses through changing the capacity of stimuli to act as reinforcers, while discriminative stimuli evoke responses through their previous correlation with higher frequencies of reinforcement.

The potential advantages of incorporating the analysis of setting events or establishing operations and stimuli into the functional analysis of challenging behaviour are considerable. For example, it is rare indeed that challenging behaviours reliably and consistently occur in response to similar situations. More commonly, while the behaviour of interest may be much more likely to occur in certain situations (e.g. during a specific type of instructional task), its actual occurrence can show considerable variability over time. In clinical practice (if not in the pages of the *Journal of Applied Behavior Analysis*), behavioural variability is the rule, people have good days and bad days. In theory, the identification of the setting events which account for such variability could allow, through their modification, for the development of highly effective nonintrusive approaches to intervention which, in effect, undercut the motivational basis underlying the challenging behaviour (Carr *et al.*, 1990*a*, *b*).

For example, a functional assessment may indicate that a person's aggression is maintained by escape from social demands. Further analysis may help identify those setting events *which establish demands as aversive stimuli* and, consequently, negative reinforcers. These could include such diverse factors as fatigue, illness, sedation, hangover, caffeine ingestion, the nature of preceding activities, the presence of preferred competing activities, the pacing or style of demands. The modification of any setting events which might be identified could, therefore, prevent social demands acquiring aversive properties and hence reduce aggression by undercutting its motivational base. This possibility is illustrated by Carr *et al.* (1976). In the study described in Chapter 4, rates of self-injury were immediately and significantly reduced by embedding demands in the context of a story (see Fig. 4.6). In all probability, these startling results reflect the operation of setting events.

Evidence of the potential operation of setting events comes from a number of disparate sources including reports of relationships between challenging behaviours and such factors as classroom density (McAfee, 1987), caffeine intake (Podboy & Mallery, 1977), resting EEG rhythms (Chaney,

---

* Establishing stimuli are defined as stimuli which evoke a response through establishing another stimulus as a conditioned reinforcer for that response. That is, the establishing stimulus establishes the reinforcing property of a previously neutral stimulus – which thereby evokes behaviours previously associated with that type of reinforcement.

Forbes & Leve, 1989), sleep patterns (Espie, 1992), seizure activity (Gedye, 1989a, b), bi-polar mood swings (Lowry & Sovner, 1992), imposed reduction diets (Talkington & Riley, 1971), awakening late (Gardner et al., 1984; Kennedy & Itkonen, 1993), menstrual cycle (Taylor et al., 1993a, b), critical comments from others (Gardner et al., 1986), the route taken to school (Kennedy & Itkonen, 1993), type of music played in public spaces (Harris, Bradley & Titus, 1992) and temporally distant social interactions (Gardner et al., 1986). Other potentially important areas of research include the analysis of biobehavioural states (Guess et al., 1990, 1993) and the evaluation of the effects of deprivation/satiation condition upon performance (Vollmer & Iwata, 1991).

To date, however, incorporating the analysis of setting events within a functional assessment remains the exception rather than the rule. As Wahler and Fox (1981) pointed out, to do so poses significant methodological, conceptual and professional challenges, as setting events may include complex phenomena which are either difficult to experimentally manipulate (e.g. menstrual cycle) or are temporally distant from the specific behaviour–consequence interaction under scrutiny (e.g. sexual abuse establishing physical contact with carers as a negative reinforcer). As such, possible approaches to their analysis would clearly run counter to the predilection of behaviour analysts for demonstrating experimental control over behaviour.

However, a number of correlational approaches have been used to identify either general aspects of the contextual control of challenging behaviour (e.g. Touchette, MacDonald & Langer, 1985) or more specific setting events which set the occasion for the challenging behaviour to occur (e.g. Gardner et al., 1984, 1986).

Touchette et al. (1985) described the use of a scatter plot to identify temporal and contextual variations in the rate of challenging behaviour. This simple technique involves the graphical display of partial-interval observational data over successive days to identify those times of day or settings associated with high rates of challenging behaviour.

Figure 6.6, for example, displays data collected by care staff over a 59-day period relating to the severe self-injurious behaviour displayed by a 19 year-old woman with severe learning disabilities. Each black square indicates that more than ten episodes of severe self-injury had occurred in the 30-minute recording period, each grey square indicates that between one and ten episodes of severe self-injury had occurred in the 30-minute recording period. As can be seen, episodes of severe self-injury were more frequent between the times of 10:00 am. and 12:00 pm. This corresponded with attendance at a day programme. Subsequent descriptive and experimental analyses suggested that the young woman's self-injury was maintained by

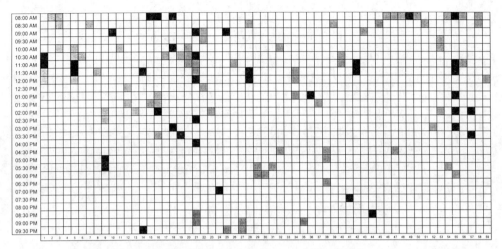

Fig. 6.6. Scatter plot of Natasha's self-injurious head hitting.

negative reinforcement involving avoidance of, and escape from, demands.

Gardner *et al.* (1984, 1986) described the use of conditional probabilities to identify setting events which set the occasion for aggression to occur. Over a one-month period they identified a range of antecedent conditions which elicited aggression in a young man with learning disabilities. These included staff reminders, corrections, repeated prompts, demands, praise and teasing by peers. The conditional probability of aggression following such events ranged from 0.01 (aggression following praise) to 0.32 (aggression following teasing). In addition, they collected information regarding a range of potential setting events including weekend visits from his family, difficulty in getting up in the morning, the presence of a particular member of staff and arguments with peers prior to arriving at his day programme. Their results indicated that: (1) 81% of all aggressive outbursts occurred on the 43% of days which included one of these settings events; (2) the mean rate of occurrence of the recorded antecedent conditions was 21.7 per day for days including setting events, compared with 8.3 per day on the remaining days; and (3) the overall conditional probability of antecedent events eliciting aggression was 0.17 for days including setting events, compared with 0.07 on the remaining days (Gardner *et al.*, 1984, 1986).

More recently, Kennedy and Itkonen (1993) reported strong correlations between: (1) awakening late and the subsequent high rates of multiple challenging behaviours displayed by a 22 year-old woman with moderate learning disabilities; and (2) the specific route taken to college and the multiple challenging behaviours of a 20 year-old woman with severe learning disabilities.

Generating hypotheses

The primary objectives of descriptive analyses are to generate hypotheses regarding the processes maintaining the person's challenging behaviour, including the identification of setting events or establishing operations which set the occasion for the behaviour to occur (Lalli & Goh, 1993). As indicated in the introduction to this book, the relationship between hypothesis formulation and data collection is interactive. Descriptive analyses are based upon hypotheses regarding the kinds of processes which may underlie challenging behaviours. Nevertheless, a mid-point stage in a functional assessment requires the specification of more precise hypotheses regarding:

☐ the process(es) responsible for maintaining the person's challenging behaviour(s);

☐ the contextual control of these processes;

☐ the inter-relationships between different forms of challenging behaviour shown by the person.

As noted in Chapter 4, these relationships may be complex. Maintaining factors may vary across behaviours, time and settings. In addition, challenging behaviours may be multiply controlled. It is appropriate, therefore, to attempt to identify the processes underlying each form of the person's challenging behaviours and to examine the extent to which this underlying process is constant across contexts.

Table 6.2 illustrates the types of context–behaviour–consequence relationships which may be indicative of various underlying processes.

As indicated above, a whole host of variables may influence the extent to which these underlying processes are operational in particular contexts. These include aspects of the individual's bio-behavioural state, preceding interactions and aspects of the current context for behaviour.

☐ *Bio-behavioural state* includes such factors as alertness, fatigue and sleep/wake patterns (e.g. Espie, 1992; Green *et al.*, 1994; Guess *et al.*, 1990, 1993), hormonal changes (Taylor *et al.*, 1993*a*), drug effects (e.g. Taylor *et al.*, 1993*b*), caffeine intake (Podboy & Mallery, 1977), resting EEG rhythms (Chaney *et al.*, 1989), seizure activity (Gedye, 1989*a, b*), bi-polar mood swings (Lowry & Sovner, 1992), and imposed reduction diets (Talkington & Riley, 1971)

☐ *Preceding interactions* include such factors as preceding compliance (Harchik & Putzier, 1990; Horner *et al.*, 1991; Mace *et al.*, 1988), task repetition (Winterling *et al.*, 1987), critical comments from others (Gardner *et al.*, 1986), temporally distant social interactions (Gardner *et*

Table 6.2. *Relationships between antecedents, challenging behaviours and consequent events which may suggest particular underlying processes*

Socially-mediated positive reinforcement

Does the person's challenging behaviour sometimes result in their receiving more or different forms of contact with others (e.g. while the episode is being managed or while they are being 'calmed down') or having access to new activities?

Is the behaviour more likely when contact or activities are potentially available but not being provided, e.g. situations in which carers are around but are attending to others?

Is the behaviour less likely in situations involving high levels of contact or during preferred activities?

Is the behaviour more likely when contact or activities are terminated?

Socially-mediated negative reinforcement (escape or avoidance)

Do people respond to the behaviour by terminating interaction or activities?

Is the behaviour more likely in situations in which demands are placed upon the person or they are engaged in interactions or activities they appear to dislike?

Is the behaviour less likely when disliked interactions or activities are stopped?

Is the behaviour less likely in situations involving participation in preferred activities?

Is the behaviour more likely in those situations in which they *may* be asked to participate in interactions or activities they appear to dislike?

Positive automatic reinforcement (sensory stimulation, perceptual reinforcement or opioid release)

Is the behaviour more likely when there is little external stimulation?

Is the behaviour less likely when the person is participating in a preferred activity?

Does the behaviour appear to have no effect upon subsequent events?

Negative automatic reinforcement (de-arousal)

Is the behaviour more likely when there is excessive external stimulation or when the individual is visibly excited or aroused?

Is the behaviour less likely when the individual is calm or in a quiet, peaceful environment?

Does the behaviour appear to have no effect upon subsequent events?

---

al., 1986), the route taken to a setting (Kennedy & Itkonen, 1993), and time of awakening (Gardner *et al.*, 1984; Kennedy & Itkonen, 1993).

☐ The *current context* for behaviour includes such factors as noise, temperature, levels of demand and positive comments from staff (e.g. Kennedy, 1994), crowding (McAfee, 1987), student preference (e.g. Cooper *et al.*, 1992; Foster-Johnson *et al.*, 1994) or choice over activities (Dunlap *et al.*, 1994; Dyer, Dunlap & Winterling, 1990), the amount of non-contingent reinforcement available in the setting (e.g. Hagopian, Fisher & Legacy, 1994; Vollmer *et al.*, 1993), and the nature of surrounding activities (Carr *et al.*, 1976).

Hypothesis testing: functional (experimental) analysis

The functional (experimental) analysis of challenging behaviour involves the demonstration, through the experimental manipulation of environmental conditions, of the stimulus control of challenging behaviour. Experimental control is demonstrated if important aspects of the challenging behaviour (e.g. its rate, duration or intensity) systematically vary as a function of the environmental manipulation. The methods employed in functional analyses, therefore, form a sub-set of single subject experimental designs (Barlow & Hersen, 1984). Most frequently, functional analyses employ either withdrawal designs (e.g. Carr *et al.*, 1976; Carr & Durand, 1985*a*, *b*) or alternating treatment (multielement) designs (e.g. Iwata *et al.*, 1982; Iwata *et al.*, 1990*c*).

Iwata *et al.* (1990*a*, *b*) made a distinction between two approaches to functional analysis: a general model in which the effects of a number of contexts of general importance are evaluated (e.g. Iwata *et al.*, 1982; Iwata *et al.*, 1994*b*), and a hypothesis-driven model in which specific hypotheses derived from prior descriptive analyses are tested (e.g. Emerson *et al.*, 1990; Mace & Lalli, 1991).

The general model of functional analysis is illustrated in the work of Brian Iwata and his colleagues in the development and use of 'analogue assessment' procedures for evaluating the behavioural processes underlying self-injurious behaviour.

As described in Chapter 4, Iwata *et al.* (1982), used an alternating treatment designed to examine the effect of social context on self-injurious behaviour. They recorded the rates of self-injury under four different conditions. The conditions were selected as representing three *general* cases of the types of contexts under which self-injury maintained by operant processes may occur ('social disapproval', 'academic demand' and 'alone') and one control condition.

☐ In the *social disapproval* condition an adult was present throughout but did not interact with the child except to express concern or mild disapproval (e.g. 'don't do that') on the occurrence of self-injury. It is assumed that self-injury maintained by positive social reinforcement is more likely to occur under this condition.

☐ In the *academic demand* condition an adult was present throughout and encouraged the child to complete an educational task using a graduated (ask–show–guide) prompting procedure. However, the adult withdrew their attention for 30 seconds contingent on the child's self-injury. This condition was assumed to be discriminative for self-injury maintained by negative social reinforcement.

☐ In the *alone* condition no adults or materials were present. This condition was assumed to be discriminative for behaviours maintained by automatic or perceptual reinforcement.

☐ The *control* condition consisted of a stimulating environment in which social attention was delivered contingent upon the non-occurrence of self-injury.

Each condition lasted for 15 minutes and was presented on at least four occasions, the order of presentation being randomised. Visual inspection of the consistency of responding across conditions was used as evidence of behavioural function. Figures 6.1, 6.2 and 6.7 illustrate the use of this procedure.

Over the past decade, this approach has been used increasingly in the functional assessment of self-injurious behaviours (e.g. Day *et al.*, 1988; Derby *et al.*, 1992, 1994; Durand & Crimmins, 1988; Hagopian *et al.*, 1994; Lerman *et al.*, 1994; Iwata *et al.*, 1994*b*; Oliver, 1991, 1993; Steege *et al.*, 1989, 1990; Wacker *et al.*, 1990*a, b*; Vollmer, Marcus & LeBlanc, 1994; Zarcone *et al.*, 1994) and has been extended to different forms of challenging behaviour including aggression (e.g. Derby *et al.*, 1992; Emerson, 1990; Hagopian *et al.*, 1994; Mace *et al.*, 1986; Paisey *et al.*, 1991; Emerson *et al.*, in press*b*; Wacker *et al.*, 1990*a*), pica (Mace & Knight, 1986), bizarre speech (Mace & Lalli, 1991) and stereotypy (e.g. Derby *et al.*, 1994; Mazaleski *et al.*, 1994; Sturmey *et al.*, 1988; Emerson *et al.*, in press*b*). In addition to the types of conditions listed above, studies have also examined covariation between the target behaviour and a variety of environmental conditions including continuous social attention (Oliver, 1991), delayed access to food (Durand & Crimmins, 1988), contingent access to individually defined reinforcers (Day *et al.*, 1988), medical examination (Iwata *et al.*, 1990*a*) and response cost (Steege *et al.*, 1989).

The hypothesis driven model of functional analysis and the use of withdrawal designs is exemplified in the work of Carr and colleagues (see Chapter 4, and Carr & Durand, 1985*a*; Carr *et al.*, 1976; Day *et al.*, 1994).

The value of alternating treatment designs, or their derivatives (e.g. Wacker *et al.*, 1990*a*), and withdrawal designs in conducting a functional analysis are that:

1. they provide a direct, reliable and standardised method for identifying functional relationships;

2. they require only brief changes to the person's environment, which is of particular value when sustaining systematic environmental changes which may be impractical and/or unethical;

3. they are particularly suitable for examining the effects of stimulus conditions which may be conceptually important but which occur only rarely in the person's normal setting (e.g. demands in institutional settings);

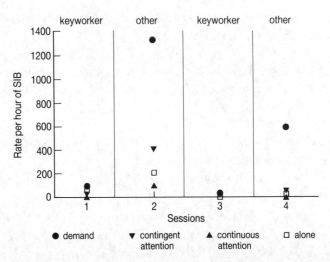

Fig. 6.7. Rate of occurrence of Natasha's self-injurious head hitting across experimental conditions.

4. they involve a high degree of quantitative precision;

5. they provide a practical method of testing hypotheses regarding the role of setting events or establishing operations in the contextual control of challenging behaviour (e.g. Carr *et al.*, 1976).

Indeed, while care needs to be taken to minimise unwanted multiple treatment interference within alternating treatment designs (Barlow & Hersen, 1984; McGonigle *et al.*, 1987), the sensitivity of the designs to interactional or sequence effects should be considered a strength rather than a weakness (Higgins-Hains & Baer, 1989).

The possibility of using a brief alternating treatment design to investigate the role of setting events is simply illustrated in Fig. 6.7. This shows the rate of self-injury shown by a 19 year-old woman with severe learning disabilities under typical analogue conditions of 'social disapproval', 'academic demand' and 'alone'. Sessions one and three involved interaction with the young woman's keyworker, sessions two and four involved interaction with another member of her residential care team. As can be seen, while the function of her self-injury appeared to be to escape from demands, this was only apparent if the demands were made by the 'other' member of staff. This suggests that the identity of the person making the demands acted as an establishing operation in making the (same) demands aversive.

The use of experimental procedures does, however, have a number of limitations (Halle & Spradlin, 1993; Iwata *et al.*, 1990c; Mace, 1994b; Oliver, 1991). In general, they are demanding of resources and expertise both of which may be in short supply in many settings (Durand & Crimmins, 1988: although see Derby *et al.*, 1992; Northup *et al.*, 1991). In such instances the opportunity costs involved in conducting a detailed experimental analysis need to be balanced against the likely benefits accruing from such an activity. For individuals with seriously challenging behaviours, investment in rigorous analysis may well be justified given the personal and social consequences of introducing inefficient or ineffective treatments. In addition, the resources and commitment required are likely to be less than that required during intervention (Iwata, *et al.*, 1990c). As such, functional analyses may provide a valuable behavioural test of staff compliance.

More serious is the possibility that experimental analyses may overlook important variables which may be operating in the person's natural environment. These could include, for example, the operation of situationaly specific or idiosyncratic reinforcers, discriminative stimuli or setting events, and all examples of elicited behaviour (Emerson & Howard, 1992; Romanczyk *et al.*, 1992). This could lead to the assessment process either failing to identify maintaining contingencies (lack of internal validity) or to it providing results which may not generalise beyond the analogue conditions (lack of external validity) (Carr, 1994; Halle & Spradlin, 1993; Iwata *et al.*, 1990c; Mace, 1994b; Oliver, 1991).

These potential limitations argue for the use of hypothesis-driven approaches to functional analysis in which experimental analysis is preceded by a detailed descriptive or structural analysis (Carr, 1994).

Summary

In the sections above, some of the more common descriptive and experimental approaches to the functional assessment of challenging behaviour have been reviewed. Table 6.3 summarises some of the key advantages and disadvantages of these approaches (see also Durand, 1990).

As can be seen, there is a clear (and unsurprising) relationship between the ease of use of different approaches and the detail, reliability and validity of the information generated. While structured interviews are easy to use and comprehensive, the information generated must be treated with considerable caution. The combination of descriptive analyses (e.g. scatter plots, structured observation) with hypothesis-driven experimental analyses is demanding of resources, but may provide clear, reliable and valid information. Of course, functional assessments are often conducted in situations with limited resources and under conditions in which there may be an obvious need to proceed as quickly as possible.

In deciding whether to invest more resources and time in further assessment it is important to keep in mind the aim of the assessment process,

Table 6.3. *Descriptive and experimental approaches to functional assessment*

	Advantages	Disadvantages
Structured interviews (e.g. O'Neill *et al.*, 1990)	Ease of use Comprehensive Applicable to low frequency behaviours	Unknown (but probably poor) reliability and validity
Rating scales (e.g. Durand & Crimmins, 1992)	Ease of use Focus on specific maintaining factors Applicable to low frequency behaviours	Poor reliability and validity
ABC charts (e.g. Pyles & Bailey, 1990)	Ease of use Provide some information about event–behaviour–event sequences Applicable to low frequency behaviours	Often poor reliability and validity Difficult to interpret
Scatter plot (e.g. Touchette *et al.*, 1985)	Ease of use Provide easily interpretable information about broad aspects of contextual control Can be reliable Applicable to low frequency behaviours	Do not provide detailed information of maintaining contingencies
Setting event questionnaire (e.g. Gardner *et al*, 1986)	Ease of use Provide easily interpretable information about broad aspects of contextual control Can be reliable Applicable to low frequency behaviours	Do not provide information about maintaining contingencies
Structured partial-interval record (e.g. Lalli *et al*, 1993)	Can be highly reliable Provide detailed information about immediate event–behaviour–event sequences Precise measurement	More demanding of resources Difficult to apply to low frequency behaviours May have difficulty in distinguishing between positive and negative reinforcement, hence questionable validity

Table 6.3. (cont.)

Structured real-time record with sequential analysis (e.g. Emerson et al., in press a)	Can be highly reliable Provide extremely detailed information about immediate event–behaviour–event sequences Sound statistical basis for decision-making Precise measurement	More demanding of resources Difficult to apply to low frequency behaviours
Standardised experimental analysis (e.g. Iwata, Pace, Dorsey et al., 1994b)	Provide experimental demonstration of stimulus control Precise measurement	More demanding of resources Difficult to apply to low frequency behaviours May overlook important variables operating in natural environment
Brief standardised experimental analysis (e.g. Derby et al., 1992)	Provide experimental demonstration of stimulus control Precise measurement	Difficult to apply to low frequency behaviours Limited internal validity May overlook important variables operating in natural environment
Hypothesis-driven experimental analysis (e.g. Carr et al., 1976)	Links to descriptive analyses Provide experimental demonstration of stimulus control Precise measurement	More demanding of resources Difficult to apply to low frequency behaviours

i.e. to identify the processes maintaining or underlying the person's challenging behaviour.

The role of specific techniques is to generate and test hypotheses about potential processes. Thus, the value of any particular approach is determined by its effect in terms of reducing uncertainty about the processes underlying the person's challenging behaviour. At times these may become painfully obvious through the use of simple descriptive techniques. In such a situation investing additional resources in order to achieve a minimal reduction in uncertainty may be unjustified.

In other situations, however, the use of simple descriptive techniques will reveal complex and confusing patterns of contextual control over the person's challenging behaviour. In such instances, to intervene prior to more detailed analysis would be ethically unjustifiable. As was discussed in the last chapter, failure to match intervention to analysis may be either ineffective or potentially harmful.

ASSESSING EXISTING SKILLS, COMPETENCIES AND POTENTIAL REINFORCERS

The constructional approach looks for solutions to problems in the 'construction of repertoires (or their reinstatement or transfer to new situations) rather than the elimination of repertoires' (Goldiamond, 1974, p.14). As a result, three additional aims of an initial assessment will be:

☐ to evaluate the broad range of skills and competencies the person possesses and to identify any additional impairments which may limit the establishment of new behaviours;

☐ to identify discrepancies between the person's current behaviour in key situations and what may be considered a more appropriate response;

☐ to identify potential reinforcers which may be needed to help establish new behaviours.

General competencies

A large number of questionnaires and checklists have been developed to help assess the general competencies or adaptive behaviours of people with severe learning disabilities (Browder, 1991; Hogg & Raynes, 1986; Leland, 1991; Nihira, Leland & Lambert, 1993). In addition to specific instruments, a number of more comprehensive overviews are available to provide guidance to practitioners regarding the assessment of adaptive behaviours (e.g. Browder, 1991), including texts which focus upon the application of such methods to people with challenging behaviour (e.g. Evans & Meyer, 1985; Meyer & Evans, 1989; Zarkowska & Clements, 1994).

Over the past decade a number of authors have suggested that challenging behaviours may be conceptualised as examples of socially inappropriate communication strategies or interactional styles (Carr & Durand, 1985*b*; Carr *et al.*, 1993; Day, Johnson & Schussler, 1986; Donnellan *et al.*, 1984, 1988; Durand, 1986, 1990; Evans & Meyer, 1985; Meyer & Evans, 1989). Furthermore, as indicated above, evidence has begun to accrue to suggest that some challenging behaviours may be rapidly eliminated by providing the individual with an alternative communicative response which serves the same function as the challenging behaviour (see Chapter 7).

As such, the evaluation of the person's communicative competencies and style is of particular significance. Donnellan *et al.* (1984) described an observational procedure for recording 'ongoing impressions regarding the possible communicative function(s) of the behavior(s) of interest' (p.205). The instrument consisted of a matrix of 31 behaviours, ranging from aggression to complex speech, and 31 possible functions which the behaviours may have served, 27 of which involved social interaction or communication (e.g. requests for attention, declarations about hurt feelings). While no information is provided regarding either the levels of inter-observer agreement obtained or the validity of the instrument in identifying actual behaviour–environment interactions, such an approach may have clinical utility in helping structure informal or qualitative observations.

Discrepancy analysis

One of the specific aims of a functionally-based constructional approach to remediating challenging behaviour is to identify skill deficits specific to conditions known to evoke challenging behaviour. Evans and Meyer (1985) suggested that 'discrepancy analysis' be employed to identify the skill deficiencies (and hence targets for intervention) associated with the person's challenging behaviour. A discrepancy analysis involves the comparison of the individual's performance in a problematic situation with that of a non-handicapped (or more competent) peer. On the basis of such a qualitative comparison, specific skill deficiencies may be identified as targets for intervention (Browder, 1991; Meyer & Evans, 1989). Such an approach has many similarities with some procedures for assessing the social validity of intervention outcomes and targets (Schwartz & Baer, 1991).

Identifying potential reinforcers

The establishment or generalisation of alternative responses to challenging behaviours may require the use of additional extrinsic reinforcers. For example, one possible strategy to reduce challenging behaviours maintained by perceptual reinforcement is to provide access to, and teach the use of, alternative reinforcing materials or activities (Mace & Roberts, 1993; Vollmer, 1994). Of course, a functional assessment may well identify some extremely powerful reinforcers and contingencies – those maintaining the challenging behaviour itself. Approaches to intervention based on the notion of functional displacement (Carr, 1988), seek to use these contingencies to support alternative behaviours (see Chapter 7).

In other situations, however, the reinforcers maintaining the challenging behaviour may be unclear or not readily accessible by other means (e.g. β-endorphin release). In these cases the identification of alternative reinforcers assumes a greater significance. There are three possible approaches for identifying potential reinforcers for people with severe learning disabilities: indirect approaches involving informant interviews; theory-driven approaches; and empirical approaches.

Indirect approaches involve soliciting judgements from key informants regarding the potentially reinforcing properties of stimuli. As noted above, however, the validity of such ratings is highly questionable (Green *et al.*, 1988, 1991). Nevertheless, indirect approaches have an obvious role to play in selecting potential stimuli for empirical evaluation (Newton *et al.*, 1993).

Theory-driven approaches seek to identify potential reinforcers on the basis of predictions from either the Premack Principle (Premack, 1959) or molar equilibrium theory (Timberlake, 1980). The Premack Principle suggests that the opportunity to engage in high probability behaviours can be used to reinforce the performance of low probability behaviours. Molar equilibrium theory extends this notion to suggest that, in effect, the opportunity to engage in any behaviour shown by the organism under a free-operant baseline can be used to reinforce or punish the performance of any other behaviour, depending upon the constraining conditions imposed (see Chapters 4 and 7). An interesting application of these approaches was reported by Charlop, Kurtz and Casey (1990). They demonstrated that the opportunity to engage in high probability stereotypy following completion of an academic task acted as a more powerful reinforcer than food for autistic children. Furthermore, they reported no negative side effects of this procedure (Charlop *et al.*, 1990).

Finally, *empirical approaches* seek to identify reinforcers by examining their actual impact upon behaviour (Berg & Wacker, 1991). A number of strategies have been employed to do this including:

☐ measuring approach responses to individual stimuli selected from an array (e.g. Green *et al.*, 1988, 1991; Pace *et al.*, 1985; Sigafoos & Dempsey, 1992; Steege *et al.*, 1989);

☐ measuring approach responses in a forced-choice situation (e.g. Fisher *et al.*, 1992; Parsons & Reid, 1990);

☐ evaluating the extent to which stimuli presented contingently would increase the rate of motor behaviours for people with profound multiple handicaps (e.g. Wacker *et al.*, 1985; Wacker *et al.*, 1988).

The available evidence suggests that the use of forced choice situations may increase the predictive power of reinforcer selection based on approach behaviours (Fisher *et al.*, 1992). This empirical approach has recently been extended to the identification of negative reinforcers or punishers (Fisher *et al.*, 1994). A number of recent studies have illustrated procedures for teaching choice-making to people with more severe disabilities (e.g. Kennedy & Haring, 1993; Reichle, Sigafoos & Piché, 1989; Wacker *et al.*, 1985, 1988).

EVALUATING THE RISKS, COSTS AND BENEFITS OF INTERVENTION

At a number of points throughout the book attention has been drawn to the need to address the social validity of intervention. It has been argued that:

☐ challenging behaviour needs to be understood in its social context, including the impact it may have on broader aspects of the quality of life of the person, their family and friends, co-residents and co-workers, care staff and the public;

☐ socially valid interventions should involve procedures acceptable to the main stakeholders in the intervention process;

☐ socially valid interventions should also result in socially significant outcomes. These need to be framed in a broader social context than is usually the case and may involve a trade-off between procedural acceptability and the speed and magnitude of outcome.

These observations indicate the need for the assessment process to collect baseline information on a range of potential outcomes in order for the risks, costs and benefits of intervention to be thoroughly evaluated. As has been indicated, however, it is important that the process is individualised and focuses upon the *legitimate outcomes of intervention.* This requires, among other things, that the goals of intervention are separated from more general life planning processes.

Let us take, for example, the situation of a young woman, living in a small house with two other women with severe learning disabilities, who shows

Table 6.4. *Assessing the risks, costs and benefits of socially significant intervention outcomes*

Outcomes	Potential approaches
Potential benefits to the person	
Reductions in rate, duration, intensity of challenging behaviour	Observational methods (see *Journal of Applied Behaviour Analysis*, 1967 onwards)
	Structured interview with person and/or informants
	Analysis of incident reports
Reductions in injuries received	Medical inspection
	Analysis of hospital/medical contacts
	'Blind' rating of photographs
	Rating scales
	Structured interview with person and/or informants
Reduced use or restrictive management practices	Analysis of medication records
	Recording of time spent in restraint/seclusion
	Analysis of records detailing restriction of liberty
	Analysis of risk-taking policies for person
Increased participation in domestic, vocational and recreational community-based activities	Direct observation
	Diaries
	Structured interview with person/informants
Increased and/or more appropriate social contact with co-residents/workers and care staff	Direct observation
	Diaries
	Structured interview with person/informants
Increased and/or more appropriate social contact with non-disabled peers, family and acquaintances	Diaries
	Structured interview with person/informants
Increased personal life satisfaction	Ratings/observation of positive effect
	Structured interview with person/informants
Potential risks/costs to person	
Psychological or physical distress caused by intervention procedure	Observation of negative affect (e.g. negative vocalisations, screaming, escape)
Restrictions imposed on lifestyle by intervention procedure	Analysis of programme documentation (e.g. restriction of free access to positive reinforcers, restriction of movement due to requirement to attend therapeutic activities)
Replacement of challenging behaviour with other/new challenging behaviours	Observational methods (see *Journal of Applied Behaviour Analysis*, 1967 onwards)
	Structured interview with person and/or informants
Reduced participation and/or social contacts	See above

Table 6.4. (*continued*)

Outcomes	Potential approaches
Potential benefits to others	
Reductions in injuries received	Medical inspection
	Analysis of hospital/medical contacts
	'Blind' rating of photographs
	Rating scales
	Structured interview with person and/or informants
Increased participation in domestic, vocational and recreational community-based activities	See above
Increased and/or more appropriate social contact with co-residents/workers and care staff	See above
Increased and/or more appropriate social contact with non-disabled peers, family and acquaintances	See above
Increased personal life satisfaction	See above
	Rating of stress
	Formal measures of quality of life
Potential risks/costs to others	
Injuries received as a result of the intervention process	See above
Psychological distress caused by intervention process	Structured interview
Restrictions on liberty imposed by intervention process	See above
Financial costs resulting from intervention process	Analysis of programme documentation
	Structured interview
Reduction in participation, social relationships, etc.	See above

self-injurious behaviour. None of the women attends any sort of day programme. Indeed, most of the people served by that particular agency have very restricted lives. In terms of lifestyle, the young woman does not stand out from her peers.

In this instance, it would appear that her challenging behaviour is not functionally related to her poor lifestyle. Rather, her social and physical isolation stem from the failing of the wider service agency. It would seem inappropriate, then, to judge the success of an intervention programme to reduce self-injury on the basis of such general lifestyle variables as earned income, social and physical integration.

Possible approaches to evaluating the broader outcomes of intervention which have been established as being functionally related to the person's challenging behaviour are illustrated in Table 6.4 (see also Meyer & Janney, 1989).

SUMMARY

In the sections above, some of the key techniques and issues involved in the assessment of challenging behaviour have been examined. It has been argued that the assessment process will need to:

☐ identify and prioritise socially significant targets for intervention;

☐ determine the processes underlying the challenging behaviour(s) shown by the person;

☐ assess general and specific aspects of the person's existing skills and competencies;

☐ identify potential reinforcers;

☐ collect information which will allow the attainment of the legitimate targets of intervention to be evaluated.

In the next chapter, behavioural approaches to intervention will be considered.

7 BEHAVIOURAL APPROACHES

In this chapter, a range of behavioural approaches for reducing challenging behaviour will be examined. It is not the intention, however, to provide a comprehensive meta-analysis of this vast area. Instead, attention will be directed to those approaches which may form important components of the emerging technology of effective 'non-aversive' behavioural support. Particular consideration will be given to approaches which are constructional, functionally based and socially valid.

Those who are looking for more comprehensive or detailed reviews of specific areas are referred to the plethora of publications relating to this topic which have appeared over the last decade (e.g. Carr *et al.*, 1990*b*; Cataldo, 1991; Cipani, 1989; Durand & Crimmins, 1991; Emerson, 1992, 1993; Gardner & Cole, 1989, 1990; Gorman-Smith & Matson, 1985; Helmstetter & Durand, 1991; Hile & Vatterott, 1991; Jones, 1991; Kiernan, 1985, 1993; Konarski *et al.*, 1992; Luiselli, Matson & Singh, 1992; Lundervold & Bourland, 1988; Mace *et al.*, 1991; Matson & Taras, 1989; Mulick, Hammer & Dura, 1991; O'Brien & Repp, 1990; Oliver, 1993; Oliver & Head, 1990; Reichle & Wacker, 1993; Repp & Singh, 1990; Rojahn & Sisson, 1990; Schlosser & Goetze, 1992; Schroeder, 1991; Schroeder *et al.*, 1990*b*, 1991; Scotti *et al.*, 1991*b*).

The contents of the chapter have been organised in terms of the general rationale behind particular approaches to intervention. Thus, approaches will be discussed which are based on:

☐ manipulating antecedent stimuli or changing the context to prevent the occurrence of challenging behaviour;

☐ behavioural competition or response covariation;

☐ disruption of maintaining contingencies; and punishment or other default technologies.

In practice, of course, intervention programmes are likely to consist of a number of distinct approaches. The chapter will, therefore, be concluded by an examination of multi-component strategies including self-management and self-control.

PREVENTION: CHANGING THE CONTEXT IN WHICH CHALLENGING BEHAVIOURS OCCUR

The results of a functional assessment should indicate: (1) contexts or settings in which the challenging behaviour is significantly more likely to occur; (2) personal or environmental setting events which may either activate or abolish the contingencies maintaining the person's challenging behaviour; and (3) the nature of the contingencies themselves.

This knowledge opens up two possibilities for either preventing or reducing the occurrence of challenging behaviours by manipulating antecedent variables. First, and very simply, the person's activities could be re-scheduled or re-arranged so as to avoid those situations in which challenging behaviours are most likely to occur. Secondly, the underlying motivational basis for the challenging behaviour may be altered through the modification of setting events.

Rescheduling activities

Touchette *et al.* (1985) described the use of a scatter plot (see Chapter 6) to identify the settings associated with high rate aggression shown by a 14 year-old girl with autism and severe learning disabilities. The results of this descriptive analysis indicated that the majority of episodes of aggression were associated with certain activities, in particular her attendance at pre-vocational and community living classes. Following the re-scheduling of her weekly timetable, in which activities associated with low rates of aggression were substituted for these class activities, the girl's aggression was rapidly reduced to near zero levels. Similarly, Touchette *et al.* (1985) demonstrated the rapid elimination of the serious self-injurious behaviour shown by a 23 year-old man with autism following the re-allocation of care staff. In both examples, it proved possible over time to gradually re-introduce (or fade in) the activity or person which had been associated with high rates of challenging behaviour while maintaining the treatment gains.

Using a similar approach, the assessment of participant preferences are taken into consideration when designing educational or vocational curricula in order to reduce or prevent the occurrence of challenging behaviour (e.g. Cooper *et al.*, 1992; Dunlap *et al.*, 1991, 1993, 1994; Dyer, 1987; Dyer *et al.*, 1990; Foster-Johnson *et al.*, 1994). For example, Foster-Johnson *et al.* (1994) used an observational procedure to assess preference for curricular activities with three children with learning disabilities (cf. Dyer, 1987). Subsequent experimental analysis using a withdrawal design revealed higher rates of challenging behaviour during non-preferred activities and, for two of the three participants, higher rates of desirable behaviours during the preferred activities. Approaches to determining student preference are described in Chapter 6. In addition, a number of recent studies have ill-ustrated procedures for teaching choice-making to people with more severe disabilities (e.g. Kennedy & Haring, 1993; Reichle *et al.*, 1989; Wacker *et al.*, 1985, 1988).

Such an approach has obvious attractions for the treatment of challenging behaviour which is under clear contextual control, in that: (1) it can result in rapid and marked reductions in the challenging behaviour; and (2) it may be relatively easy to sustain since it requires organisational change rather than day-to-day implementation by carers or care staff. Its primary disadvantages, however, are that (1) the settings which evoke behaviour may be either important for the person's health and safety, development or quality of life (e.g. interaction with other people, requests to participate in an activity) or (2) it may be difficult to avoid the eliciting circumstances.

Modification of setting events

A wide range of antecedent manipulations have been shown to decrease the rate of various types of challenging behaviour. It is probable that a number of these have their effect by reducing the potency of the reinforcers responsible for maintaining challenging behaviour. That is, they involve the modification of establishing operations or stimuli which set the occasion for the behaviour to occur. A number of specific techniques and general approaches are outlined below.

Generalised environmental enrichment and non-contingent reinforcement

A number of studies have indicated that generally enriching the environment by, for example, increasing interaction or introducing materials into barren environments may lead to a reduction in the rate of challenging behaviours. Thus, for example, increasing social contact (Baumeister *et al.*, 1980; Mace & Knight, 1986), providing toys (Favell *et al.*, 1982; Finney, Russo & Cataldo, 1982; Horner, 1980), visual stimulation (Forehand & Baumeister, 1970), leisure activities (Sigafoos & Kerr, 1994) and music (Mace, Yankanich & West, 1989) have been associated with increased compliance (Nordquist, Twardosz & McEvoy, 1991), and reduced rates of stereotypy (Baumeister *et al.*, 1980; Forehand & Baumeister, 1970; Horner, 1980; Mace & Knight, 1986; Mace *et al.*, 1989) and self-injury (Favell *et al.*, 1982; Finney *et al.*, 1982). Similarly, moving from materially and socially deprived institutional settings into enriched community-based residential provision is commonly associated with a reduced rate of stereotypic (although not more seriously challenging) behaviour (Emerson & Hatton, 1994).

These results are consistent with predictions made from behavioural theory. As McDowell (1982) has pointed out, Herrnstein has demonstrated that a hyperbolic relationship exists between the rate of response contingent reinforcement and behaviour. The relationship is moderated, however, by the rate of background or response-independent reinforcement *. One implication of this observation is that a particular rate of reinforcement will sustain a greater response rate in an impoverished environment than in an enriched environment. Put another way, increasing the rate of 'free' or response independent reinforcement should decrease response rate for a given rate of contingent reinforcement. Thus, the rate of behaviours maintained by positive reinforcement (external or automatic) should reduce as the background level of reinforcement increases.

As was noted in Chapter 4, however, other studies have indicated that increasing the level of stimulation in the environment through visual displays (Duker & Rasing, 1989), television (Gary, Tallon & Stangl, 1980) and crowding (McAfee, 1987) can lead to increased rates of stereotypy (Duker & Rasing, 1989; Gary et al., 1980), aggression (McAfee, 1987) and decreased task performance (Duker and Rasing, 1989). The results suggest that, for the individuals concerned, the environmental enrichment may be associated with increased rates of negative reinforcement (e.g. over-arousal, increased rates of negative peer contact). The contradictory nature of the results highlights the importance of basing interventions on prior functional assessment, since the same environmental changes may have very different effects on topographically similar behaviours (cf. Duker & Rasing, 1989; Nordquist et al., 1991).

A more specific illustration of reducing the rate of challenging behaviour by increasing the rate of background reinforcement is provided by studies of the effects of non-contingent (or response-independent) reinforcement and reinforcer satiation. In these studies the background rate of the *specific reinforcer maintaining the challenging behaviour* is increased. Of course, if the background rate of reinforcement is sufficiently high, it will abolish the deprivational condition which establishes the stimulus as reinforcing and consequently eliminate the challenging behaviour. That is, it should prevent maintaining stimuli acting as reinforcers in that particular context.

Mace and Lalli (1991), for example, demonstrated that the bizarre 'delusional and hallucinatory' speech of a 46 year-old man with moderate learning disabilities was maintained by attention. Subsequently, the provision of non-contingent attention on a conjunctive fixed-time, DRO schedule** resulted in the immediate reduction of bizarre speech to near zero levels. More recently, Hagopian et al. (1994) examined the effects of dense and lean

* See Martens and Houk (1989) for an applied demonstration of the predictive power of Herrnstein's mathematical formulation of the law of effect.
** A conjunctive FT–DRO schedule results in the reinforcer being presented after a set period of time has elapsed (FT component) as long as the target behaviour was not occurring (DRO component).

schedules of non-contingent reinforcement on the attention-maintained aggressive, disruptive and self-injurious behaviour shown by four, five year-old identical quadruplets with learning disabilities and pervasive developmental disorder. They reported that: (1) the dense (FT-10 s) schedule resulted in greater reductions in disruptive behaviour (virtual elimination) than the lean (FT-5 min) schedule; (2) it was possible to gradually fade from the dense to lean schedule over a period of 55–85, 20 minute sessions while maintaining treatment gains; (3) once established on the FT-5 min schedule, it was possible to generalise treatment gains to the home setting using the children's mother as the therapist. These gains were maintained at one and two month follow-up (see also Vollmer *et al.*, 1993).

An example of the use of non-contingent negative reinforcement was probably provided by Gaylord-Ross, Weeks and Lipner (1980). They substantially reduced the rate of escape-maintained self-injury by scheduling frequent breaks in tasks which had previously elicited challenging behaviour.

Satiation involves allowing free access to the reinforcer maintaining challenging behaviour for a specified period of time. This technique has been used successfully to reduce rumination (the regurgitation and chewing of food). Rast *et al.* (1981) and Rast, Johnston and Drum (1984) demonstrated that rumination in people with profound learning disabilities could be prevented if they were allowed to eat until they were full. Given that the participants in these studies were underweight, increased calorific intake was in itself beneficial.

The value of approaches based on the use of non-contingent reinforcement are that: (1) they are relatively simple to implement; (2) they appear to have few side-effects; and (3) they may prevent the development of deprivational conditions which set the occasion for challenging behaviour to occur (Vollmer *et al.*, 1993). One general concern, however, is that while functionally based, such procedures are not constructional. That is, no new behaviours are established or generalised to the settings in which the person had learned a strategy for accessing particular stimuli. Indeed, the procedure results in an overall loss of opportunities for the person with severe disabilities to exert control over their environment. Given the generalised importance of our ability to exercise control (Bannerman *et al.*, 1990), and the very limited opportunities for control available to people with severe disabilities, perhaps the use of non-contingent reinforcement *on its own* should be advocated with some caution.

Changing the nature of preceding activities

The nature of preceding activities may have a significant impact on people's responses to ongoing events. Krantz and Risley (1977), for example, identified some effects of the scheduling of activities upon disruptive behaviour in a preschool setting. They reported that levels of disruption during a story-telling period were markedly reduced if the activity was preceded by a rest period rather than by a period of vigorous activity. In a similar vein, Wahler (1980) presented data to suggest that aversive interactions between low-income parents and their relatives or workers from service agencies set the occasion for subsequent aversive interactions between parents and children.

Studies have examined a number of types of preceding activities on subsequent rates of challenging behaviour. These include studies of the effects of:

☐ behavioural momentum in increasing compliance and reducing challenging behaviours associated with non-compliance;

☐ choice-making;

☐ task variety and stimulus fading;

☐ exercise; and

☐ a variety of idiosyncratic setting events.

Mace *et al.* (1988) described the application of the phenomenon of *behavioural momentum* to the reduction of challenging behaviour. Behavioural momentum refers to the temporary but marked increase in response probability for a response class following a period of reinforcement. That is, following repeated reinforcement, behaviour appears to gain a 'momentum' which makes it temporarily resistant to change. Mace *et al.* (1988) applied the notion of behavioural momentum to increase compliance in four men with learning disabilities. They first identified requests which either elicited high (high probability requests) or low (low probability requests) rates of compliance. They reported that compliance with low probability requests was significantly increased by preceding them with a series of high probability requests. Subsequent studies have also demonstrated that this procedure is effective in reducing challenging behaviours associated with non-compliance. For example, preceding a request to take medication (which often led to challenging behaviour) with a series of requests to 'give me five' resulted in increased compliance and reduced challenging behaviour (Harchik & Putzier, 1990). It would appear that the generalised response class of complying with requests had gained a momentum from prior reinforcement which 'carried over' to the more problematic request. A number of studies since then have illustrated the viability of this procedure across a range of settings (e.g. Davis *et al.*, 1992; Horner *et al.*, 1991; Mace & Belfiore, 1990; Singer, Singer & Horner, 1987).

In the previous section the effects of basing educational curricula on participant preferences were discussed. A small number of studies have also suggested that the actual act of choice-making may be important in increasing participation (Bambara, Ager & Koger, 1994; Mithaug & Mar, 1980; Parsons *et al.*, 1990) and reducing challenging behaviour (Dyer *et al.*, 1990). Dunlap *et al.*, (1994), for example, attempted to untangle the effects of the act of choosing and the results of choosing (gaining access to preferred activities) in a study involving three young boys with severe emotional and behavioural difficulties. They found that, when the children chose tasks, they showed greater engagement and less challenging behaviour than when simply presented with identical tasks at other times. While this obviously does not account for momentary fluctuations in preferences, it does suggest that the act of choosing itself may be important (cf. Bannerman *et al.*, 1990).

Previous exposure to tasks associated with high rates of challenging behaviour may either increase or decrease challenging behaviour when the task in next presented. Winterling *et al.* (1987) reported that increasing task variety (and decreasing repetition) was associated with immediate and significant reductions in aggression and tantrums for three young people with learning disabilities and autism. These results are consistent with the suggestion that *repeated exposure* to the task within a short period of time acted as an establishing operation, leading to subsequent presentations acting as negative reinforcers.

Alternatively, a small number of studies have examined the potentially therapeutic effects of *stimulus fading* (e.g. Heidorn & Jensen, 1984; Kennedy, 1994). Stimulus fading refers to the temporary withdrawal and gradual re-introduction of stimuli which set the occasion for challenging behaviour. For example, Touchette *et al.* (1985) reported that, once challenging behaviour had been eliminated by rescheduling activities, it had been possible to gradually re-introduce the activities whilst maintaining treatment gains (see above). More recently, the technique of stimulus fading has been combined with the use of negative extinction in the treatment of escape-motivated self-injurious behaviour. The results of these studies suggest that, while stimulus fading may help avoid the occurrence of an extinction burst (Zarcone *et al.*, 1993), it does not necessarily appear to increase the effectiveness of the extinction procedure itself (Zarcone *et al.*, 1993; although see also Pace *et al.*, 1993).

The technique of stimulus fading is, of course, procedurally similar to the techniques of systematic desensitisation and reinforced graded practice in the treatment of fears and phobias (cf. Marks, 1987). This, when combined with the suggestion that conditioned arousal may be implicated in the maintenance of self-injury (Romanczyk, 1986; Romanczyk *et al.*, 1992), suggests that the effectiveness of stimulus fading may be increased if combined with procedures incompatible with arousal (e.g. relaxation, massage, eating). While there have been no tests of this specific hypothesis, a few case studies have reported the beneficial effects of including relaxation training or massage as a component of more complex treatment packages (Bull & Vecchio, 1978; Dossetor, Couryer & Nicol, 1991; Steen & Zuriff, 1977). Steen and Zuriff (1977), for example, describe the use of relaxation training and reinforced practice* during the phased removal of restraints from a 21 year-old woman with severe learning disabilities. Prior to intervention she had been kept in full restraint (involving tying her ankles and wrists to her bed) for the previous three years in an attempt to control her self-injurious finger biting, and the scratching of her legs, face and scalp. Within 115 sessions over a total time of 17 hours, her self-injury was virtually eliminated.

More recently, Kennedy (1994) combined the stimulus fading of instructor demands with high rates of non-contingent praise to reduce the escape-motivated challenging behaviour of two 20 year-old men and one 20 year-old woman with severe learning disabilities. He also reported that, for two of the participants, a repetition of the preliminary functional assessment after intervention indicated that teacher demands no longer served as antecedents to challenging behaviour.

Numerous studies have reported that physical exercise may result in reductions in stereotypic (Bachman & Fuqua, 1983; Bachman & Sluyter, 1988; Baumeister & MacLean, 1984; Kern et al., 1982; Kern, Koegel & Dunlap, 1984), self-injurious (Baumeister & MacLean, 1984; Lancioni et al., 1984) and aggressive or disruptive behaviours (Jansma & Combs, 1987; McGimsey & Favell, 1988; Tomporowski & Ellis, 1984, 1985) during subsequent activities. Greater reductions in challenging behaviour have been reported for more strenuous activities (e.g. jogging compared with ball games, Kern et al., 1984). These results cannot be accounted for by overall reductions in activity since some studies also report increases in the amount of time spent on task and work performance (e.g. Kern et al., 1982). Schroeder and Tessel (1994) suggest that the results may reflect the impact of exercise on dopamine turnover. Whatever the mechanism, the accumulated evidence points to a consistent, although not inevitable (e.g. Larson & Miltenberger, 1992), effect of strenuous aerobic exercise on subsequent activity.

Finally, as we saw in Chapter 6, Gardner et al. (1984, 1986) and Kennedy and Itkonen (1993) have presented data to link idiosyncratic, temporally distant events (e.g. difficulty getting up, the choice of route to school) with a significantly increased probability of challenging behaviour. Figure 7.1, from Kennedy and Itkonen (1993), shows the effect of travelling to college via the

* Equivalent to a DRO schedule.

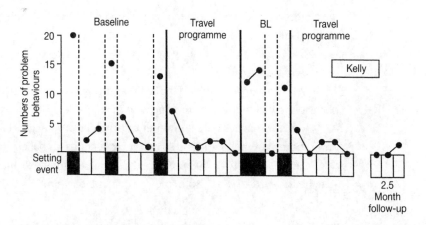

Fig. 7.1. Results for Kelly in Study 2. The data are presented as the frequency of problem behaviour per school day. Closed rectangles arrayed along the horizontal axis indicate the occurrence of a setting event. (From Kennedy & Itkonen, 1993).

'city route' (dark squares) versus the 'highway route' (light squares) on the frequency of subsequent aggressive and disruptive behaviours shown by Kelly, a 20 year-old woman with severe learning disabilities, cerebral palsy and visual impairments. The 'travel program' consisted solely of travelling by the 'highway route'. As can be seen, marked and systematic changes were associated with choice of route. The 'intervention' resulted in rapid and significant reduction in challenging behaviour, these gains being maintained two and a half months later. Clearly, descriptive and experimental analyses are essential for identifying the operation of such idiosyncratic setting events.

Embedding: changing the nature of concurrent activities

A number of studies have indicated that challenging behaviour may be substantially reduced by changing the nature or context of concurrent activities. The use of the phenomenon of 'behavioural momentum' to increase compliance and reduce challenging behaviours associated with non- compliance has been discussed above. As was demonstrated in Chapter 4, changing relatively superficial aspects of the context in which requests are made had an immediate and dramatic effect on the severe self-injury shown by an eight year-old boy with learning disabilities and childhood schizophrenia. Similarly, Carr and Newsom (1985), Carr, Newsom and Binkoff (1980) and Kennedy (1994) have shown that increasing the rate of positive reinforcers in 'high risk' situations may significantly reduce escape-motivated challenging behaviour. In addition, Carr *et al.* (1980), described evidence that combining experimenter demands with access to toys and food immediately reduced to near zero rates, the aggression shown by a nine year-old boy with severe learning disabilities and autism.

Summary

Table 7.1 summarises some of the main approaches to reducing challenging behaviour which rely on the modification of antecedent or contextual factors.

Such approaches have a number of potential advantages. First, they can bring about extremely rapid and significant reductions in challenging behaviour (e.g. Carr *et al.*, 1976, 1980; Kennedy, 1994; Kennedy & Itkonen, 1993; Touchette *et al.*, 1985). Both the speed and magnitude of the reported

Table 7.1. *Antecedent manipulations: changing the context in which challenging behaviours occur*

Method	Examples
General Approaches	
Increase the rate of general stimulation available in the setting	Baumeister *et al.* (1980); Horner (1980)
Non-contingent exercise	Bachman & Fuqua (1983); Kern *et al.* (1982, 1984)
Increase opportunities for choice-making	Dyer *et al.* (1990)
Functionally based approaches	
Avoid antecedents which set occasion for challenging behaviour	Touchette *et al.* (1985)
Base activities on participant preferences	Foster-Johnson *et al.* (1994)
Gradually re-introduce antecedents which set occasion for challenging behaviour (stimulus fading)	Zarcone *et al.* (1993)
Increase task variety	Winterling *et al.* (1987)
Embed antecedents which set occasion for challenging behaviour in reinforcing context	Carr *et al.* (1976, 1980)
Precede antecedents with requests which normally elicit compliance (behavioural momentum)	Mace *et al.* (1988)
Non-contingent reinforcement satiation	Hagopian *et al.* (1994) Rast *et al.* (1984)
Modify idiosyncratic setting events	Gardner *et al.* (1986); Kennedy & Itkonen (1993)

changes compare well with more traditional approaches to intervention (Carr *et al.*, 1990*b*). Indeed, if the intervention is successful in removing those setting events which establish the reinforcing potential of the stimuli maintaining the person's challenging behaviour, we would expect the intervention to *immediately eliminate* the challenging behaviour. To date, however, such dramatic effects have only been reported for escape-motivated challenging behaviour where preliminary descriptive or experimental analyses have been able to identify clear environmental setting events. Little attention has been paid to the analysis and modification of bio-behavioural states as potential setting events.

Secondly, approaches based on the modification of antecedent events may be relatively easy to implement and sustain over time. Such approaches place less reliance on altering the nature of carers' responses to episodes of challenging behaviour, responses which may be powerfully determined by the dynamics of the challenging behaviour itself (Taylor & Carr, 1993, 1994). Failure to sustain 'successful' intervention programmes and the re-emergence of challenging behaviour has been one of the enduring problems faced by applied behavioural approaches.

Finally, studies to date have not reported any negative 'side-effects' of intervention. Again, this is consistent with the underlying rationale of the approach. If the motivational bases for challenging behaviour can be removed, there is no particular reason why new challenging behaviours should emerge to replace those eliminated.

BEHAVIOURAL COMPETITION AND RESPONSE COVARIATION

The second set of approaches to intervention which will be examined are all based on the notion that decreases in challenging behaviour may be brought about indirectly through increasing the rate of other behaviours. Two sets of procedures which share this common aim will be discussed:

☐ the use of *functional displacement* to replace challenging behaviour with a more appropriate member of the same response class (Carr, 1988); and

☐ other procedures involving the *differential reinforcement* of other, alternative or incompatible behaviours.

Before discussing these techniques, however, some of the concepts and evidence underlying this set of approaches will be briefly reviewed.

As discussed in Chapter 4, a behavioural perspective is primarily concerned with the discovery of *functional relationships* between behaviours, and between behaviour and environmental variables. It also views the behaviours shown by a person as the product of a *dynamic system* of elements which may interact in complex and unforeseen ways. Early behavioural studies illustrated the possible complexity of such behaviour–behaviour (or response–response) relationships. Sajwaj, Twardosz and Burke (1972), for example, examined the effects and 'side-effects' of differential reinforcement and extinction procedures on the excessive talking of a child with learning disabilities. They reported that, as the intervention was successfully implemented in one setting, the child's behaviour deteriorated in a second setting. In addition, the occurrence of different appropriate and challenging behaviours shown by the child appeared to be positively or negatively correlated to varying extents.

The concern with the discovery of functional relationships between behaviours led to the notion of *response classes*. Response classes are topographically distinct behaviours which have the same functional relationship to environmental events. So, for example, pressing a light switch with your thumb or index finger has the same environmental effect. As such, these two behaviours are members of the same response class. It was also suggested that different forms of challenging behaviour may be members of the same or different response classes, and that a behaviour's membership of a response class may vary over time and across settings. Intervention through functional displacement (Carr, 1988) seeks to establish and/or differentially reinforce socially appropriate members of response classes containing challenging behaviour.

Other concepts have also been developed to describe the organisation of behaviour (see Evans *et al.*, 1988; Parrish & Roberts, 1993; Schroeder & MacLean, 1987; Scotti *et al.*, 1991*a*; Voeltz & Evans, 1982; Wahler & Graves, 1983). The most important of these are *behavioural clusters, keystone behaviours* and *response chains*.

The *behavioural cluster* is a theoretically neutral term which refers to behaviours which tend to occur together in the same context. So, for example, writing an essay, drinking coffee and gazing out of the window may form a cluster of behaviours centred around the *keystone or pivotal behaviour* of writing. That is, knowledge of the keystone behaviour allows us to predict the occurrence of other behaviours in the cluster. Wahler (1975), in a classic study, examined the correlation of 19 categories of child behaviour and six categories of social–environmental events across two settings for two boys. He identified a number of naturally covarying behavioural clusters which were all specific to a particular setting. Clusters were, however, stable over time and across experimental phases. So, for example, the self-stimulatory behaviour of one participant was positively correlated with social contact at home, and with sustained attention to classroom work at school. Wahler (1975) suggested that such analyses may indicate ways in which covert or low frequency behaviours may be treated indirectly and may help identify keystone behaviours whose modification may be associated with more widespread positive change. Evidence in support of such suggestions had been provided earlier by Wahler *et al.* (1970). They reported two examples in which stuttering had spontaneously improved following intervention for oppositional behaviour. In the framework we have been discussing, oppositional behaviour may be considered a keystone behaviour of a cluster containing stuttering.

Response chains are sequences of behaviour where each step in the chain is dependent upon the occurrence of the previous 'link'. Taking a bath, for example, includes a chain of behaviours (putting the plug in, running the water ....) in which the completion of each step sets the occasion for the next step in the sequence. Performance of the complete chain is maintained by end-point reinforcing contingencies. It is possible that some examples of challenging behaviours which occur together may form response chains (Parrish & Roberts, 1993; Scotti *et al.*, 1991*a*). If this were the case, then intervention focused on initial components in the chain should have generalised benefits in also preventing the occurrence of later links.

Functional displacement

As noted above, intervention through functional displacement seeks to establish and/or differentially reinforce socially appropriate members of response classes containing challenging behaviour. That is, it does not aim to alter either the antecedents which set the occasion for the behaviour to occur, or the contingencies maintaining the challenging behaviour. Rather, it seeks to introduce a new behaviour (or increase the rate of a pre-existing behaviour) which will tap in to the existing contingencies and displace the challenging behaviour.

The seminal study in this area was conducted by Carr and Durand (1985*a*). In their first experiment they used a withdrawal design to undertake a thorough functional analysis to determine the processes underlying the disruptive behaviours (aggression, tantrums, self-injury, non-compliance) shown by four children with learning disabilities (Jim, Eve, Tom and Sue). Jim and Eve's disruptive behaviours appeared to be maintained by negative reinforcement involving escape from difficult tasks. Tom's disruptive behaviours appeared to be maintained by positive reinforcement involving teacher attention. Sue's disruptive behaviours appeared to be maintained by both negative reinforcement involving escape from difficult tasks *and* positive reinforcement involving teacher attention.

In Experiment II, Carr and Durand taught the children 'relevant' and 'irrelevant' communicative responses to the situations which elicited their challenging behaviour. The relevant response was functionally equivalent to the child's challenging behaviour. This involved either asking the teacher for help, by saying 'I don't understand', during difficult tasks (Jim, Eve and Sue) or asking the teacher for feedback, by asking 'Am I doing good work?', during easy tasks (Tom and Sue). The irrelevant response was functionally unrelated to the child's challenging behaviour. This involved either asking the teacher for feedback during difficult tasks (Jim, Eve and Sue) or asking the teacher for help during easy tasks (Tom and Sue). The results of this study demonstrated immediate and dramatic reductions in each of the children's challenging behaviours when the child was pre-trained on the relevant (functionally equivalent) communicative response (Fig. 7.2). Training on the irrelevant communicative response had no effect.

Two studies serve to illustrate the use of functional displacement to reduce the challenging behaviour shown by people with more severe disabilities. Steege et al. (1990) taught two young children with severe multiple disabilities to press a microswitch which activated a tape recording to request a break from self-care activities. Use of this assistive device was associated with significant reductions in their escape-motivated self-injurious behaviour. Bird et al. (1989) described the use of functional communication training to eliminate the severe escape-maintained challenging behaviours of two men (Gregg and Jim) with severe learning disabilities. Gregg was taught to exchange a token for a short break from vocational tasks. Jim was taught to use the manual sign 'break'. In addition to rapid and marked reductions in challenging behaviour, spontaneous communication increased in a range of settings and, interestingly, both men spent more time on-task than they had previously as well as actually requesting work. This suggests that one effect of the intervention was to decrease the aversiveness of the negatively reinforcing tasks. This is, of course, consistent with the extensive literature which suggests that *perceived control* over potentially aversive events is an important moderator of the level of stress experienced (cf. Bannerman et al., 1990).

A number of other studies have demonstrated the viability of the procedure across a number of settings, participants and challenging behaviours (e.g. Campbell & Lutzker, 1993; Day et al., 1994; Duker, Jol & Palmen, 1991; Durand & Carr, 1987, 1991, 1992; Durand & Kishi, 1987; Fisher et al., 1993; Horner & Budd, 1985; Horner & Day, 1991; Horner et al., 1990a, b; Northup et al., 1991; Smith, 1985; Smith & Coleman, 1986; Sprague & Horner, 1992; Wacker et al., 1990b; for a recent review see Durand et al., 1993). In addition, studies have indicated that the treatment gains achieved may generalise across settings and therapists (Durand & Carr, 1991) and may be maintained over time (Durand & Carr, 1992).

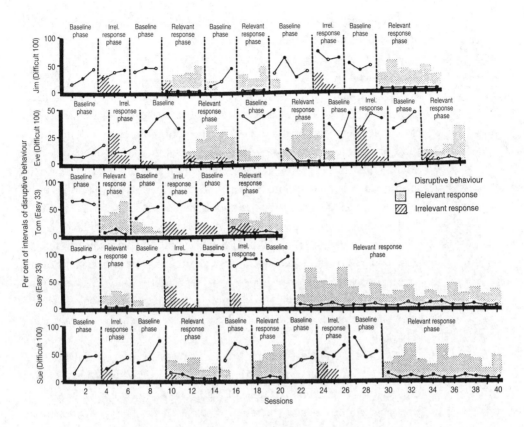

Fig. 7.2. Per cent intervals of disruptive behaviour during baseline, relevant response, and irrelevant response phases. Open circles depict sessions conducted by an informed experimenter; filled circles, sessions conducted by naive experimenters. The level of relevant verbal responses is indicated by stippled bars and that of irrelevant verbal responses, by hatched bars. (From Carr & Durand, 1985a, b).

Studies have also begun to identify the conditions under which functional displacement is more or less likely to occur. Carr (1988) suggested that functional displacement is likely to occur if the replacement response is truly equivalent and is also a relatively more 'efficient' response than the person's challenging behaviour (see also Durand et al., 1993). He defined response efficiency as a complex construct reflecting the combined effects of response effort and the rate, delay and quality of reinforcement contingent upon the response. Indeed, much basic research on behavioural choice has identified these variables as predicting allocation between two concurrently available responses (Davison & McCarthy, 1988; Mace & Roberts, 1993; McDowell, 1988, 1989). These experimental results have also been extended to applied studies which have indicated that such variables as the rate of reinforcement (Martens & Houk, 1989; Martens et al., 1992; Neef et al., 1992), reinforcer quality (Neef et al., 1992), response effort (Horner, Sprague et al., 1990b) and the immediacy of reinforcement (Neef, Mace & Shade, 1993) predict behaviour in real-life settings.

Horner *et al.* (1990*a, b*) examined the effect of response effort on the displacement of escape-motivated aggression in a 14 year-old boy with learning disabilities and cerebral palsy. They demonstrated that, while training in an alternative response which required substantial effort (spelling out 'help please' on a personal communicator) had no impact on aggression, training in a low effort response (pressing one key to elicit the message 'help please') resulted in marked reductions in aggression and an increased use of appropriate communication. Similarly, Horner and Day (1991) in three separate studies demonstrated the importance of response effort (signing a whole sentence compared with signing one word), the schedule of reinforcement (FR3 compared with FR1) and the immediacy of reinforcement (20-second delay compared with 1-second delay) in predicting whether a functionally equivalent communicative response would replace the challenging behaviours shown by three people with severe learning disabilities. In each study only the latter alternative was associated with significant reductions in challenging behaviour.

Further support for the importance of relative response efficiency in predicting the outcomes of intervention is provided by studies which have undertaken component analyses of intervention programmes based on functional communication training*. Wacker *et al.* (1990*b*), for example, demonstrated that the combination of functional communication training with DRO and time-out contingencies for the occurrence of challenging behaviour resulted in significantly greater reductions in challenging behaviour than functional communication training alone. Fisher *et al.* (1993) reported that functional communication training alone only reduced the severely challenging behaviours shown by one of three people with severe learning disabilities. However, the combination of functional communication training and punishment of the challenging behaviour (verbal reprimand plus prompting and guiding to complete five requests or 30-second physical restraint) resulted in rapid and clinically significant reductions in all challenging behaviours.

The accumulated evidence, therefore, suggests that a range of challenging behaviours may be rapidly and substantially reduced by establishing and/or differentially reinforcing a more socially appropriate member of the response class which includes the person's challenging behaviour. In addition, it would appear that the effects of intervention may persist over time and generalise to

---

* Functional communication training is an approach to intervention based on the use of alternative communicative responses within a functional displacement framework (e.g. Carr & Durand, 1985*a*, 1985*b*; Carr *et al.*, 1993; Durand, 1990; Reichle & Wacker, 1993).

new settings (Durand & Carr, 1991, 1992). This approach is attractive in that it is functionally based, constructional and seeks to tap into contingencies of reinforcement which are known to be highly effective in maintaining behaviour over time and across settings (i.e. the contingencies maintaining challenging behaviour).

The success of this approach, however, is dependent upon the alternative response being:

☐ a true *functional equivalent* of the challenging behaviour; and

☐ relatively more efficient than the challenging behaviour.

The first requirement highlights the importance of conducting a thorough functional assessment prior to intervention. Indeed, it is only through such an assessment that the behavioural function of the person's challenging behaviour may be established. As was noted in Chapter 4, however, this may not be a simple matter, in that the processes underlying challenging behaviour may be complex (e.g. Carr & Durand, 1985*a*; Day *et al.*, 1994), and may vary over time (e.g. Lerman *et al.*, 1994), behaviours (e.g. Derby *et al.*, 1994; Emerson *et al.*, in press*a,b*) and across settings (e.g. Emerson *et al.*, in press*a*; Haring & Kennedy, 1990).

Day *et al.* (1994) illustrated some of these issues in a study of multiply controlled challenging behaviours shown by a 9 year-old girl, an 18 year-old boy and a 34 year-old woman with severe learning disabilities. For each person, their challenging behaviours (self-injury or aggression) were shown to be maintained by both escape from difficult tasks *and* access to preferred items. Teaching functionally equivalent communicative responses (signing 'want' for access to preferred items; saying 'go' or exchanging a card for escape) only brought about reductions in challenging behaviour in the appropriate condition (cf. Carr & Durand, 1985*a*).

The second requirement, that the replacement response be more efficient than the challenging behaviour, has two main implications. First, in order to maximise the impact of intervention, it would appear sensible to increase the response efficiency of the replacement behaviour while decreasing the response efficiency of the challenging behaviour. That is, it is likely to be important to combine functional displacement or functional communication training with more traditional reactive strategies (e.g. extinction, time-out) to weaken the challenging behaviour (Fisher *et al.*, 1993; Wacker *et al.*, 1990*b*). In situations in which the challenging behaviour is multiply controlled by biological and behavioural factors (e.g. self-injury maintained by extrinsic reinforcement and β-endorphin release), this may involve the combined use of behavioural and psychopharmacological treatments.

Secondly, evidence of the powerful effects of challenging behaviour on the performance of care staff (Taylor & Carr, 1993, 1994) suggests that differential response efficiency may prove difficult to maintain. Indeed, the behavioural account of the development of challenging behaviour through a process of shaping (see Chapter 4) suggests that such behaviours may, over time, have replaced more socially appropriate functionally equivalent behaviours. Thus, the problem is not that the person did not have more appropriate behaviours in his or her repertoire, but that environments have, over time, preferentially selected challenging behaviours. Decay in the implementation of 'successful' intervention programmes has long been a problem faced in applied settings (e.g. Cullari & Ferguson, 1981). If such decay results in reducing the response efficiency of the alternative behaviour (e.g. care staff not attending to socially appropriate requests for breaks or attention) it is likely that the challenging behaviour will re-emerge (e.g. Durand & Kishi, 1987). In many ways, teaching a functionally equivalent response to a service user may be considerably easier than ensuring that carers and care staff continue to listen to, and act upon, alternative methods of communication.

The primary disadvantages of functional displacement are, first, that its successful implementation requires skilled and intensive support during assessment and intervention. Secondly, it may not be appropriate in situations in which the person's challenging behaviour is maintained by either access to events which are detrimental to their health, welfare or safety (e.g. challenging behaviour maintained by sexually inappropriate contact with care staff) or, perhaps more commonly, avoidance of situations which are important to their health, welfare or quality of life (e.g. social interaction). Take, for example, the situation in which, following sexual abuse, a person with severe learning disabilities develops challenging behaviour to escape from physical or social contact with all carers. Would it be appropriate to simply provide the person with an alternative way of avoiding contact, or should the aim of intervention also be to help the person overcome their fear/distress of non-abusive contact?

Differential reinforcement

A more general set of approaches based on the notion of differential reinforcement also seeks to intervene indirectly on challenging behaviour by increasing the rate of other behaviours (Carr et al., 1990a, b; Jones, 1991; O'Brien & Repp, 1990). These include:

☐ the *differential reinforcement of other* behaviour (DRO); and

☐ the *differential reinforcement of alternative* (DRA) or *incompatible* (DRI) behaviour.

The differential reinforcement of other behaviour, also known as omission training, is a non-constructional procedure involving the delivery of a reinforcement contingent on the non-occurrence of the targeted challenging behaviour during an interval of time or, more unusually, at a specific point in time (momentary DRO). Under a DRO schedule the nature of the 'other' behaviours are not specified. Reinforcement is provided as long as the challenging behaviour does not occur. In effect, a DRO schedule is equivalent to time-out from a newly imposed contingency of positive reinforcement (Rolider & Van Houten, 1990).

The differential reinforcement of alternative or incompatible behaviour involves the delivery of reinforcement contingent on the occurrence of a specified alternative behaviour (DRA) or a behaviour which is physically incompatible with the challenging behaviour (DRI). Functional displacement is, in effect, a particular form of DRA in which the reinforcing contingency is identical to that maintaining the challenging behaviour.

Individual studies have reported marked variability in the outcomes associated with differential reinforcement procedures, with results ranging from complete suppression, through marginal improvements to increases in the rate of challenging behaviour over baseline (Carr *et al.*, 1990*b*). In general, however, it would appear that such procedures may not be particularly effective in reducing severely challenging behaviours (Carr *et al.*, 1990*b*; Lancioni & Hoogeveen, 1990; O'Brien & Repp, 1990; Scotti *et al.*, 1991*b*). There are, however, some notable exceptions to this generalisation. Luiselli *et al.* (1985), for example, used a five-minute DRO schedule involving food and tactile reinforcement to reduce to near zero levels the frequent aggression shown by a 15 year-old girl with severe learning disabilities and dual sensory impairments. As intervention progressed, the schedule was faded from 5 to 30 minutes. Russo, Cataldo & Cushing (1981) reported the use of a DRA procedure to reinforce compliance with requests among three pre-school children with learning disabilities. As compliance increased, challenging behaviours, which included aggression and self-injurious behaviour, rapidly decreased to near zero levels.

As has been discussed above, studies of behavioural choice suggest that a person's allocation of time between concurrently available alternatives (e.g. attending to a task, engaging in self-injurious behaviour, gazing out of the window) is a function of response effort and the rate, quality and immediacy of reinforcement. As such, these factors should predict the effectiveness of differential reinforcement procedures as well as functional displacement. Thus, an effective procedure should aim to ensure that:

☐ the alternative behaviour requires less effort than the person's challenging behaviour;

☐ the rate of reinforcement delivered contingent on the alternative behaviour is greater than the rate of reinforcement maintaining the challenging behaviour;

☐ reinforcement is delivered immediately upon occurrence of the alternative behaviour;

☐ the reinforcers selected are more powerful than those maintaining the challenging behaviour, preferably through the use of empirical procedures to identify reinforcer selection.

It is clear, however, that such requirements are rarely attended to in the applied research literature (O'Brien & Repp, 1990).

The effectiveness of differential reinforcement procedures may also be enhanced by selecting alternative behaviours which show a natural negative covariation with the targeted challenging behaviour. Parrish *et al.* (1986), for example, demonstrated the natural negative covariation of compliance and challenging behaviours, including aggression, property destruction, pica and disruption, among four children with learning disabilities. As compliance increased, owing to the effects of either differential reinforcement and guided compliance, challenging behaviours decreased (see also Koegel & Frea, 1993). Similarly, if challenging behaviours were suppressed using a DRO procedure, compliance increased.

These suggestions for improving the effectiveness of differential rein-forcement procedures again highlight the importance of preceding intervention with a thorough functional assessment. Carr *et al.* (1990*b*) suggested that differential reinforcement procedures may have rapid effects if the delivery of reinforcers is *discriminative* for the absence of challenging behaviour. In addition, such procedures are relatively simple to administer in that they do not require skilled performance from care staff. The main drawbacks of these procedures, however, are that reinforcer satiation may occur at brief inter-reinforcement intervals and that their implementation requires intensive monitoring of user behaviour.

MODIFICATION OF MAINTAINING CONTINGENCIES: EXTINCTION

The approaches discussed so far have not involved any *direct* alteration of the contingencies maintaining the person's challenging behaviour. Antecedent manipulations and differential reinforcement may both, of course, indirectly influence the power of the maintaining contingencies through modifying establishing operations, by increasing the rate of 'free' reinforcement or

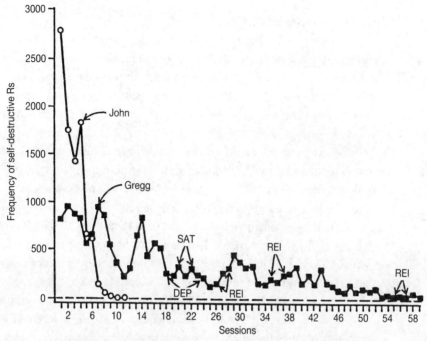

Fig. 7.3. Extinction of John's and Gregg's self-destructive behaviour, over successive days of extinction, during 90-min sessions with total number of self-destructive acts on any one day given on the ordinate. SAT stands for satiation, DEP for deprivation, and REI for reinforcement. (From Lovaas & Simmons, 1969).

reinforcement available for competing behaviours. Extinction procedures involve the direct modification of the contingencies responsible for maintaining the challenging behaviour.

Specifically, extinction procedures involve ensuring that the contingencies responsible for maintaining the person's challenging behaviour are no longer operative. Thus, for example, if functional assessment has indicated that an individual's aggression is maintained by positive social reinforcement involving attention from care staff, an extinction procedure would ensure that such positive reinforcers were no longer delivered contingent upon the person's challenging behaviour.

Lovaas and Simmons (1969), for example, used an extinction procedure to reduce the attention-maintained severe self-injurious behaviour shown by two boys with severe learning disabilities. The procedure involved leaving each boy alone in an observation room for 90 minute sessions. The results of this procedure are shown in Fig. 7.3.

As can be seen, within eight sessions (12 hours) John's self-injury had been eliminated. Prior to this, however, he had hit himself 9000 times during the extinction sessions. Gregg's self-injury clearly took much longer to extinguish. These effects were, however, situationally specific, in that treatment gains failed to generalise to other settings.

Escape extinction involves ensuring that negative reinforcers are not withdrawn contingent upon the person's challenging behaviour (e.g. preventing escape from an aversive situation contingent upon challenging behaviour). Such procedures have been used to successfully reduce escape-maintained challenging behaviour (e.g. Iwata *et al.*, 1994*a*, 1990*a*; Repp, Felce & Barton, 1988).

Sensory extinction procedures involve attempting to block the sensory or perceptual feedback from challenging behaviours maintained by automatic reinforcement (Rincover & Devany, 1982). Such procedures have been employed to reduce self-injurious and stereotypic behaviours apparently maintained by automatic reinforcement (e.g. Iwata *et al.*, 1994*a*; Rincover & Devany, 1982). As was noted in Chapter 4, however, the effectiveness of sensory extinction may be attributable to a number of factors including antecedent control and punishment (cf. Mazaleski *et al.*, 1994).

While extinction may be effective, its use does have a number of significant problems. First, it is not uncommon for the rate, intensity and variability of the behaviour to increase during the initial stages of an extinction programme (e.g. Iwata *et al.*, 1994*a*; Lovaas & Simmons, 1969), although this may be avoided by combining extinction with stimulus fading (Zarcone *et al.*, 1993). Such *extinction bursts* may place the physical safety of the person in jeopardy and are likely to be distressing to carers and care staff. As such, extinction procedures may prove unacceptable to some stakeholders. Secondly, extinction procedures need to be implemented with great consistency. Otherwise, the procedure is equivalent to simply reducing the rate of reinforcement for the person's challenging behaviour. While this may have the effect of reducing response rate (see above), it may not bring about socially or clinically significant improvement. Thirdly, as noted above, the effects of extinction procedures may not generalise to new situations. Finally, as a non-constructional approach, extinction may be associated with unwanted changes in collateral behaviours.

Given the problems associated with extinction procedures, it is highly unlikely that they would be implemented on their own. They are often, however, included as an important component in complex treatment packages (see below).

DEFAULT TECHNOLOGIES: PUNISHMENT

As was discussed in Chapter 4, in behavioural terms punishment *by definition* brings about a reduction in the rate of behaviour. Over the past three decades numerous studies have demonstrated that punishment procedures can produce socially and clinically significant reductions in severe challenging behaviours shown by people with severe learning disabilities (Axelrod & Apsche, 1983; Cataldo, 1991; Luiselli *et al.*, 1992; Matson & DiLorenzo, 1984; Matson & Taras, 1989; O'Brien, 1989; Repp & Singh, 1990). Indeed, meta-analyses of the intervention literature indicates that extinction and punishment-based procedures are the most effective approaches available, both immediately and at follow-up, if the goal is to eliminate challenging behaviour (e.g. Scotti *et al.*, 1991*b*). An illustration of the variety of punishment-based procedures which have been used by applied behaviour analysts to reduce challenging behaviours shown by people with severe learning disabilities is provided in Table 7.2.

In terms of the criteria which we suggest should underpin intervention, however, the use of punishment-based procedures poses some problems. First, they are neither constructional nor functionally based. Secondly, the procedures (if not the outcomes) are increasingly being seen as socially unacceptable (e.g. G. Allen Roeher Institute, 1988; Guess *et al.*, 1987; LaVigna & Donnellan, 1986; O'Brien, 1991; Repp & Singh, 1990). This combination of factors has led to a situation in which punishment procedures may be best viewed as 'default technologies' (Iwata, 1988). That is, approaches which should only be considered when: (a) alternative approaches have failed or are not feasible, and (b) the costs of not intervening outweigh the costs and risks associated with the use of such procedures.

In the sections below, some of the approaches to punishment which have been successfully used to reduce severely challenging behaviours will be briefly reviewed.

Response cost: time-out and visual screening

Response cost (or negative punishment) refers to the reduction in the rate of a behaviour resulting from the *withdrawal* of positive reinforcers contingent upon its occurrence. *Time-out* is a clinical procedure in which opportunity for positive reinforcement is removed or reduced for a set period following the occurrence of a target behaviour (Hobbs & Forehand, 1977). This may involve the brief seclusion of the person in a barren environment (e.g. Wolf *et al.*, 1964), removal to a less stimulating part of the current setting (e.g. Mace *et al.*, 1986) or the withdrawal of potentially positively reinforcing activities or events from the vicinity of the person (e.g. Foxx & Shapiro, 1978).

Time out has been shown to be successful in reducing challenging behaviours shown by people with severe learning disabilities (Cataldo, 1991). Mace *et al.* (1986), for example, used a time-out procedure involving sitting in a chair facing a wall for two minutes to bring about rapid and significant reductions in the aggressive and disruptive behaviours shown by three

Table 7.2. *Punishment-based approaches*

	Procedure and examples
Negative punishment	
Time-out	Contingent removal of opportunity for positive reinforcement involving either brief seclusion (e.g. Wolf, Risley & Mees, 1964), withdrawal from activity (e.g. Mace *et al.*, 1986) or withdrawal of potentially positively reinforcing activities from the vicinity of the person (e.g. Foxx & Shapiro, 1978)
Visual screening	Contingent blocking of vision (e.g. Jordan, Singh & Repp, 1989; Lutzker, 1978)
Positive punishment	
Verbal reprimand	(e.g. Baumeister & Forehand, 1972; Schutz *et al.*, 1978)
Response satiation	Implementation of 'constraining' relationships between responses (e.g. Realon & Konarski, 1993)
Overcorrection	Contingent practice of alternative 'appropriate' behaviour (e.g. Foxx & Azrin, 1973) or restitution of environment to previous state (e.g. Duker & Seys, 1977; Foxx & Azrin, 1972)
Response interruption and brief manual restraint	Blocking of challenging behaviour combined with brief manual restraint (e.g. Azrin *et al.*, 1988)
Required relaxation	Contingent 'relaxation' involving cessation of all movement (e.g. Foxx & Bechtel, 1983)
Mechanical restraint and protective clothing	Contingent application of mechanical restraints or protective clothing (e.g. Dorsey *et al.*, 1982)
Water mist	Contingent spray of water mist to face (e.g. Dorsey *et al.*, 1980; Gross, Berler & Drabman, 1982)
Aromatic ammonia	Contingent application of aromatic ammonia under nose (e.g. Tanner & Zeiler, 1975; Doke, Woelry & Sumberg, 1983)
Aversive tastes	Contingent application of aversive tastes including lemon juice (e.g. Hogg, 1982; Sajwaj, Libet & Agras, 1974), tabasco sauce (Altmeyer *et al.*, 1985) and shaving cream (Conway & Butcher, 1974)
Electric shock	contingent electric shock (e.g. Linscheid *et al.*, 1990; Lovaas & Simmons, 1969; Tate & Baroff, 1966)

children with learning disabilities. As we noted in Chapter 5, however, 'time-out' may also lead to an increase in the rate of escape-motivated challenging behaviour (e.g. Durand *et al.*, 1989; Solnick *et al.*, 1977). For such behaviours the implementation of a typical exclusionary time-out procedure is likely to negatively reinforce the targeted behaviour. Research conducted on the parameters of time-out have suggested that short durations are as effective as long durations, the use of contingent delay for release from time out (i.e. release is delayed until challenging behaviours have stopped) may be unnecessary and the effectiveness of the procedure may be enhanced by combining time-out with differential reinforcement of more appropriate behaviour (Hobbs & Forehand, 1977; Murphy & Oliver, 1987). While potentially effective, the implementation of time-out and response-cost procedures may themselves set the occasion for the occurrence of challenging behaviour as the person seeks to avoid or escape from the punishing contingency.

Visual or *facial screening* involves the brief (5–15 seconds) blocking of vision contingent upon the occurrence of challenging behaviour (Rojahn & Marshburn, 1992). This procedure has been shown to bring about rapid, significant and, at times, persistent reductions in self-injurious behaviour (e.g. Lutzker, 1978; Singh, Watson & Winton, 1986), screaming (e.g. Singh, Winton & Dawson, 1982) and stereotypy (e.g. Jordan, Singh & Repp, 1989). Similarly with the use of time-out, visual screening may set the occasion for the occurrence of challenging behaviour as the person seeks to avoid or escape from the punishing contingency (Rojahn & Marshburn, 1992).

Positive punishment

Positive punishment refers to the reduction in the rate of a behaviour resulting from the contingent presentation of a punishing stimulus. As indicated in Table 7.2, a wide range of punishing stimuli have been employed to reduce challenging behaviour. Apart from verbal reprimands, all approaches have been shown to be effective in some instances in bringing about short and medium-term reductions in severe challenging behaviour (Axelrod & Apsche, 1983; Cataldo, 1991; Luiselli *et al.*, 1992; Matson & DiLorenzo, 1984; Matson & Taras, 1989; O'Brien, 1989; Repp & Singh, 1990).

Azrin *et al.* (1988), for example, demonstrated that the combination of the differential reinforcement of incompatible behaviour (DRI), response interruption and contingent manual restraint for a two-minute period brought about rapid and significant reductions in the severe long-standing self-injurious behaviour shown by one girl, two women and six men with severe learning disabilities. Across all participants, self-injury was reduced to 11% of baseline levels. The combined treatment package was shown to be significantly more effective than its constituent components, each of which reduced self-injury to approximately 50% of baseline levels (see also Luiselli, 1992*a*; Van Houten, Rolider & Houlihan, 1992).

More controversially, Linscheid *et al.* (1990) describe the development and evaluation of the Self-Injurious Behavior Inhibiting System (SIBIS; see also Iwata, 1988; Linscheid, 1992; Linscheid *et al.*, 1994; Ricketts, Goza & Matese,

1992; Williams, Kirkpatrick-Sanchez & Iwata, 1993*a*). This is an automated device which delivers an electric shock (3.5 mA for 0.08 seconds) contingent on self-injury detected by a piezoelectric impact detector. An initial evaluation was undertaken with five people with severe learning disabilities whose self-injury met the criteria of: (1) producing obvious tissue damage; (2) having been resistant to previous attempts at intervention; (3) currently required control through protective devices and/or mediation. For four of the five participants the use of SIBIS was associated with rapid elimination of self-injury. The very high frequency self-injurious behaviour of the fifth participant was eliminated after approximately 90 sessions during which he received 3640 shocks.

The use of punishment-based procedures raises a number of issues. Several commentators have suggested that the use of punishment may be associated with unacceptably high rates of negative 'side-effects' (e.g. Guess *et al.*, 1987; LaVigna & Donnellan, 1986; Meyer & Evans, 1989). Indeed, negative outcomes associated with the use of punishment have included increases in non-targeted challenging behaviour, increased incontinence and decreased appetite (Cataldo, 1991). However, reviews of applied research have consistently noted that: (a) reporting of side-effects is often anecdotal, and (b) the reporting of positive side-effects (e.g. increased sociability, increased responsiveness, reduced medication, reduced use of restraints) consistently outweighs the reporting of negative side-effects in the applied literature (Carr & Lovaas, 1983; Cataldo, 1991; see also Linscheid *et al.*, 1990, 1994). Nevertheless, as with procedures based on negative punishment, the implementation of punishment-based procedures may set the occasion for the occurrence of challenging behaviour as the person seeks to avoid or escape from the punishing contingency (Linscheid, 1992). In addition, problems may be encountered in the maintenance of treatment gains, especially over the longer term (e.g. Murphy & Wilson, 1980).

In addition, as with the use of positive reinforcers, care needs to be taken to ensure that the stimuli selected actually do function as punishers. The danger of making assumptions about the punishing effects of specific procedures is illustrated by the effects of time-out on increasing some forms of challenging behaviour (Durand *et al.*, 1989; Solnick *et al.*, 1977) and the use of contingent mechanical restraint as a *positive reinforcer* for some people with learning disabilities (e.g. Favell *et al.*, 1981). Furthermore, evidence also exists to suggest that some 'non-aversive' approaches which involve close personal contact may be highly distressing to some people (e.g. Paisey *et al.*, 1989).

Fisher *et al.* (1994) have described empirical procedures for selecting punishing stimuli. An innovative empirical approach to defining punishing relationships is described by Realon and Konarski (1993). They employed molar equilibrium theory (Timberlake, 1980) to design punishment contingencies involving engagement in challenging behaviour (handmouthing and self-injury) and the use of leisure materials for two men with severe learning disabilities. Observation under free operant baseline conditions was used to empirically define constraining relationships between the challenging behaviour and use of leisure materials (e.g. for every episode of handmouthing the person was required to interact with leisure materials for 10 seconds). Implementation of these contingencies was predictably associated with reductions in challenging behaviour.

Finally, as noted above, punishment procedures are often viewed as abusive and degrading (O'Brien, 1991). In the UK in particular, the social unacceptability of more 'extreme' approaches to punishment (e.g. electric shock) has effectively prevented their use in clinical practice. As has been argued in Chapter 5, however, such decisions need to be informed by careful comparisons between the actual risks, costs and benefits of intervention and non-intervention. The ethics of denying a person access to a proven treatment in the knowledge that their severe self-injurious behaviour may produce permanent physical damage, and is likely to be managed by physical and/or pharmacological restraint, are questionable indeed.

SELF-MANAGEMENT AND SELF-CONTROL

In the sections above, we have described a wide range of possible approaches to intervention, all of which are implemented by carers, care staff or professionals. *Self-management* or *self-control* refers to the use of behavioural strategies to change one's own behaviour. Thus, the key defining characteristic of self-management lies in the identity of the intervenor, rather than in the specific procedures implemented. Indeed, *any* of the approaches described above could be implemented as part of a self-management approach to the reduction of challenging behaviour.

Korinek (1991) argues that the benefits of self-management include its short-term efficacy, effective maintenance and generalisation, increased independence, reduced need for supervision and enhanced motivation. However, the use of self-management procedures by people with learning disabilities has received relatively little attention (cf. Gardner & Cole, 1989; Jones, Williams & Lowe, 1993; Korinek, 1991). This is particularly so with regard to the self-management of challenging behaviour among people with severe learning disabilities.

Studies involving people with mild learning disabilities (mild or moderate mental retardation) have indicated that:

☐ self-monitoring alone may reduce self-injury, aggressive and stereotypic behaviour (Reese, Sherman & Sheldon, 1984; Rudrud, Ziarnik & Coleman, 1984; Zeigob, Klukas & Junginger, 1978);

☐ more complex self-management procedures may reduce aggressive, disruptive, stereotypic and self-injurious behaviour (Benson, Rice & Miranti, 1986; Cole, Gardner & Karan, 1985; Gardner, Clees & Cole, 1983a; Gardner et al., 1983b; Grace et al., 1988; Koegel et al., 1992; Rosine & Martin, 1983).

Two recent studies have examined the effectiveness of self-management strategies when used with autistic children with severe learning disabilities. Koegel & Koegel (1990) investigated the applicability of self-management procedures in the reduction of stereotypic behaviours shown by four children with autism. The children's mental age ranged from 2 years 9 months to 5 years 11 months. Their chronological age ranged from 9 to 14 years. Each child displayed between three and six distinct forms of stereotypic behaviour. Implementation of an externally reinforced self-monitoring procedure was associated with highly significant reductions in stereotypy for three of the children. The fourth child, who had the highest mental age, showed consistent but less pronounced reductions in stereotypy.

More recently, Pierce and Schreibman (1994) examined the effects of a pictorial self-cueing and self-reinforcement strategy on the independent performance of daily living skills (e.g. setting the table, making lunch, getting dressed). The participants were three children with autism (age range six to eight years; mental age range two years two months to three years ten months). Implementation of the self-management package was associated with an increase in independent performance and a decrease in stereotypy (see also Krantz, MacDuff & McLannahan, 1993; MacDuff, Krantz & McClannahan, 1993; Stahmer & Schreibman, 1992).

At present the applicability of self-management procedures to people with more severe disabilities is unclear. Of particular importance is the relationship between the development of language and the emergence of rule-governed behaviour, of which self-management or self-regulation is an example (Hayes, 1989; Jones et al., 1993; Whitman, 1990). Whatever the specific linguistic competencies necessary for effective self-management, it appears clear that this approach to intervention has been significantly under-utilised.

MULTI-COMPONENT STRATEGIES

The research literature has been primarily concerned with determining the efficacy of discrete approaches to intervention. In clinical practice, however, the need to bring about rapid and significant change argues for the use of complex multi-component intervention strategies (e.g. Berkman & Meyer, 1988; Carr & Carlson, 1993; Lovaas, 1987; Lovaas & Smith, 1994; McEachin, Smith & Lovaas, 1993). Indeed, the evidence which has been reviewed above suggests that the impact of such complex strategies may be significantly greater than their individual components (e.g. Azrin *et al.*, 1988; Fisher *et al.*, 1993; Wacker *et al.*, 1990*b*).

Carr and Carlson (1993), for example, employed a complex package involving choice, embedding, functional communication training, building tolerance for delay of reinforcement and the presentation of discriminative stimuli for non-problem behaviours to teach shopping skills to three adolescent boys with autism and severe learning disabilities. Following the implementation of the programme, all participants were able to shop in supermarkets and displayed virtually no challenging behaviour during this activity.

Lovaas (1987), Lovaas & Smith (1994) and McEachin *et al.* (1993) described the medium- and longer-term outcomes of an intensive behaviourally orientated educational treatment programme for a group of 19 young children with autism (mean age 32 months at intake). This involved 'two years or more of one-to-one treatment for 40 hours per week in their homes and communities from a treatment team that included families, normal peers, and teachers of normal classes, as well as staff from UCLA [University of California at Los Angeles]' (Lovaas & Smith, 1994, p.253). Follow-up of this group at age seven (Lovaas, 1987) and thirteen (McEachin *et al.*, 1993) indicated substantial gains in IQ scores, adaptive behaviours and educational achievement in comparison with a quasi-random control group. Lovaas and Smith (1994) also report that 'our preliminary data show that all but 2 of the intensively treated [children] ... are free of clinically significant problems associated with destructive behaviors. In contrast, the majority of the control [children] are medicated and living in institutional settings, where their self-injurious and assaultive behaviors present major management problems.' (Lovaas & Smith, 1994, p.253.)

SUMMARY

Table 7.3, below, summarises some of the main advantages and disadvantages of the approaches to intervention discussed in this chapter.

Table 7.3. *Summary of behavioural approaches to intervention*

Approach	Constructional?	Functionally based?	Primary advantages	Primary disadvantages
Antecedent manipulations				
Increase level of background stimulation	No	No	Simple to sustain, ease of implementation, broad-based effects, possible positive collateral changes (e.g. wakefulness), possible when maintaining factors unknown	May be ineffective for, or increase, escape-motivated challenging behaviours. May be difficult to implement initially
Non-contingent exercise	No	No	Ease of implementation, broad-based effects, possible positive collateral changes (e.g. sleeping, general health benefits), possible when maintaining factors unknown	May be ineffective for, or increase, some escape-motivated challenging behaviour
Increase opportunities for choice-making	No	No	Possible broad-based effects, possible positive collateral changes (e.g. reduced stress), possible when maintaining factors unknown	Unknown effectiveness, may be complex to implement
Schedule activities to avoid antecedents or on basis of preferences	Yes	No	Immediate and significant reductions in challenging behaviour, ease of implementation	May not be feasible to avoid antecedents, antecedents may be important for health or welfare of person, requires detailed functional assessment
Stimulus fading	No	Yes	May help reduce escape-motivated challenging behaviour elicited by conditioned arousal, may help re-introduce antecedents important to health/welfare of person	May not be feasible to control access to antecedents, relatively slow acting, requires detailed functional assessment
Increase task variety, embedding, interspersed requests (behavioural momentum)	No	Yes	Immediate and significant reductions in challenging behaviour, ease of implementation	Requires detailed functional assessment

Table 7.3. (*cont.*)

Non-contingent reinforcement and satiation	No	Yes	Immediate and significant reductions in challenging behaviour	Requires detailed functional assessment
Modify idiosyncratic setting events	No	Yes	Immediate and significant reductions in challenging behaviour Possible ease of implementation	Requires detailed functional assessment
Response covariation Functional displacement	Yes	Yes	Immediate and significant reductions in challenging behaviour	Requires detailed functional assessment, complex implementation, may involve avoidance of activities important for health/welfare of person
Differential reinforcement of other behaviour (DRO)	No	No	Possible when maintaining factors unknown	Complex or intensive implementation
Differential reinforcement of incompatible (DRI) or alternative (DRA) behaviour	Yes	?	Possible when maintaining factors unknown	Complex or intensive implementation
Modification of maintaining contingencies				
Extinction	No	Yes		Requires detailed functional assessment, complex or intensive implementation, temporary increases in rate/variety/intensity of challenging behaviour, slow acting, poor generalisation, low procedural acceptability
Punishment (default technologies)				
Time-out	No	No		Requires detailed functional assessment, complex or intensive implementation, poor generalisation, low procedural acceptability

Table 7.3. (cont.)

Approach	Constructional?	Functionally based?	Primary advantages	Primary disadvantages
Visual screening	No	No	Possible when maintaining factors unknown Immediate and significant reductions in challenging behaviour	Complex or intensive implementation, possibly poor generalisation, low procedural acceptability
Positive punishment	No	No	Possible when maintaining factors unknown, immediate and significant reductions in challenging behaviour	Complex or intensive implementation, possibly poor generalisation, low procedural acceptability

The evidence which has been reviewed in earlier chapters indicated that severely challenging behaviours may be highly persistent. To recapitulate:

☐ adults who come to the attention of specialised services have commonly shown the same challenging behaviours for a decade or more (e.g. Emerson *et al.*, 1988; Murphy *et al.*, 1993);

☐ the vast majority of people who show self-injurious behaviour at one point in time, are also likely to do so a decade later (e.g. Windahl, 1988);

☐ longer-term follow-up of 'successful' intervention programmes often report a very high rate of relapse (Griffin *et al.*, 1986*a*; Murphy & Wilson, 1980; Schroeder & MacLean, 1987) or, alternatively, indicate that challenging behaviours tend to persist, but at a much lower intensity and/or rate (e.g. Foxx, 1990; Jensen & Heidorn, 1993).

Attention was also drawn to some of the personal and social consequences which the person may experience as a result of his or her challenging behaviour. These include:

☐ physical injury, ill health and the development of secondary sensory or neurological impairments;

☐ abuse (Maurice & Trudel, 1982; Rusch *et al.*, 1986);

☐ inappropriate treatment involving the long-term prescription of neuroleptics (Buck & Sprague, 1989; Pary, 1993; Stone *et al.*, 1989), the widespread use of mechanical restraints and protective devices (Griffin *et al.*, 1986*a*) and possible exposure to unnecessarily degrading or abusive psychological treatments (Freagon, 1990);

☐ exclusion from community settings (Borthwick-Duffy *et al.*, 1987; Eyman & Call, 1977; Hill & Bruininks, 1984; Lakin *et al.*, 1983), relationships (Anderson *et al.*, 1992) and services (Jacobsen *et al.*, 1984);

☐ social and material deprivation (Emerson & Hatton, 1994; Emerson *et al.*, 1992; Mansell, 1994*a*, *b*) and systematic neglect (Cullen *et al.*, 1983; Felce *et al.*, 1987) in institutional settings.

In the light of these observations, it is important to attempt to determine the general effectiveness of behavioural approaches in bringing about socially significant and durable change. Two aspects of the nature of the available evidence militate against being able to provide a clear answer to this important question.

First, a reliance in the research literature on single-subject experimental designs, when combined with the tendency not to report treatment failures, does mean that we know little about the extent to which the results of successful interventions may be generalised across individuals, therapists and settings (Barlow & Hersen, 1984). Thus, while single-subject designs often have a very high internal validity (i.e. they can demonstrate that the observed changes are due to a particular intervention), systematic replication is required to determine whether the same results can be obtained with other participants, other therapists and in other settings. Unfortunately, such *systematic* replication is extremely rare in this field. As a result, while we are able to conclude that various behavioural procedures *can* bring about significant change, we cannot predict with any confidence the proportion of 'cases' in which this is likely to be achieved. It is important that we keep the limitations of the available evidence in mind when advocating particular approaches. For example, while functional communication training obviously *can* bring about reductions in challenging behaviour, only one study has been reported (Durand & Carr, 1992) which has involved more than four participants. Indeed, half of the sixteen studies reviewed by Durand *et al.* (1993) were based on just one or two participants.

Similarly, reliance on single-subject designs means that there is only limited knowledge with regards to the characteristics of the behaviour, participants or setting which are likely to influence the impact of an intervention. The one exception to this general rule is the gradual accumulation of evidence which illustrates the importance of basing intervention on the results of a prior functional assessment (e.g. Carr & Durand, 1985*a*; Day *et al.*, 1994; Durand *et al.*, 1989; Iwata *et al.*, 1994*a*; Kennedy & Itkonen, 1993; Repp *et al.*, 1988; Solnick *et al.*, 1977).

The second major limitation in the available evidence concerns restrictions on the range of outcomes evaluated and the length of time over which the durability of intervention gains are assessed. Attention was drawn to the former issue in Chapter 2. The failure to assess the maintenance or durability of treatment effects is highlighted by the observation that, of the 96 studies employing 'positive' behavioural approaches reviewed by Carr *et al.* (1990*b*), only five reported follow-up data for one year or more following the termination of intervention.

This means that relatively little is known regarding such factors as:

☐ collateral changes or the 'side-effects' of intervention;

☐ the contextual control of challenging behaviour and the generalisation of the effects of intervention to new settings, behaviours and people;

☐ the long-term outcomes of intervention; and

☐ the broader social validity of intervention when applied in community-based settings.

Nevertheless, the accumulated evidence does indicate that be approaches *can* be effective in bringing about rapid, significant and w reductions in severely challenging behaviours and that such changes *may* be associated with a range of positive 'side-effects' (cf. Carr *et al.*, 1990*b*; Cataldo, 1991; Lovaas & Smith, 1994), *may* generalise to new settings (e.g. Durand & Carr, 1991) and *may* be maintained over long periods of time (e.g. Foxx, 1990; Jensen & Heidorn, 1993; Lovaas & Smith, 1994; McEachin *et al.*, 1993).

The above observations do, however, point to what must be considered to be two of the key priorities for future research in this area. These are:

☐ epidemiological studies of the natural history of challenging behaviour over prolonged periods of time; and

☐ the systematic replication of the long-term evaluation of multiple outcomes associated with different approaches to intervention.

Finally, consideration of the early onset and apparently high degree of persistence of severely challenging behaviours points to the desirability of developing preventative interventions and ensuring that intensive support is provided as early as possible once challenging behaviours have begun to emerge (Dunlap, Johnson & Robbins, 1990; Kiernan, 1994; Lovaas & Smith, 1994; Schroeder, Bickel & Richmond, 1986). This issue will be considered further in the final chapter.

8   PSYCHOPHARMACOLOGY

In this chapter, the evidence relating to psychopharmacological approaches to reducing challenging behaviour will be reviewed briefly. It is beyond the scope of the present book to provide a comprehensive review of the area. To do so would also unnecessarily duplicate existing reviews (e.g. Aman, 1991; Aman & Singh, 1988, 1991; Baumeister & Sevin, 1990; Gadow & Poling, 1988; Singh, Singh & Ellis, 1992; Thompson et al., 1994a; Thompson et al., 1991). The intention of this review is to pay particular attention to approaches based on current understanding of the neurobiological bases of challenging behaviour (see Chapter 4).

The importance of gaining a basic understanding of psychopharmacological approaches is underscored by three factors. First, as was indicated in Chapter 4, there is growing evidence to suggest that alterations in dopaminergic, serotoninergic and opioid neurotransmitter systems may play a role in the aetiology of some forms of challenging behaviour. This recent research opens up the possibility of developing a functionally based approach to psychophar-macological interventions which may complement behavioural approaches. Secondly, an appreciation of the behavioural mechanisms of drug action (Thompson et al., 1994a) is likely to be of value when developing behavioural approaches for people in receipt of psychoactive medication.

Finally, psychopharmacological interventions constitute the most common form of treatment received by people with severe learning disabilities and challenging behaviour. North American studies suggest that between 26% and 40% of all residents of community-based facilities, and between 38% and 50% of all residents of institutional facilities, receive psychotropic medication for challenging behaviour (Buck & Sprague, 1989; Pary, 1993; Stone et al., 1989; Thompson et al., 1991). It is estimated that between one-half and two-thirds of people with severe learning disabilities and challenging behaviour receive psychotropic medication (Davidson et al., 1994; Meador & Osborn, 1992). In the UK, the results of the survey undertaken in 1987 by Kiernan and colleagues indicated that anti-psychotic medication was prescribed for 52% of people with challenging behaviour (Kiernan & Qureshi, 1993; Qureshi, 1994). Such a high prevalence of the use of psychopharmacological interventions suggests that all professional and clinical staff involved should posses a basic appreciation of the effects and side-effects of the more common approaches.

In Chapter 4, some of the evidence was discussed which related to the role of three different classes of neurotransmitters in the aetiology of challenging behaviour: dopamine, serotonin (5-hydroxytryptamine) and the opioid peptides (in particular β-endorphin). In the sections below, some of the implications of this evidence for psychopharmacological intervention will be considered. The evidence concerning other psychopharmacological agents will then be reviewed briefly. Throughout the discussion, attention will be drawn to the link between neurobiological processes and challenging behaviour and the behavioural mechanism of drug action (Thompson *et al.,* 1994*a*).

DOPAMINE ANTAGONISTS

As noted in Chapter 4, the dopaminergic system is closely involved in the regulation of motor activity. It contains two main groups of dopamine receptors (D1 and D2), each of which contains further subtypes. Evidence which suggests that abnormalities in the D1 receptor subsystem may be implicated in the development and maintenance of at least some forms of self-injurious behaviour includes:

☐ the association between Lesch–Nyhan syndrome and injurious self- biting;

☐ animal studies which have shown that destruction of dopamine pathways is associated with severe self-biting;

☐ the association between isolation rearing of rhesus monkeys, self-injurious behaviour and long-term alterations in dopamine receptor sensitivity and destruction of dopaminergic pathways.

Commonly prescribed anti-psychotic medications (e.g. chlorpromazine, thioridazine) are known to suppress dopaminergic activity. They are the most commonly prescribed medications for people with challenging behaviour (Kiernan & Qureshi, 1993; Thompson *et al.,* 1991). There have been literally hundreds of studies evaluating the effects of such agents on the challenging behaviours shown by people with learning disabilities (see Sprague & Werry, 1971; Singh *et al.,* 1992; Thompson *et al.,* 1991). While there is, not surprisingly, convincing evidence that such agents may reduce challenging behaviour which is associated with an underlying mental illness (e.g. Williams *et al.,* 1993*a, b*), evidence regarding their general effectiveness is much less clear.

   In summarising the results of their recent review, Thompson *et al.* (1991) concluded that 'administration of neuroleptic drugs can result in beneficial effects in treating certain behavioral disorders in some people with mental retardation. It is difficult to specify which individuals and which behavioral disorders will benefit from neuroleptic drugs. Previous reviews ... reached similar conclusions' (Thompson *et al.*, 1991, p.396–7, see also Singh *et al.*, 1992). Such a conclusion is not surprising when we consider the neurobiological and behavioural bases of action of common antipsychotics.

As has been shown, the accumulating evidence suggests links between self-injurious behaviour and supersensitivity of D1 receptors, and between stereotypy and D2 receptor activity (Cooper & Dourish, 1990; Schroeder & Tessel, 1994). Commonly prescribed antipsychotic agents are dopamine antagonists which are relatively specific to D2 receptor types. They are extremely unlikely, therefore, to have any *specific* effects on either aggression or self-injurious behaviour. Evidence of a link between stereotypy and D2 pathways, however, does suggest that such agents may have a more specific effect on stereotyped behaviour. This conclusion has been tentatively drawn by both Aman and Singh (1988) and Thompson *et al.*, (1991).

However, as was indicated in Chapter 4, there is some preliminary evidence to suggest that D1 antagonists (e.g. clozapine, fluphenazine) may have a more specific effect on self-injurious behaviour (e.g. Goldstein *et al.*, 1985; Gualtieri & Schroeder, 1989). Gualtieri and Schroeder (1989), for example, reported positive outcomes for 10 out of 15 participants with self-injurious behaviour in a placebo-controlled trial of low dose fluphenazine.

Thompson *et al.*, (1991) and Thompson *et al.* (1994*a*) reviewed some of the behavioural effects of antipsychotics. They pointed to two general effects of this class of agents. First, they appear to have a general 'ahedonic' effect involving a reduction in the efficacy of positive reinforcers (Wise, 1982), an effect which is most marked for behaviours maintained by low rates of reinforcement. Secondly, antipsychotics weaken avoidance behaviour at dosage levels which have no effect on escape. These observations suggest that antipsychotics may be expected to have a general effect on challenging behaviour which is maintained by operant processes. In particular, they may reduce avoidance-maintained behaviours, and behaviours maintained by lean schedules of positive reinforcement. Given the moderating effects of the background rate of reinforcement on the relationship between the rate of reinforcement and response rate (McDowell, 1982), this effect may be more pronounced in enriched environments. The observations would also suggest, however, that use of these drugs may be expected to have generalised suppressive effects on other learned behaviours, including adaptive behaviours (Thompson *et al.*, 1994*a*).

It should also be noted that the use of antipsychotics is known to be associated with a range of adverse side-effects. These include sedation, blurred vision, nausea, dizziness, weight gain, opacities of the cornea, grand mal seizures, a range of extrapyramidal syndromes including parkinsonism, akathisia, acute dystonic reaction and tardive dyskinesia, and death through neuroleptic malignant syndrome (Boyd, 1993; Gadow & Poling, 1988; Gross *et al.*, 1993; Thompson *et al.*, 1991).

SEROTONIN AGONISTS

The serotoninergic system is closely linked with a number of processes including arousal, appetite control, anxiety and depression. Disturbances in the system have been linked with insomnia, depression, disorders of appetite control and obsessive compulsive disorders (cf. Bodfish & Madison, 1993). With regard to potential behavioural mechanisms, Thompson *et al.* (1994*a*) suggest that serotonin activity may regulate reactivity to aversive stimuli and moderate the effectiveness of punishment on suppressing behaviour. As was discussed in Chapter 4, evidence is accumulating to point to a link between serotonin and aggression, and, perhaps, serotonin and self-injurious behaviour. This evidence includes:

☐ animal studies which show that lesions in areas which contain serotoninergic neurones or inhibit serotonin synthesis can lead to an increase in aggression. Similarly, interventions which increase serotonin synthesis or administration of serotonin agonists lead to a reduction in aggression;

☐ studies of non-disabled people which suggest a negative correlation between levels of serotonin or its metabolites in the cerebral spinal fluid or blood plasma and aggression.

This evidence suggests that serotoninergic agonists (e.g. buspirone) or reuptake inhibitors (e.g. fluoxetine) may have an impact on reducing aggression and possibly other forms of challenging behaviour. Indeed, some evidence is beginning to accumulate to suggest that fluoxetine (Prozac) may reduce aggression and self-injurious behaviour in people with severe learning disabilities (Bodfish & Madison, 1993; Cook *et al.*, 1992; Markowitz, 1992; Sovner *et al.*, 1993). Bodfish and Madison (1993), for example, reported that fluoxetine (at a dosage of 40 mg/day) significantly reduced self-injurious and aggressive behaviours which had a 'compulsive' nature in seven out of ten participants. None of the six participants who showed 'non-compulsive' aggression or self-injury responded positively. These results are particularly interesting in that they appear to point to possible aetiological factors which may discriminate between responders and non-responders. Bodfish and Madison (1993) argue that some forms of self-injurious behaviour may, in fact, be examples of obsessive–compulsive disorder. They may be distinguished by the person also showing other compulsive behaviours (e.g. ordering, touching, hoarding) which interfere with ongoing activities and the person being resistant to change. If these preliminary results are replicated, they suggest a means of identifying and treating a functionally distinct class of self-injury which may be maintained more by neurobiological processes than by environmental contingencies.

Similarly, buspirone, a serotonin agonist, has been associated with reduced aggression and self-injury in a small number of participants, an effect which may be enhanced by the introduction of a serotonin rich diet (Gedye, 1990, 1991; Ratey *et al.*, 1991).

Reported side-effects of serotonin reuptake inhibitors include the development of grand-mal seizures, possibly due to their effect of blocking gamma aminobutyric acid (GABA), a neurotransmitter which has anticonvulsant properties (Gedye, 1993).

β-ENDORPHIN ANTAGONISTS

β-endorphin, one of the opioid peptide neurotransmitters, has significant analgesic and antinocicoptive (blocking of pain receptors) properties, can be associated with a euphoric mood state, and may lead to physical dependence (Singh *et al.*, 1993*b*). Sandman and his colleagues (e.g. Sandman, 1990/1991) have proposed two models in which β-endorphin activity may be related to self-injurious behaviour. In the *congenital opioid excess* model it is proposed that excess opioid activity leads to permanently raised pain thresholds. In the *addiction* hypothesis it is proposed that self-injurious behaviour leads to the release of β-endorphin which, through its analgesic, antinocicoptive and euphoria-inducing properties, acts as an automatic reinforcer for the self-injury. Over time, it is suggested, physical dependence (with associated withdrawal symptoms) may develop.

There is accumulating evidence to support a link between β-endorphin and self-injurious behaviour. For instance:

☐ levels of β-endorphin are raised in the cerebral spinal fluid of people with severe learning disabilities who self-injure when compared with appropriate controls (Sandman *et al.*, 1990*b*);

☐ levels of β-endorphin are raised in the cerebral spinal fluid of people with severe learning disabilities following an episode of self-injury (Sandman, 1990/91);

☐ suggestive associations have been reported between self-injurious behaviour and paradoxical responses to sedatives (Sandman & Barron, 1992), diet (Neri & Sandman, 1992) and the menstrual cycle (Taylor *et al.*, 1993*a*).

The strongest evidence of an association between β-endorphin and self-injurious behaviour, however, comes from experimental and clinical studies which have examined the impact of the endorphin antagonists naloxone hydrochloride and, more recently, naltrexone hydrochloride (Nalorex) on self-injurious behaviour shown by people with severe learning disabilities (for recent reviews, see Ricketts *et al.*, 1993; Singh *et al.*, 1992).

A number of studies have reported significant reductions in self-injurious behaviour associated with the administration of naltrexone hydrochloride (e.g. Barrett, Feinstein & Hole, 1989; Bernstein *et al.*, 1987; Crews *et al.*, 1993; Herman *et al.*, 1987; Kars *et al.*, 1990; Knabe, Schulz & Richard, 1990; Lienemann & Walker, 1989; Ryan *et al.*, 1989; Sandman, Barron & Coleman, 1990*a*; Taylor *et al.*, 1991; Thompson *et al.*, 1994*b*; Walters *et al.*, 1990). However, it is clear that such positive results are not inevitable as a number of studies have also reported treatment failures, clinically insignificant results or occasional worsening of self-injury (e.g. Barrera *et al.*, 1994; Johnson, Johnson & Sahl, 1994; Kars *et al.*, 1990; Knabe *et al.*, 1990; Luiselli, Beltis & Bass, 1989; Ricketts *et al.*, 1992; Zingarelli *et al.*, 1992). A number of factors may account for these variations in outcome. These include:

☐ *dose-dependent effects*, in that a number of studies have reported positive outcomes only for specific dose levels, other dosages having either no effect or leading to an increase in self-injurious behaviour. Unfortunately, the relationships between dosage and outcome have been inconsistent, in that studies have reported greater effects with both lower (e.g. Barrera *et al.*, 1994; Herman *et al.*, 1987; Ricketts *et al.*, 1992; Sandman, Barron & Coleman, 1990*a*) and higher dosages (e.g. Barrera *et al.*, 1994; Bernstein *et al.*, 1987; Knabe *et al.*, 1990; Ryan *et al.*, 1989; Sandman *et al.*, 1990*b*);

☐ *behavioural topography*, Thompson *et al.* (1994*b*) presented data to suggest that particular forms of self-injury may respond differently to naltrexone with hand-to-head hitting, head-to-object hitting and self-biting showing more positive changes than eye, nose and throat poking and face slapping. These relationships held up within individuals, as well as across participants, and may be related to the extent to which specific behaviours lead to the release of β-endorphin;

☐ *behavioural function*, as we have seen in Chapter 4, there is extensive evidence to suggest that self-injurious behaviour may be maintained by a variety of factors. It is plausible to propose, therefore, that forms of self-injurious behaviour which are maintained by powerful operant contingencies, and especially those which may be less painful or less effective in leading to the release of β-endorphin, may be less likely to be reduced by administration of naltrexone. To date, this hypothesis has yet to be tested.

β-endorphin antagonists may also influence the response efficiency of self-injurious behaviour (Oliver, 1993). That is, by blocking the release of β-endorphin they may increase the 'cost' of responding by making the behaviour more painful. As has been discussed, decreasing response efficiency may lead to a behaviour being replaced by a functionally equivalent response (Horner & Day, 1991). It also points to the potential for integrating psychopharmacological and behavioural approaches, in that decreasing the response efficiency of the challenging behaviour is an important component of intervention based on the notion of functional displacement.

Very few side-effects have been reported with naltrexone hydrochloride, although there appears to be some risk of hepatic toxicity due to an increase in liver enzymes (Thompson *et al.*, 1994*b*). Reports of behavioural 'side-effects' include *increased* attention and learning (Taylor *et al.*, 1993*b*).

OTHER APPROACHES

A number of studies have examined the effects of other classes of psychoactive agents on the challenging behaviour shown by people with learning disabilities (for more detailed reviews, see Aman & Singh, 1988; Gadow & Poling, 1988; Thompson *et al.*, 1991; Singh *et al.*, 1992).

Anxiolytics and sedatives/hypnotics

There is little evidence to suggest that anxiolytics, such as the benzodiazepines, or sedatives/hypnotics (e.g. chloral hydrate) have any clinically significant effect on challenging behaviour (Gadow & Poling, 1988; Thompson *et al.*, 1991; Singh *et al.*, 1992). Indeed, there is growing evidence to suggest that 'paradoxical' responding to these classes of drugs may occur among people with learning disabilities who show self-injurious and stereotypic behaviour (Sandman & Barron, 1992). Thompson *et al.* (1991) and Thompson *et al.* (1994*b*) suggested that this may be due to the effects of benzodiazepines and sedative hypnotics in blocking the suppressive effects of punishment contingencies, which may be acting to reduce the occurrence of challenging behaviour.

Anti-manics

Lithium carbonate has been used to reduce symptoms of mania in bipolar affective disorder for a considerable number of years. A number of poorly controlled case studies have reported that reductions in aggressive, disruptive and self-injurious behaviours may be associated with administration of lithium (Singh *et al.*, 1992; Thompson *et al.*, 1991). It is unclear, however, whether these positive results are reflected in the reduction in challenging behaviour specifically associated with mania or indicate more general effects.

Stimulants

A few early studies suggested that stimulants (e.g. D-amphetamine, methyl-phenedate) may have a general effect on reducing hyperactivity and improving intellectual functioning among people with learning disabilities (e.g. Bell & Zubek, 1961). Later studies have failed to replicate these effects (Aman & Singh, 1988; Gadow & Poling, 1988; Singh *et al.*, 1992; Thompson *et al.*, 1991).

Monoamine oxidase inhibitors and tricyclic anti-depressants

Again, there is little evidence to suggest that either MAOI or tricyclic antidepressants have any general effect on reducing challenging behaviour (Singh *et al.*, 1992; Thompson *et al.*, 1991). Indeed, one of the more recent studies reported increased irritability, agitation and non-compliance to be associated with administration of imipramine (Aman *et al.*, 1986; although see also Hittner, 1994).

Anticonvulsants

Clearly, anticonvulsants may have an important role to play in situations in which challenging behaviours may be attributed to seizure activity (cf. Gedye, 1989*a*, *b*). In addition, a small number of often poorly controlled studies have reported marked reductions in challenging behaviour associated with administration of carbamazepine (e.g. Langee, 1989; Reid, Naylor & Kay, 1981). Of greater importance, however, is the occurrence of challenging behaviours as side-effects of anticonvulsants at higher doses (Thompson *et al.*, 1991).

Antihypertensives

Again, a small number of poorly controlled case studies have suggested that propanadol and other beta-blockers may be associated with significant reductions in self-injury and aggressive behaviours (Singh *et al.*, 1992).

SUMMARY AND CONCLUSIONS

Virtually every review of psychopharmacological approaches to reducing challenging behaviour among people with learning disabilities has commented upon the methodological inadequacies of the majority of studies which have been conducted in this field (Aman, 1991; Aman & Singh, 1988, 1991; Baumeister & Sevin, 1990; Gadow & Poling, 1988; Ricketts *et al.*, 1993; Singh & Aman, 1990; Singh *et al.*, 1992; Sprague & Werry, 1971; Thompson *et al.*, 1991). These methodological flaws make interpretation of much of the data highly problematic.

Nevertheless, a number of promising directions are evident, many of which stem from the integration of neurobiological theorising and psycho-pharmacological intervention (Baumeister & Sevin, 1990). Thus, for example, although the data is as yet scarce, D1 antagonists, serotonin reuptake inhibitors and β-endorphin antagonists may all have specific effects which are predictable from neurobiological models of challenging behaviour.

As was stressed in Chapter 4, however, it is highly likely that the factors underlying challenging behaviours are complex and varied. Thus, for example, it is quite clear that some examples of self-injurious behaviour appear to be primarily maintained by operant processes (which may in themselves be complex). On the other hand, it does appear that β-endorphin release is also implicated in some examples of self-injury (see above). There is also, of course, evidence that both serotoninergic and dopaminergic systems may play a role in the expression of self-injurious behaviour.

In Chapter 5 an argument was made for the adoption of a functional perspective. In the light of the preceding discussion, this would imply that one task of analysis would be to attempt to identify the biological, as well as the behavioural, processes underlying challenging behaviour. Markers for the operation of biological processes may include such factors as covariation of challenging behaviour with mood state (e.g. Lowry & Sovner, 1992; Sovner *et al.*, 1993), co-occurrence with compulsive behaviours (e.g. Bodfish & Madison, 1993), behavioural topography (Thompson *et al.*, 1994*b*) and environmental independence. The selection of an appropriate intervention, whether behavioural, psychopharmacological or combined, could then proceed on the basis of evidence rather than personal preference, availability or fashion. To date, however, such a hope has yet to be realised.

9 LONGER-TERM MANAGEMENT

In Chapter 3 attention was drawn to the apparent chronicity and persistence of severely challenging behaviours. The research which was summarised indicated that:

☐ adults with challenging behaviours, who come to the attention of specialised services, have often shown those particular behaviours for a decade or more (e.g. Emerson *et al.*, 1988; Murphy *et al.*, 1993);

☐ the vast majority of people who show challenging behaviour at one point in time, are also likely to do so a decade later (e.g. Windahl, 1988);

☐ longer-term follow up of 'successful' intervention programmes often report a very high rate of relapse (Griffin *et al.*, 1986*a*; Murphy & Wilson, 1980; Schroeder & MacLean, 1987).

In addition, the few instances of successful long-term maintenance of treatment gains which have been reported in the literature indicate that, although the intensity and/or rate may be significantly reduced, challenging behaviours tend to persist (e.g. Foxx, 1990; Jensen & Heidorn, 1993; Williams *et al.*, 1994).

Foxx (1990) reported a ten-year follow-up of 'Harry', a man with severe learning disabilities and severe self-injurious behaviour. At the time of the initial intervention, Harry was 22 years old. His self-injury, which had started in infancy, was managed through the use of hinged arm splints and a face mask. Assessment suggested that self-injury was negatively reinforced by escape from social demands, and positively reinforced by access to restraints. Intervention focused on: (1) the fading of restraints from arm splints and a face mask to spectacles and, later, a baseball cap; (2) reinforcing compliance during high demand situations with praise, physical contact, drinks and access to restraints; and (3) punishing self-injury through the implementation of a brief five-minute time-out period, without restraints. These procedures rapidly reduced 'Harry's' self-injury to very low levels, made use of mechanical restraint unnecessary and enabled him to participate in a much wider range of community-based activities. The achievements were all maintained over the following ten years (Foxx, 1990; Foxx & Dufrense, 1984). However, the data presented also indicated that 'Harry's' self-injury and need to self-restrain still persisted, albeit at a very low level, and that his self-injury partially re-emerged after seven years in response to his placement in a supported work setting.

Jensen and Heidorn (1993) also reported a ten-year follow-up of the treatment of severe self-injurious behaviour shown by a 27 year-old man with severe learning disabilities. By the time of the initial intervention he had blinded himself through his self-injurious eye poking which appeared to have emerged in response to an untreated eye infection. He also rubbed his head on walls, floors and other objects and dug his nails into his forehead and nose. These behaviours resulted in him losing cartilage from his nose and developing a large lesion above his eye. The man's self-injury was (ineffectively) managed by use of physical restraints for up to 17 hours per day. Assessment indicated that his self-injury was multiply controlled. In low demand situations it appeared to be maintained by socially mediated positive reinforcement. In high demand situations it appeared to be maintained by escape from demands. Intervention, therefore, combined DRO, escape extinction and stimulus fading (Heidorn & Jensen, 1984). Ten year follow-up data indicated significant reductions in actual injury, minimal rate of self-injury, discontinuation of the use of restraint and reduction in medication. Again, however, his self-injury did persist, albeit in a different form and at a much lower rate. As Jensen and Heidorn state, 'in recent years he is reported to pick at his skin and then pick or scratch at the scabs. He reportedly can pick at one scab for several months at a time ... occasionally he will become agitated and put his thumb in his eye, make loud vocalisations, and drop to the floor on his knees' (Jensen & Heidorn, 1993).

These two case studies and the preceding observations raise a number of important issues regarding the longer-term management of severely challenging behaviours, and the maintenance of treatment gains. These will be discussed below in relation to the requirements for practical long-term support and sustaining the implementation of intervention processes.

LONG-TERM SUPPORT

While reports of long-term successes are extremely heartening (see also Lovaas & Smith, 1994), the existing literature does indicate that relatively few people with challenging behaviour are likely to obtain access to such specialised support (Kiernan & Alborz, 1994; Oliver et al., 1987; Qureshi, 1994). It also indicates that, in the absence of intensive intervention, severe challenging behaviour may be highly persistent over time (see above). This suggests that the effective management or prevention of episodes of challenging behaviour is likely to be of crucial importance if some of the adverse personal and social consequences of such behaviours are to be avoided.

As we saw in Chapter 2, these adverse consequences can include:

☐ secondary infections, physical disfigurement, loss of sight or hearing, additional neurological impairments and even death;

☐ inappropriate long-term medication and/or restraint;

☐ exposure to unnecessarily degrading or abusive psychological treatments;

☐ families seeking alternative residential provision for their son or daughter;

☐ ill health among carers;

☐ exclusion from community-based services and admission or re-admission to institutional settings;

☐ abuse by carers and care staff.

Below, some of the issues relevant to preventing secondary consequences will be discussed briefly. These include the development of effective approaches to the physical management of episodes of challenging behaviour and the development of practical support to families and residential settings.

Managing episodes of challenging behaviour

Self-injurious behaviour

Griffin *et al.* (1986*a*), Luiselli (1992*b*), Richmond *et al.* (1986) and Spain, Hart and Corbett (1984) discussed the use of mechanical and physical restraint to either prevent the occurrence, or minimise the physical consequences, of self-injury. This included the use of devices such as arm splints, face masks, helmets and gloves. While generally only considered as a last resort, Griffin *et al.* (1986*a*) and Richmond *et al.* (1986) argued that such methods should be given greater attention given that: (1) restraint appears to be quite frequently used in practice; and (2) failure to do so may place the person at considerable physical risk if either insufficient resources are available to implement an intensive intervention programme, or the person's self-injury appears intractable.

Protective equipment can be used in two main ways (Luiselli, 1992*b*).

☐ *Mechanical restraint* involves the use of devices such as rigid arm splints to prevent the occurrence of the self-injurious behaviour. At its most extreme, this may involve full immobilisation (e.g. Tate, 1972; Tate &

Baroff, 1966). Some of the adverse effects associated with the use of mechanical restraint include: reduced opportunity to participate in habilitative activities; stigmatisation; reduced interaction with care staff; development of alternative self-injurious behaviours; muscular atrophy, demineralisation of the bones; shortening of tendons; and the risk of injury resulting from the process of the restraints being applied (Griffin *et al.*, 1986; Jensen & Heidorn, 1993; Luiselli, 1992*b*; Richmond, *et al.*, 1986; Rojahn, Schroeder & Mulick, 1980; Spreat *et al.*, 1986). In addition, restraint may become highly reinforcing for the person (e.g. Favell *et al.*, 1981; Foxx & Dufrense, 1984; Smith *et al.*, 1992; for a recent review on the issue of self-restraint, see Schroeder & Luiselli, 1992). There is, evidence, however, that reliance on mechanical restraints or self-restraint can be accomplished by *restraint fading* combined with differential reinforcement (e.g. Foxx & Dufrense, 1984; Pace *et al.*, 1986). In addition, some of the more detrimental effects of mechanical restraint can be minimised by the use of devices which interrupt, rather than totally prevent, the self-injurious behaviour (e.g. hinged or inflatable arm splints).

☐ *Response prevention* involves the use of protective equipment such as helmets (e.g. Spain *et al.*, 1984) to prevent or reduce the risk of injury resulting from self-injurious behaviour. While less restrictive than mechanical restraint, such protective devices may still result in similar social consequences as more extreme mechanical restraint (e.g. decreased interaction with care staff; see Mace & Knight, 1986). The use of such devices may, however, bring about reductions in self-injury, either by exerting discriminative control over the behaviour (e.g. Dorsey *et al.*, 1982) or by leading to sensory extinction (e.g. Rincover & Devany, 1982).

Aggressive and disruptive behaviour

The management of episodes of aggressive or disruptive behaviour will require the physical intervention of carers and staff in order to either protect themselves or others, remove the person from the vicinity of others or objects, or remove others or objects from the vicinity of the person. This is likely to be relevant during the implementation of both non-aversive and aversive interventions (Altmeyer *et al.*, 1987; Cataldo, 1991; McGee *et al.*, 1987). Unfortunately, the issues involved in physically managing aggressive and disruptive behaviours shown by people with severe learning disabilities have received little attention in the research literature. Spreat *et al.* (1986) reported that unplanned restraint is more likely to result in injury to both care staff and service users than planned restraint, an observation which highlights the need for appropriate planning and training for carers and care staff in all aspects of the physical management of aggression (e.g. Harvey & Schepers, 1977; McDonnell, Dearden & Richens, 1991). It is also clear that episodes of disturbed behaviour may be frightening and disturbing for carers and staff (e.g. Bersani & Heifetz, 1985; Bromley & Emerson, in press; Hastings, 1993; Kiernan & Alborz, 1994). This suggests the importance of providing support and counselling for victims or witnesses of serious aggressive or disruptive behaviours.

Service supports

As was noted in the introductory chapter, much has been written over recent years regarding some of the general issues involved in providing community-based supports for people with challenging behaviours (e.g. Allen *et al.*, 1991; Blunden & Allen, 1987; Department of Health, 1989, 1993; Emerson *et al.*, 1994; Fleming & Stenfert Kroese, 1993; Lowe & Felce, 1994a; Kiernan, 1993; Kiernan & Alborz, 1994; Forrest *et al.*, 1995; Russell, 1995). Obviously, the timely and sensitive provision of appropriate technical and practical support to families and service settings has a major role to play in minimising any adverse personal and social consequences arising from a person's challenging behaviour. Rather than repeating in detail the recommendations and proposals of previous reports, attention will be drawn to some of the issues which appear to be of particular concern.

As has been shown, challenging behaviours are a major source of stress to parents, and are often cited by parents as the main reason for them seeking residential care for their son or daughter (e.g. Quine & Pahl, 1985; Tausig, 1985). Unfortunately, it would appear that, in the UK at least, families caring for an individual with challenging behaviour can expect little effective support from service agencies (e.g. Kiernan & Alborz, 1994; Qureshi, 1992). Forms of advice and support which may reduce the strain experienced by carers and potentially prevent inappropriate moves to residential care include:

☐ information concerning the causes, 'meaning' and prognosis of their child's challenging behaviour;

☐ consistent, practical and effective advice regarding the behavioural and medical management of challenging behaviour;

☐ practical support with regard to implementing advice given by professional staff;

☐ help in dealing with stress arising from the task of caring;

☐ access to a range of options for respite care.

A detailed discussion of issues related to providing services to families in the UK was provided by Russell (1995) and Kiernan and Alborz (1994).

With regard to residential provision, it is clear that the majority of people with severe learning disabilities and challenging behaviour are, and can be, supported in non-specialised community-based residential provision, i.e. within services not specifically designed to meet the needs of people with challenging behaviour (Department of Health, 1993; Emerson & Hatton, 1994; Felce, Lowe & de Paiva, 1994). The outcomes associated with such services are consistently better than those seen in institutional and medium-sized residential provision (Emerson & Hatton, 1994). However, such services often lack effective managerial and professional support and, as a result, they may be highly susceptible to breakdown in response to short-term crises (Mansell *et al.*, 1994*a*; Mansell, Hughes & McGill, 1994*b*).

For the small number of people who display extreme forms of challenging behaviour, appropriate support can be provided in small community-based settings designed to meet the specific needs of known individuals (Emerson, 1990). Typically, such settings will avoid congregating people who display challenging behaviour together (McGill, Emerson & Mansell, 1994). As with the less specialised settings outlined above, the outcomes associated with such services appear superior to those associated with either institutional settings (e.g. Mansell, 1994) or specialised treatment units (e.g. Emerson *et al.*, 1992). Again, however, such services often lack the necessary levels of managerial and professional support, leaving them susceptible to breakdown (Mansell *et al.*, 1994*b*; McGill *et al.*, 1994).

For both non-specialised and specialised community-based services, better outcomes appear to be associated with those services which employ an 'active support' model (Emerson & Hatton, 1994). This approach is based on the use of behavioural principles to design supportive physical and social environments for people with severe disabilities (Felce, 1991).

Finally, as noted in the preceding paragraphs, despite the marked growth of peripatetic community-based support teams for people with challenging behaviour, there still remains a considerable shortage of professional support for people with challenging behaviour (Kiernan & Alborz, 1994; Lowe & Felce, 1994*a*; Mansell *et al.*, 1994*a*; Russell *et al.*, 1995). As a result, challenging behaviours may persist unnecessarily.

SUSTAINING PROGRAMME IMPLEMENTATION

The evidence which has been reviewed so far suggests that intervention programmes may need to be sustained over considerable periods of time.

This does not mean that significant reductions in challenging behaviour are not possible over the short term. On the contrary, most of the approaches to providing effective behavioural support which were discussed in Chapter 7 have been shown, under certain circumstances, to bring about rapid and meaningful reductions in challenging behaviour. However, maintaining these gains, generalising them to new settings and achieving broader 'life-style' outcomes are unlikely to occur without continued support. As Anderson *et al.* (1993) point out:

> *patterns of severe challenging behaviors do not simply "disappear". Long-term support plans must create and maintain settings and programmatic contexts in which these behaviors are made and continue to be ineffective, inefficient, or irrelevant. Only then will near-zero levels of challenging behaviors occur and be maintained in all settings relevant to a person's life (Anderson et al., 1993, p.368).*

Such a requirement does, of course, pose a major challenge (cf. Hastings & Remigton, 1993). It should not, however, surprise us. The behavioural approach suggests that challenging behaviours have been shaped over time, and are currently being maintained by powerful contingencies of reinforcement. We should expect, therefore that, unless intervention brings about a *lasting change* in the maintaining contingencies, intervention gains are highly unlikely to prove durable. As we have seen, establishing alternative behaviours is only likely to be effective if the person's challenging behaviour is made 'ineffective, inefficient, or irrelevant'. Intervention, therefore, needs to be seen as an ongoing process, rather than as a time-limited episode of 'treatment'.

This perspective forces us to consider ways in which intervention can bring about sustained changes in the behaviours of carers and care staff who are likely to be primarily involved in programme implementation. It requires us to examine issues related to resources, the contingencies operating on carers and care staff and the beliefs and attitudes they hold about the person's challenging behaviours.

Resources

A very basic (and obvious) requirement for successfully sustaining the implementation of behavioural programmes is that carers and care staff have access to the resources required by the task in hand. Two aspects of resources will be briefly considered: the skills or competencies of carers and care staff; and the time available for carers and care staff to work with service users.

Skills and competencies

Obviously, carers and/or care staff will not be able to implement a programme of intervention successfully unless they possess the requisite skills and competencies. Fortunately, a considerable amount is known regarding effective and efficient ways of imparting skills such as verbal and physical guidance, teaching procedures, the use of reinforcement, goal setting and the recording and monitoring of behaviour (Anderson *et al.*, 1993; Baumgart & Ferguson, 1991; Cullen, 1992; Egel & Powers, 1989; Hogg & Mitler, 1987; McClannahan & Krantz, 1993; Reid & Green, 1990; Parsons, Reid & Green, 1993; Reid, Parsons & Green, 1989*a*).

Similarly, an increasing number of approaches have been documented for training clinical practitioners in the areas of programme development, implementation, review and modification (e.g. Anderson *et al.*, 1993; McGill & Bliss, 1993; see also *Journal of Applied Behavior Analysis*, **24**, Issue 4). To date, however, no systematic evaluation of the effectiveness of such programmes has been reported. In the UK, at least, access to more advanced practitioner training programmes is highly restricted. As a result, the majority of practitioners providing community-based support for people with challenging behaviour in the UK have received only minimal specialised training (Forrest *et al.*, 1995; McGill & Bliss, 1993).

One consistent conclusion, which has been drawn from reviews of the behavioural training literature, is that training *per se* has little impact on subsequent performance (Cullen, 1992; Reid & Green, 1990; Reid *et al.*, 1989*a*). This leads us to examine other variables which are likely to determine whether the skills available to carers and care staff are used appropriately.

Time available

Again, it is very obvious that the successful implementation of behavioural approaches is dependent upon carers and/or care staff having the necessary time available. A number of studies have examined the relationship between resources, such as staff : user ratios, and staff performance in a range of residential settings. This research literature indicates that the relationship between resources and performance is far from straightforward. The available evidence suggests that:

☐ the amount of contact received by users is largely unrelated to overall staff : user ratios (e.g. Felce *et al.*, 1991; Hatton *et al.*, 1994), although users who are supported in small groups of 1 to 4 by one or two staff do receive more contact from staff (e.g. Felce *et al.*, 1991);

☐ increasing the ratio of staff to users in a setting does not necessarily lead to users receiving more support (e.g. Seys & Duker, 1988);

☐ in highly staffed residential settings for people with challenging behaviour the majority of staff time is spent on activities not involving direct contact with users (e.g. Emerson *et al.*, 1992).

The evidence outlined above does not, of course, deny the importance of human resources. Rather, it points to the reasonably obvious conclusion that an adequate level of resources may be a necessary, but is certainly not a sufficient, condition for sustaining programme implementation. Nevertheless, it will be of obvious importance to ensure that the requirements for successful implementation, including all monitoring and record-keeping activities, are, and will continue to be, available in the appropriate settings (cf. Berg & Sasso, 1993). This is likely to be particularly important when working with families (cf. Kiernan & Alborz, 1994).

Rules and contingencies

The field of organisational behaviour management has demonstrated repeatedly that control may be exercised over behaviour in the workplace by:

☐ expectations concerning required job performances;

☐ monitoring of behaviour in the workplace; and

☐ providing feedback to staff in the light of the relationship between expectations and performance (see, for example, Cullen, 1992; Reid *et al.*, 1989*a*, *b* and *Journal of Applied Behavior Analysis*, **25**, Issue 3).

Techniques based on this framework have been employed repeatedly in demonstration projects to significantly improve the performance of direct-care staff in services for people with severe learning disabilities (Cullen, 1992; Krantz, MacDuff & McClannahan, 1993; Reid *et al.*, 1989*a*, *b*). While clearly effective, at least in the short term, the general approach suffers from two major weaknesses. First, studies have largely failed to address the nature of the contingencies maintaining existing staff behaviour (cf. Hastings & Remington, 1994*a*, *b*). That is, while they have repeatedly shown that new powerful 'bolt-on' contingencies can change staff behaviour, little has been learned about why staff act in the way they do in the absence of these artificially imposed contingencies. This is, of course, highly reminiscent of the 'behaviour modification' approach to challenging behaviour which was dominant for so many years. This failure to base intervention on a prior *analysis* of the factors maintaining inappropriate staff performance is, at least in part, responsible for the field's reliance on highly artificial, hierarchical and bureaucratic procedures for ensuring staff *compliance* with the organisation's aims. Secondly, and following on from this, many of the specific techniques which have been shown to be effective in the North American literature (e.g. public posting of feedback, reinforcement of appropriate staff performance with lottery tickets) are likely to be procedurally unacceptable in the UK, particularly in agencies committed to notions of participative management (although see Burgio, Whitman & Reid, 1983).

A behaviour *analytic* approach to understanding and changing the behaviour of care staff or carers toward someone with challenging behaviour would need to consider the nature of the contingencies maintaining existing behaviour. These would involve a consideration of the impact of the behaviour of service users on the behaviour of carers or care staff, aspects of control exercised by other family members (for carers) or colleagues (for care staff), influences from outside the immediate setting (e.g. neighbours, friends and relatives), as well as any control exerted by the management systems operating within services.

As we have seen, care staff often report strong emotional reactions to episodes of challenging behaviour (Bromley & Emerson, in press; Hastings, 1993). In addition, experimental studies have shown that the behaviour of the person with challenging behaviour may exert considerable control over the approach and avoidance behaviour of care staff (Carr *et al.*, 1991; Taylor & Carr, 1993, 1994; Taylor & Romanczyk, 1994). In general, escape-maintained challenging behaviours are likely to elicit avoidance by staff, attention-maintained challenging behaviours are likely to elicit approach by staff.

Furthermore, it seems plausible to assume that a range of 'informal' rules and contingencies exert a powerful influence on the behaviour of carers and care staff. That is, peer groups and family members define what should be done, monitor each other's performance against these (often implicit or unstated) aims, and provide effective (if not always constructive) feedback. Unfortunately, however, these informal rules and contingencies may support practices which are either irrelevant to, or at odds with, the explicit aims of the service or the advice of consulting professional staff. Thus, for example, the costs of not icing a birthday cake for the sister of someone with challenging behaviour may outweigh the benefits of recording the details of an episode of challenging behaviour. In service settings, it is often possible to identify processes of socialisation by which new staff are taught the 'tricks of the trade' by members of the existing staff group. These may involve, for example, communicating a clear understanding that it is easier and simpler all round if staff do things for users, rather than support the participation of users in everyday activities. While it may be possible in theory to use behavioural concepts to 'engineer' more appropriate informal cultures within the workplace (cf. McClannahan & Krantz, 1993), such studies have yet to be reported.

As was suggested in Chapters 4 and 7, it is likely to be important to view the operation of contingencies resulting from the behaviour of users, peers and managers within the context of rule-governed behaviour, which would incorporate an analysis of the effects of the beliefs and attitudes or *self-generated rules* held by carers and staff on their behaviour (Hastings, 1993; Hastings & Remington, 1994*a*). As Hastings and Remington (1994*a*) explained, in behaviour analysis

rules are verbal formulations of contingencies. They describe relationships between behavioral and environmental events that would normally need to be learned through direct experience. For example, the rule, 'When reinforcement is withdrawn, the to-be-extinguished behavior increases', describes a relationship between behavior and its consequences that is not immediately obvious. A person who is told the rule, and uses it, can thereby operate as if he or she had experienced many extinction procedures (Hastings & Remington, 1994a, p.284).

Hastings and Remington went on to describe some of the sources, forms and characteristics of the rules which may, in part, determine the behaviour of care staff. A very similar framework could be used to understand the behaviour of family members toward a person with challenging behaviour. Hastings and Remington (1994*a, b*) and Hastings (1993) defined some of the important characteristics of such an approach. First and foremost, if staff/carer behaviour is rule governed, it then becomes important to determine: (1) the content of the rules which are influencing behaviour; (2) their sources; and (3) the nature of the contingencies maintaining rule following.

With regard to content, rules are likely to vary widely with regard to their specificity. These may range from the type of highly specific performance-related instructions commonly encountered in behavioural teaching programmes (e.g. 'on the first trial guide the person's hand toward the ...'), to much more general beliefs about the nature of challenging behaviour (e.g. 'it reflects a lack of bonding') which will require considerable 'translation' before it can provide a more specific guide to action. It is interesting to note, therefore, that Bromley and Emerson (in press) reported that the most common staff beliefs concerning the causes of challenging behaviour relate to either the person's internal psychological state (e.g. frustration, boredom) or to very broad environmental factors (e.g. previous deprivation, lack of staff), i.e. to factors which have relatively weak implications for specific staff performance.

As was suggested above, rules may be either self-generated (i.e. generalised from other areas of life), or externally supplied by managers, professionals or peers. Importantly, viewing staff/carer behaviour as potentially rule governed switches attention from the contingencies operating on specific staff behaviours to the contingencies maintaining more general classes of rule-following. Thus, rule-governed behaviour is not independent of the environment, although it may be insensitive to momentary changes in the contingencies it describes (Hastings & Remington, 1994*a, b*). The contingencies maintaining rule following will be dependent upon the nature of the rule but could include such factors as: positive reinforcement (e.g. praise) for *rule following* from peers, managers and professionals; avoidance of the withdrawal of positive reinforcers (e.g. having pay docked); escape from, or avoidance of, the presentation of punishing stimuli (e.g. peer censure); and 'automatic reinforcement' arising from the confirmation of the rule's predictions.

Summary

In the sections above, attention has been drawn to some of the research and concepts which will help to inform a behavioural analysis of the behaviour of families and direct-care staff in caring for someone with challenging behaviours. It would appear that such an analysis is essential if intervention plans are to be sustained over lengthy periods of time. This would require the assessment of service or family settings prior to the implementation of an intervention plan to address such questions as ...

☐ What skills will be required to implement the intervention? Do the people who will be carrying out the intervention have the required skills? If not, can those skills be taught, generalised and maintained?

☐ What other resources will be required to implement the intervention? Do the people who will be implementing the intervention have adequate time and resources to carry it out effectively? What other demands upon their time are likely to interfere with implementation? Can the programme be made more 'user-friendly' by requiring less intensive input? Can additional resources be secured?

☐ Are performance expectations clear? How will compliance with these expectations be monitored? How will feedback be given?

☐ What other rules may the participants be following? Are these likely to reinforce or be in conflict with the programme requirements? How can the following of conflicting rules be weakened? How can the following of concordant rules be strengthened?

At present, extremely little research is available to guide practice in these areas. In particular, little is known regarding the characteristics of organisations which achieve the successful and sustained implementation of behavioural approaches. Drawing upon their experiences over the last two decades at the Princeton Child Development Institute, McClannahan and Krantz (1993) speculated that success in the area is dependent upon such factors as: (1) a non-departmentalised organisational structure; (2) providing effective and comprehensive staff training, primarily through modelling by trainers and supervisors; (3) providing support for multilateral reciprocal feedback for *all* members of staff; (4) ongoing performance-based evaluation of all staff; (5) involving all staff in the design and use of routine evaluation of programme outcomes and processes; (6) setting personal and organisational goals in areas which are likely to tap into powerful naturally occurring sources of group reinforcement.

10   CHALLENGES AHEAD

In this, the concluding chapter, an attempt will be made to draw together some of the key themes and issues which have arisen at various points in the book. In particular, those areas of research will be highlighted which will need to be explored in much more detail over the next decade if applied behavioural approaches are to continue to make a significant contribution to practice. These include issues regarding the development of more comprehensive approaches to understanding challenging behaviour, refining approaches to assessment, developing and evaluating effective approaches to intervention and the implementation of behavioural approaches in applied settings.

UNDERSTANDING CHALLENGING BEHAVIOUR

In Chapter 4, attention was drawn on a number of occasions to the importance of developing more comprehensive models of challenging behaviour. It is clear from the evidence which has been reviewed in this book that a wide range of cultural, social, behavioural and biological processes are involved in the development, maintenance and treatment of challenging behaviour. So, for example, cultural and social processes are involved in the definition of behaviour as challenging and in shaping people's reactions to challenging behaviour. As we have seen, reciprocal behavioural processes may be responsible for shaping the development of challenging behaviour. They are clearly implicated in the maintenance of some examples of challenging behaviour and have provided a framework for developing powerful approaches to treatment. Similarly, biological processes are clearly involved in the development, maintenance and treatment of some examples of challenging behaviour.

To date, however, much of the theorising about challenging behaviour has taken place within, rather than across, these potentially complementary frameworks. More recently, a number of researchers have begun to sketch out some of the possible links between cultural, social, behavioural and biological processes (e.g. Guess & Carr, 1991; Oliver, 1993; Murphy, 1994; Thompson *et al.*, 1994a).

Guess & Carr (1991), for example, presented a three-stage model of the development of stereotypic and self-injurious behaviours, which drew together the concepts of behaviour states (Guess *et al.*, 1990, 1993), homeostatic mechanisms for modulating levels of arousal (cf. Murphy, 1982), and operant processes. They suggested that stereotyped behaviours first emerge as part of a biologically determined behavioural state condition which occurs relatively independently of environmental processes. As a result of developmental and learning processes, the child may learn to use such behaviours to self-regulate levels of stimulation. That is, stereotypy may form a component of a homeostatic process by which optimal levels of stimulation or arousal are maintained. Finally, reciprocal behavioural processes (Taylor & Carr, 1993, 1994) gradually shape more complex and/or intense forms of stereotypy, some of which are likely to become injurious. During this final stage of the process, they suggested that the operant properties of the behaviour become dominant. While not without its own omissions, particularly with regard to the potential significance of the neurobiological substrate of stereotypy and self-injury (cf. Baumeister, 1991; Mulick & Meinhold, 1991), this does represent a coherent framework for integrating evidence from disparate sources.

Similarly, in the UK, Murphy (1994) and Oliver (1993) have begun to identify some of the components of integrated bio-behavioural models of self-injury (Oliver, 1993; Oliver & Head, 1990) and challenging behaviours in general (Murphy, 1994). Oliver (1993) discussed the interactions between predisposing factors (e.g. degree of learning disability, additional sensory impairments, specific conditions), mediating conditions (e.g. handicap in expressive communication) and maintaining processes (operant, β-endorphin release) in the development of self-injurious behaviour. Murphy (1994) considered possible interactions between biological, behavioural and social-ecological processes in the development of challenging behaviour in general.

To date, however, research examining some of the propositions arising from more complex models is extremely scarce. There is an obvious need to rectify this omission. Profitable areas of enquiry are likely to include observational studies of the emergence of challenging behaviours (e.g. Murphy, Hall & Oliver, 1995), the role of biological setting events in accounting for variation in challenging behaviours maintained by operant processes, and the interaction between operant processes and endorphin activity in the maintenance of self-injurious behaviour.

It will also, of course, be important to ensure that behavioural models themselves continue to be refined and developed. Indeed, the field of applied behavioural analysis in general has been frequently criticised for failing to take account of more recent developments in basic operant theory (e.g. Epling & Pierce, 1983; Michael, 1980; Pierce & Epling, 1980; Remington, 1991*a*).

Recent developments in analysis and intervention studies of challenging behaviour which run counter to this general trend include the growth in applied studies on implications of the matching law (Martens & Houk, 1989; Martens *et al.*, 1992; Neef *et al.*, 1992, 1993), the application of the phenomenon of behavioural momentum to intervention (Mace *et al.*, 1988), analyses of the role of schedule-induction (Emerson & Howard, 1992; Emerson *et al.*, in press*b*), the use of molar equilibrium theory to identify reinforcement contingencies (Aeschleman & Williams, 1989; Diorio & Konarski, 1989; Realon & Konarski, 1993) and application of the notion of rule-governed behaviour to the analysis of staff behaviour (Hastings & Remington, 1994*a*). Nevertheless, there clearly remains considerable scope for integrating these and other factors into applied models and practices.

Romanczyk, for example, has argued the case for paying much greater attention to respondent processes and issues of arousal in behavioural accounts of self-injurious behaviour (Romanczyk, 1986; Romanczyk *et al.*, 1992). As has been shown, some forms of stereotypic and self-injurious behaviours may be examples of schedule-induced behaviors. These issues are also likely to be important in developing more comprehensive behavioural accounts of aggressive and disruptive behaviours (cf. Archer, 1989/1990; Berkowitz, 1988; Mulick *et al.*, 1991).

In addition, the current focus in intervention on constructional approaches in general, and functional displacement in particular, suggest that much more needs to be learned about the properties of complex behavioural systems in complex environments (cf. Mace, 1994*a*, *b*; Remington, 1991*a*,; Schroeder & MacLean, 1987; Scotti *et al.*, 1991*a*) and in the operation of motivational processes which underlie challenging behaviour (Emerson, 1993).

REFINING ASSESSMENT

The further development of two aspects of the assessment process is likely to be particularly important in improving future understanding and practice in the treatment of severely challenging behaviours. These aspects are the conceptual expansion of functional assessment and the evaluation of the social validity of intervention outcomes.

The conceptual expansion of functional assessment

First, it has been argued that there are both logical and empirical grounds for adopting a functionally based approach to intervention (Carr *et al.*, 1990*a*; Mace & Roberts, 1993; Mace *et al.*, 1991). That is, the benefits of intervention are likely to be maximised and the risks and costs minimised, if intervention is based on knowledge of the processes maintaining the person's challenging behaviour. Indeed, such an assumption would appear to be axiomatic to 'good practice' in this field.

This does, of course, presuppose the existence of assessment techniques which are capable of identifying underlying processes. As was shown in Chapter 6, however, existing approaches are marked by a number of limitations. These include:

☐ the low, or unknown, reliability and validity of approaches based on informant reports (e.g. Thompson & Emerson, in press; Zarcone *et al.*, 1991);

☐ the logical flaws associated with simple approaches to observation (e.g. ABC charts);

☐ issues relating to the applicability of more complex observational and experimental techniques to low frequency challenging behaviours;

☐ the resource requirements and, to a certain extent, unknown validity of these more complex approaches (cf. Lerman & Iwata, 1993; Emerson *et al.*, in press*b*).

Acknowledgement of these limitations indicates certain obvious areas for future research and development. So, for example, attention needs to be paid to determining the nature of information which can be reliably obtained from third parties, and the extent to which this information generalises across settings, informants, users and forms of challenging behaviours. The resource requirements of more complex observational methods could be significantly reduced by harnessing recent developments in information technology, including the development of 'user-friendly' software for data capture and analysis. Much more needs to be known about the comparative and ecological validity of differing experimental and observational approaches to assessment.

While not denying the importance of these technical developments, perhaps the most important challenge ahead lies in broadening functionally based approaches to assessment to include the analysis of motivational factors (Michael, 1982, 1993), multiple response repertoires (Scotti *et al.*, 1991*a*), rule-governed behaviour (Jones *et al.*, 1993), and the interaction of these with such non-operant processes as respondent behaviour (Romanczyk *et al.*, 1992), schedule induction (Emerson & Howard, 1992) and the neurobiological substrate of challenging behaviour (Schroeder & Tessel, 1994).

As was indicated in Chapter 6, the technology provided by existing experimental and complex observational approaches to assessment is well suited to addressing some of these issues. Thus, for example, observational approaches can be used to investigate the impact of contextual variables (e.g. setting, biological state) on behaviour–environment relationships (see Fig.

4.8; Emerson *et al.*, in press*a*). One of the great values of alternating treatment designs, the basis of many experimental approaches, is their sensitivity to contextual factors (Higgins-Hains & Baer, 1989). The possibility of using experimental approaches to evaluate the effect of setting on operant processes was illustrated in Fig. 6.7 (see also Carr *et al.*, 1976). Similarly, both observational and experimental approaches have clear potential for facilitating the incorporation of the analysis of behaviour–behaviour relationships into functional assessment (see Figs 4.7, 6.1, 6.2; Derby *et al.*, 1994; Emerson *et al.*, in press*a*).

The analysis of the roles of rules and non-operant processes in the maintenance of challenging behaviours, however, involves technical as well as conceptual challenges. Assessing the content and nature of rules will require the development of valid approaches for interviewing people with severe learning disabilities as well as establishing ways of evaluating the actual impact of such rules on behaviour. These developments are long overdue. For too long the individual with learning disabilities has been viewed as the passive subject of the assessment and intervention process.

Analysis of the effect of respondent processes will require the use of independent means of measuring aspects of arousal (Romanczyk *et al.*, 1992). Perhaps most challenging of all, however, will be the development of a means to assess the contribution of biological processes to the maintenance of challenging behaviour. Possible approaches would include the combination of traditional experimental and observational methods to determine the relative environmental independence of the behaviour, with the assessment of markers for the operation of neurobiological processes (e.g. site of self-injury, Thompson *et al.*, 1994*b*; response to sedatives/hypnotics, Sandman & Barron, 1992) or controlled trials of mechanism-specific medication (e.g. naltrexone). Clearly, much more needs to be learned about the role of neurobiological processes and their interaction with operant processes before routine practice could incorporate such methods with any degree of confidence.

Assessing the social validity of intervention outcomes

At a number of points throughout the book, attention has been drawn to the significant personal and social costs associated with challenging behaviour. The widespread failure of published studies to evaluate the wider risks, costs and benefits associated with particular approaches to intervention (cf. Meinhold & Mulick, 1990) has also been highlighted. To address these issues would not require significant technical developments. Indeed, there already exists a range of reasonably well-validated user-friendly approaches to evaluating changes in such areas as physical injury, general health, participation and broader aspects of quality of life (cf. Emerson & Hatton, 1994; Meyer &

Evans, 1993*a*; Meyer & Janney, 1989; Schalock, 1990; Schwartz & Baer, 1991). Incorporating the routine measurement of 'meaningful outcomes' into behavioural research would, however, require a significant conceptual shift and changes in professional practice in such areas as publication standards (Meyer & Evans, 1993*b*). Again, such changes are long overdue.

DEVELOPING AND EVALUATING EFFECTIVE INTERVENTIONS

In the concluding section of Chapter 7, some of the difficulties involved in drawing conclusions regarding the general efficacy of behavioural techniques were discussed. The problems arise from the combination of: (1) failure to systematically replicate the results of studies involving small numbers of participants; (2) the tendency not to publish the 'treatment failures'; and (3) limitations with regard to the range of outcomes evaluated (see above) and the length of time over which the durability of treatment is assessed. As was indicated, this does mean that relatively little is known regarding such factors as: collateral changes associated with intervention; variables controlling the extent to which intervention effects may generalise to new settings, behaviours and people; and the long-term outcomes of intervention. Obviously, attending to these shortcomings in the literature must be considered key priorities for future research.

Nevertheless, it would be counter-productive to express too great a caution regarding the efficacy of behavioural approaches. After all, the accumulated evidence does indicate that behavioural approaches *can* be effective in bringing about rapid, significant and widespread reductions in severely challenging behaviours and that such changes *may* be associated with a range of positive 'side-effects' (cf. Carr *et al.*, 1990*b*; Cataldo, 1991; Lovaas & Smith, 1994), *may* generalise to new settings (e.g. Durand & Carr, 1991), and *may* be maintained over long periods of time (e.g. Foxx, 1990; Jensen & Heidorn, 1993; Lovaas & Smith, 1994; McEachin *et al.*, 1993).

If the aim of intervention is to bring about significant and durable change whilst minimising the risks and costs associated with intervention, four general approaches would appear to constitute what might be considered 'most promising practice'. These are: functionally based interventions; the modification of setting events; intervention based on the notions of response covariation and functional displacement; and the possibilities of intensive early intervention.

Functionally based intervention

As has been stated on numerous occasions throughout this book, there are logical and empirical grounds for adopting a functionally based approach to intervention (Carr *et al.*, 1990; Mace & Roberts, 1993; Mace *et al.*, 1991). Indeed, as was suggested in the preceding section, a clear consensus has now emerged that such an approach is axiomatic to the idea of 'good practice' in the field. In many ways, the most remarkable thing about such a suggestion is that it still needed to be made after three decades of applied behavioural research. One of the challenges ahead will be to develop appropriate interventions for challenging behaviours under the multiple control of behavioural and biological processes.

We should not, however, deceive ourselves into believing that designing functionally based interventions will be possible in all cases. In all probability, there will be occasions in which it is simply not possible, given the available knowledge and resources, to identify the processes underlying some examples of severely challenging behaviours. Hopefully, these will be infrequent. Such a possibility does, however, point to the need to allow the carefully sanctioned use of 'default technologies' in such situations (Iwata, 1988).

Modifying setting events

Chapter 7 included a review of some of the recent developments in intervention based on the modification of setting events, i.e. interventions which alter the motivational bases of challenging behaviour. Most commonly, this has involved changing aspects of the context in which escape-motivated challenging behaviours are most likely to occur by, for example:

☐ facilitating participant choice and/or substituting preferred tasks for non-preferred tasks (e.g. Cooper *et al.*, 1992; Dunlap *et al.*, 1991, 1993, 1994; Dyer, 1987; Dyer *et al.*, 1990; Foster-Johnson *et al.*, 1994);

☐ enriching the environment by, for example, increasing interaction or introducing materials into barren environments (e.g. Favell *et al.*, 1982; Horner, 1980; Mace & Knight, 1986; Sigafoos & Kerr, 1994);

☐ reducing the general level of stimulation (Duker & Rasing, 1989) or crowding (McAfee, 1987) present in the setting;

☐ increasing the rate of non-contingent reinforcement (e.g. Gaylord-Ross *et al.*, 1980; Hagopian *et al.*, 1994; Mace & Lalli, 1991; Vollmer *et al.*, 1993);

☐ using the phenomenon of behavioural momentum to increasing compliance and reducing challenging behaviours associated with non-compliance (e.g. Davis *et al.*, 1992; Harchik & Putzier, 1990; Horner *et al.*, 1991; Mace & Belfiore, 1990; Mace *et al.*, 1988; Singer *et al.*, 1987);

☐ stimulus fading (e.g. Heidorn & Jensen, 1984; Kennedy, 1994);

☐ embedding requests in a different context (Carr & Newsom, 1985; Carr *et al.*, 1976, 1980; Kennedy, 1994);

☐ preceding activities with physical exercise (e.g. Bachman & Fuqua, 1983; Bachman & Sluyter, 1988; Baumeister & MacLean, 1984; Kern *et al.*, 1982, 1984; Lancioni *et al.*, 1984; McGimsey & Favell, 1988); and

☐ the modification of a variety of idiosyncratic setting events (e.g. Gardner *et al.*, 1984, 1986; Kennedy & Itkonen, 1993).

While the processes underlying these effects are open to various interpretations, it appears likely that at least some of them involve either (1) the modification of the establishing operations which potentiate the capacity of neutral stimuli to act as negative reinforcers and hence elicit escape-motivated challenging behaviour, or (2) the modification of the establishing operations which potentiate the capacity of neutral stimuli to act as positive or negative reinforcers for competing behaviours. There would appear to be enormous scope for developing such approaches to intervention. This may be particularly the case in relation to escape-motivated challenging behaviour.

The logic of such an approach is in many ways radically different from traditional behavioural approaches in that it seeks to determine how escape-motivating stimuli acquire their aversive capacity and, on the basis of this information, redesign settings or provide the person with new behaviours so that their environments are less 'challenging'. This stands in stark contrast to more traditional behavioural approaches which seek to either render challenging behaviours non-functional or punish them out of existence. Realising the potential of these approaches will, of course, be dependent on incorporating the analysis of setting events into functionally based assessments (see above), and broadening the range of assessment to include both biological states and temporally distant interactions (Wahler & Fox, 1981). It is, perhaps, rather disconcerting that, despite a decade or more of exhortation to do so, applied behaviour analysts show little inclination to rise to this challenge.

Response covariation and functional displacement

Also in Chapter 7, a summary was presented of recent evidence regarding the efficacy of approaches to intervention based on the notions of response covariation and functional displacement (cf. Reichle & Wacker, 1993). Approaches based on the idea of functional displacement (Carr, 1988) have a number of powerful attractions. In particular, by tapping into existing contingencies which are known to have often maintained the person's (challenging) behaviour over long periods of time and across many settings, such approaches offer the hope of bringing about rapid, significant, durable generalised change. That this *can* be achieved has already been demonstrated (cf. Durand *et al.*, 1993). The generalised applicability of the approach, however, remains to be determined. Two particular challenges to the successful widespread application of this approach include: the refinement of functionally based approaches to assessment (see above); and potential problems of sustaining significant differences in the relative efficiency of the alternative response in comparison with the person's challenging behaviour (see below and Chapters 7 and 9). Indeed, if behavioural accounts of the gradual shaping of challenging behaviour in natural environments are substantiated (cf. Murphy *et al.*, 1995; Taylor & Carr, 1993, 1994), we may well predict that, in the absence of carefully planned *long-term* implementation, challenging behaviours are likely to emerge owing to their powerful effects on carer and staff behaviour.

Prevention and early intervention

Finally, consideration of the early onset and apparently high degree of persistence of severely challenging behaviours points to the desirability of developing preventative interventions and ensuring that intensive support is provided as early as possible once challenging behaviours have begun to emerge (Dunlap *et al.*, 1990; Kiernan, 1994; Lovaas & Smith, 1994; Schroeder *et al.*, 1986).

Prevention

To date, there is no direct evidence that the development of challenging behaviours can be prevented. There are, however, both strong arguments and circumstantial evidence to suggest that the possibility of prevention is worthy of serious consideration. As has been shown, many examples of challenging behaviour appear to be maintained by operant processes, and can be reduced by interventions which either undercut the motivational basis for such behaviours or support the emergence of alternative functionally equivalent behaviours. This suggests that preventative approaches based on either (1) reducing exposure to potentially eliciting conditions or (2) ensuring that more efficient functional equivalent behaviours already exist in the person's repertoire *may* act to reduce the incidence of challenging behaviour.

Examples of the former approach would include reducing exposure to conditions of sensory, material and social deprivation, high levels of unpredictable stressors, repeated illnesses, abuse, repeated changes of carers and rigid external controls (McGill & Toogood, 1994; Schroeder *et al.*, 1986). Examples of the latter approach would involve the use of intensive support to develop socially appropriate ways of expressing choice and controlling access to, and escape from, potentially salient events through the use of assistive devices (e.g.

Wacker *et al.*, 1988) and general approaches to language and social development (cf. Dunlap *et al.*, 1991; Kiernan, 1994). It would, of course, be possible to target such preventative interventions, given the information available from epidemiological studies regarding 'risk factors' associated with variations in the prevalence of challenging behaviour (see Chapter 3).

Unfortunately, while there has been much general interest in the impact of broad based early intervention programmes over the last three decades, no data are available to determine whether such programmes have reduced the incidence of challenging behaviours among children with severe learning disabilities. There is some evidence, however, to suggest that these programmes may be effective in accelerating language development in the short term, improving social performance and reducing delinquency later in life among children who have a mild learning disabilities or are socially disadvantaged (see Kiernan, 1994; Meisels & Shonkoff, 1990; Westlake & Kaiser, 1991).

There is also evidence that children with autism who have received highly intensive early intervention services show significantly less challenging behaviour on follow-up than similar children who did not receive such services (Lovaas, 1987; McEachin *et al.*, 1993; Lovaas & Smith, 1994). What is not known, however, is whether this is due to a reduction in the incidence of challenging behaviour or effective treatment of challenging behaviours as they emerged (i.e. reduced persistence). These studies will be considered in the section below.

Early intervention

Dunlap *et al.* (1991) and Kiernan (1994) reviewed the evidence and arguments in support of the proposition that intervention is more likely to be effective if it occurs as soon as possible during the emergence of challenging behaviour. These arguments include:

☐ increased receptivity to learning, given that many (but not all) challenging behaviours may begin to develop in early childhood;

☐ the simplicity of the learning histories associated with challenging behaviours maintained by operant processes;

☐ increased commitment among carers and care staff;

☐ the potentially greater ease of physically managing the behaviour, given that challenging behaviours may begin to develop in early childhood when the individual is still physically maturing.

Evidence to support these propositions is extremely limited, being based on a small number of studies which report negative correlations between the success of, often broadly based, intervention programmes and the child's age at point of entry (cf. Dunlap *et al.*, 1991; Kiernan, 1994; Westlake & Kaiser, 1991). So, for example, Fenske *et al.* (1985) reported that positive outcomes in a specialised programme for children with autism were achieved for six of the nine children who entered before five years of age, but for only one of the nine who entered after this age.

As noted above, the *potential* benefits of intensive home-based early intervention are illustrated by the results of a long-term follow-up of 19 autistic children reported by Lovaas and his colleagues (Lovaas, 1987; Lovaas & Smith, 1994; McEachin *et al.*, 1993; Smith, McEachin & Lovaas, 1993b). At the time of entry to the programme (before 46 months of age) most children were demonstrating severe tantrums and all showed 'extensive ritualistic and stereotyped behavior'. The programme involved '40 or more hours per week of one-to-one behavioral treatment for 2 or more years' (McEachin *et al.*, 1993, p.361). A comparison group of 19 autistic children received less intensive support. At the time of the follow-up, the children in the experimental group were between 9 and 19 years of age. At that time they were showing significant gains over the comparison groups with respect to IQ, adaptive and challenging behaviour. Lovaas and Smith (1994) report that

> *our preliminary data shows that all but 2 of the intensively treated experimental subjects ... are free from clinically significant problems associated with destructive behaviors. In contrast, the majority of the control group subjects are medicated and living in institutional settings, where their self-injurious and assaultive behaviors present major management problems. Should these initial observations be substantiated in further follow-ups, it may mean that permanent reductions in destructive behaviors displayed by autistic children may come only from intensive home- and community-based intervention, with a comprehensive focus, administered while the children are in their pre-school years (Lovaas & Smith, 1994).*

Such dramatic results are, of course, highly unusual and obviously need to be replicated. They do, however, illustrate the possible potential of focused *intensive* early intervention on bringing about significant and durable reductions in challenging behaviour.

THE IMPLEMENTATION OF BEHAVIOURAL APPROACHES

The widespread adoption and consistent implementation of behavioural procedures to bring about significant and durable reductions in challenging behaviours constitutes, perhaps, the single greatest challenge for this area of applied behaviour analysis. There exists an enormous gap between our knowledge concerning effective approaches and the routine availability of such approaches in our educational, health and social services (cf. Department of Health, 1993; Kiernan, 1993). As Lovaas (1993) pointed out, there currently exists a 25-year delay between knowledge and application. Such concerns are not, however, specific to this field. Stolz (1981), for example, has questioned why behavioural technologies in general, which have been shown to be effective in addressing socially important problems, 'mostly lie unnoticed in our ever-proliferating professional journals' (Stolz, 1981, p.492).

The answers to such questions undoubtably lie in broader analyses of the role of social research on the processes of policy-making and implementation (e.g. Bulmer, 1982, 1986; Weiss & Bucuvalas, 1980). The concerns expressed by behaviour analysts, as well as their proposed solutions, often appear to reflect a belief in what have been termed knowledge-driven or problem-solving (Weiss, 1979), engineering (Bulmer, 1982, 1986) or instrumental (Beyer & Trice, 1982) approaches to policy-making and implementation. These essentially rationalist approaches suggest either a logical flow from basic research, through applied research and development, to application (the knowledge-driven model), or that those involved in making or implementing policy engage in rational searches for scientific information when confronted with a social problem (the problem-solving model). Neither model, of course, reflects the reality of the policy-making and implementation process. Rather, such processes may be more accurately characterised as involving a process of 'partisan mutual adjustment' (Bulmer, 1986), as accommodations are made between key stakeholders.

If this analysis is correct, it has a number of implications for the dissemination and adoption of behavioural approaches. First, recognition needs to be given to the potentially important role of behavioural concepts (rather than technologies) in shaping the grounds of the debate surrounding policy formulation and implementation. Indeed, most commentators in this area have suggested that ideas or concepts derived from social research may have a significantly greater impact than either data or technologies (e.g. Beyer & Trice, 1982; Bulmer, 1982, 1986; Weiss, 1979; Weiss & Bucuvalas, 1980). Thus, for example, the concept of 'institutionalisation' appears to have had an effect on policy debates far in excess of that justified by the data upon which the idea was based. This suggests that, in order to maximise the impact of behavioural approaches, the behavioural community will need to become more proficient at communicating ideas and concepts, rather than assuming data will 'speak for itself'.

Secondly, recognition of the inherently 'political' nature of the process of policy-making and implementation indicates the importance of identifying, influencing and building alliances with key stakeholders or interest groups (e.g. managers and administrators, political groups, advocacy organisations and professional associations). Here, influence is likely to be maximised if, for example, information is transmitted in the preferred medium's terminology and addresses key issues of concern for that group (e.g. personal contact, written and visual information, visits to model programmes); and the stakeholder(s) perceives there to be a pressing problem whose potential solutions fall within the range of behavioural technologies (cf. Fixsen & Blase, 1993; King, 1981; Stolz, 1981).

Whatever means are required, it is clear that systematic widespread adoption of behavioural procedures has the potential to make a significant impact on the considerable personal and social costs associated with challenging behaviour. For, as LaVigna and Donnellan have pointed out *some of the greatest abuses against learners in our mental health/education delivery systems come not from inappropriate utilization of behavioral intervention but from the lack of application of such technology in situations that clearly warrant it* (LaVigna & Donnellan, 1986, p.12).

REFERENCES

Aeschleman, S.R. & Willliams, M.L. (1989). A test of the response deprivation hypothesis in a multiple-response context. *American Journal on Mental Retardation*, **93**, 345–53.

Allen, D., Banks, R. & Staite, S. (1991). *Meeting the Challenge: Some Perspectives on Community Services for People with Learning Difficulties and Learning Disabilities.* King's Fund: London.

Allison, P.D. & Liker, J.K. (1982). Analyzing sequential categorical data on dyadic interaction: A comment on Gottman. *Psychological Bulletin*, **91**, 393–403.

Altmeyer, B.K., Locke, B.J., Griffin, J.C., Ricketts, R.W., Williams, D.E., Mason, M. & Stark, M.T. (1987). Treatment strategies for self-injurious behavior in a large service delivery network. *American Journal on Mental Deficiency*, **91**, 333–40.

Altmeyer, B.K., Williams, D.E. & Sams, V. (1985). Treatment of severe self-injurious and aggressive biting. *Journal of Behavior Therapy and Experimental Psychiatry*, **16**, 159–67.

Aman, M.G. (1991). Pharmacotherapy in the developmental disabilities: New developments. *Australia and New Zealand Journal of Developmental Disabilities*, **17**, 183–99.

Aman, M.G. & Singh, N.N. (1988). *Psychopharmacology of the Developmental Disabilities.* Springer-Verlag: New York.

Aman, M.G. & Singh, N.N. (1991). Pharmacological intervention. In *Handbook of Mental Retardation* (2nd ed) (ed. J.L. Matson & J.L. Mulick). Pergamon: New York.

Aman, M.G., White, A.J., Vaithianathan, C. & Teehan, C.J. (1986). Preliminary study of imipramine in profoundly retarded residents. *Journal of Autism and Developmental Disorders*, **16**, 263–73.

Anderson, D.J., Lakin, K.C., Hill, B.K. & Chen, T.H. (1992). Social integration of older persons with ‡Mental Retardation– in residential facilities. *American Journal on Mental Retardation*, **96**, 488–501.

Anderson, J.L., Albin, R.W., Mesaros, R.A., Dunlap, G. & Morelli-Robbins, M. (1993). Issues in providing training to achieve comprehensive behavioral support. In *Communicative Alternatives to Challenging Behavior*, pp.317–342 (ed. J. Reichle & D.P. Wacker). P. H. Brookes: Baltimore.

Archer, J. (1989/1990). Pain-induced aggression: an ethological perspective. *Current Psychology: Research and Reviews*, **8**, 298–306.

Axelrod, S. (1987a). Functional and structural analyses of behavior: approaches leading to the reduced use of punishment procedures? *Research in Developmental Disabilities*, **8**, 165–78.

Axelrod, S. (1987b). Doing it without arrows: a review of LaVigna and Donnellan's 'Alternatives to punishment: solving behavior problems with non-aversive strategies'. *The Behavior Analyst*, **10**, 243–51.

Axelrod, S. (1990). Myths that (mis)guide our profession. In *Perspectives on the Use of*

Nonaversive and Aversive Interventions for Persons with Developmental Disabilities, pp.59–72 (ed. A.C. Repp & N.N. Singh). Sycamore: Sycamore, IL.

Axelrod, S. & Apsche, J. (1983). *The Effects of Punishment on Human Behavior.* Academic Press: New York.

Azrin, N.H. & Foxx, R.M. (1971). A rapid method of toilet training the institutionalized retarded. *Journal of Applied Behavior Analysis*, **4**, 89–99.

Azrin, N.H., Besalal, V.A., Jamner, J.P. & Caputo, J.N. (1988). Comparative study of behavioral methods of treating severe self-injury. *Behavioral Residential Treatment*, **3**, 119–52.

Bachman, J.E. & Fuqua, R.W. (1983). Management of inappropriate behaviors of trainable mentally impaired students using antecedent exercise. *Journal of Applied Behavior Analysis*, **16**, 477–84.

Bachman, J.E. & Sluyter, D. (1988). Reducing inappropriate behaviors of developmentally disabled adults using antecedent aerobic dance exercises. *Research in Developmental Disabilities*, **9**, 73–83.

Baer, D.M. (1993). To disagree with Meyer and Evans is to debate a cost–benefit ratio. *Journal of the Association for Persons with Severe Handicaps*, **18**, 235–6.

Baer, D.M., Wolf, M.M. & Risley, T.R. (1968). Some current dimensions of applied behavior analysis. *Journal of Applied Behavior Analysis*, **1**, 91–7.

Baer, D.M., Wolf, M.M. & Risley, T.R. (1987). Some still-current dimensions of applied behavior analysis. *Journal of Applied Behavior Analysis*, **20**, 313–27.

Bailey, J. & Meyerson, L. (1969). Vibration as a reinforcer with a profoundly retarded child. *Journal of Applied Behavior Analysis*, **2**, 135–37.

Bailey, J.S. & Pyles, A.M. (1989). Behavioral diagnostics. In *The Treatment of Severe Behavior Disorders* (ed. E. Cipani). American Association on Mental Retardation: Washington, DC.

Bailey, J.S., Shook, G.L., Iwata, B.A., Reid, D.H. & Repp, A.C. (1987). *Behavior Analysis in Developmental Disabilities 1968–1985 from the Journal of Applied Behavior Analysis.* Society for the Experimental Analysis of Behavior: Lawrence, KS.

Bakeman, R. & Gottman, J.M. (1986). *Observing Interaction: An Introduction to Sequential Analysis.* Cambridge University Press: Cambridge.

Balsam, P.D. & Bondy, A.S. (1983). The negative side effects of reward. *Journal of Applied Behavior Analysis*, **16**, 283–96.

Bambara, L.M., Ager, C. & Koger, F. (1994). The effects of choice and task preference on the work performance of adults with severe disabilities. *Journal of Applied Behavior Analysis*, **27**, 555–6.

Bannerman, D.J., Sheldon, J.B., Sherman, J.A. & Harchik, A.E. (1990). Balancing the right to habilitation with the right to personal liberties: the rights of people with developmental disabilities to eat too many doughnuts and take a nap. *Journal of Applied Behavior Analysis*, **23**, 79–89.

Barlow, D.H. & Hersen, M. (1984). *Single Case Experimental Designs.* Pergamon: Oxford.

Barrera, F.J., Teodoro, J.M., Selmeci, T. & Madappuli, A. (1994). Self-injury, pain and the endorphin theory. *Journal of Developmental and Physical Disabilities*, **6**, 169–92.

Barrett, R.P, Feinstein, C, & Hole, W.T. (1989). Effects of Naloxone and Naltrexone on self-injury: a double blind, placebo-controlled analysis. *American Journal on Mental Retardation*, **93**, 644–51.

Bates, W., Smeltzer, D. & Arnoczky, S. (1986). Appropriate and inappropriate use of psychotherapeutic medications for institutionalized mentally retarded persons. *American Journal of Mental Deficiency*, **90**, 363–70.

Baumeister, A.A. (1991). Expanded theories of stereotypy and self-injurious responding: commentary on 'Emergence and maintenance of stereotypy and self-injury'. *American Journal on Mental Retardation*, **96**, 321–3.

Baumeister, A.A. & Forehand, R. (1972). Effects of contingent shock and verbal command on body rocking of retardates. *Journal of Clinical Psychology*, **28**, 586–90.

Baumeister, A.A. & MacLean, W.E. (1984). Deceleration of self-injurious and stereotypic responding by exercise. *Applied Research in Mental Retardation*, **5**, 385–93.

Baumeister, A.A. & Sevin, J.A. (1990). Pharmacologic control of aberrant behavior in the mentally retarded: toward a more rational approach. *Neuroscience and Biobehavioral Reviews*, **14**, 253–62.

Baumeister, A.A., MacLean, W.E., Kelly, J. & Kasari, C. (1980). Observational studies of retarded children with multiple stereotyped movements. *Journal of Abnormal Child Psychology*, **8**, 501–21.

Baumgart, D. & Ferguson, D.L. (1991). Personnel preparation: directions for the next decade. In *Critical Issues in the Lives of People with Severe Disabilities* (ed. L.H. Meyer, C.A. Peck, & L. Brown). P.H. Brookes: Baltimore.

Bell, A. & Zubek, J.P. (1961). Effects of Deanol on the intellectual performance of mental retardates. *Canadian Journal of Psychology*, **15**, 172–5.

Bellamy, G.T., Horner, R.H. & Inman, D. (1979). *Vocational Habilitation of Severely Retarded Adults: A Direct Service Technology*. University Park Press: Baltimore.

Benson, B.A. (1990). Emotional problems I: anxiety and depression. In *Handbook of Behavior Modification with the Mentally Retarded* (ed. J.L. Matson). Plenum: New York.

Benson, B.A., Rice, C.J. & Miranti, S.V. (1986). Effects of anger management training with mentally retarded adults in group treatment. *Journal of Counselling and Clinical Psychology*, **54**, 728–9.

Bentall, R.P., Lowe, C.F. & Beasty, A. (1985). The role of verbal behavior in human learning: II. Developmental differences. *Journal of the Experimental Analysis of Behavior*, **43**, 165–81.

Berg, W. & Sasso, G.M. (1993). Transferring implementation of functional assessment procedures from the clinic to natural settings. In *Communicative Alternatives to Challenging Behavior*, pp.317–342 (ed. J. Reichle & D.P. Wacker). P. H. Brookes: Baltimore.

Berg, W. & Wacker, D. (1991). The assessment and evaluation of reinforcers for individuals with severe mental handicap. In *The Challenge of Severe Mental Handicap: A Behaviour Analytic Approach* (ed. B. Remington). Wiley: Chichester.

Berkman, K.A. & Meyer, L.H. (1988). Alternative strategies and multiple outcomes in the remediation of severe self-injury: going 'all out' nonaversively. *Journal of the Association for Persons with Severe Handicaps*, **13**, 76–86.

Berkowitz, L. (1988). Frustrations, appraisals, and aversively stimulated aggression. *Aggressive Behavior*, **14**, 3–11.

Berkson, G. (1983). Repetitive stereotyped behaviors. *American Journal of Mental Deficiency*, **88**, 239–46.

Bernstein, G.A., Hughes, J.R., Mitchell, J.E. & Thompson, T. (1987). Effects of narcotic antagonists on self-injurious behavior: a single case study. *Journal of the*

American Academy of Child and Adolescent Psychiatry, **26**, 886–9.

Bersani, H.A. & Heifetz, L.J. (1985). Perceived stress and satisfaction of direct-care staff members in community residences for mentally retarded adults. *American Journal of Mental Deficiency,* **90**, 289–95.

Beyer, J.M. & Trice, H.M. (1982). The utilization process: a conceptual framework and synthesis of empirical findings. *Administrative Science Quarterly,* **27**, 591–622.

Bihm, E.M., Kienlen, T.L., Ness, M.E. & Poindexter, A.R. (1991). Factor structure of the motivation assessment scale for persons with mental retardation. *Psychological Reports,* **68**, 1235–8.

Bijou, S.W. (1966). A functional analysis of retarded development. In *International Review of Research in Mental Retardation* (Volume 1) (ed. N. Ellis). Academic Press: New York.

Bijou, S.W. & Baer, D.M. (1978). *Behavior Analysis of Child Development.* Prentice-Hall: Englewood Cliffs, NJ.

Bijou, S.W., Peterson, R.F. & Ault, M.H. (1968). A method to integrate descriptive and experimental field studies at the level of data and empirical concepts. *Journal of Applied Behavior Analysis,* **1**, 175–91.

Bird, F., Dores, P.A., Moniz, D. & Robinson, J. (1989). Reducing severe aggressive and self-injurious behaviours with functional communication training. *American Journal on Mental Retardation,* **94**, 37–48.

Blunden, R. & Allen, D. (1987). *Facing the Challenge: An Ordinary Life for People with Learning Difficulties and Challenging Behaviours.* King's Fund: London.

Bodfish, J.W. (1990). Research on the ecobehavioral analysis of stereotypic and self-injurious behaviours of the mentally retarded, Sixteenth Annual Convention for the International Association for Behavior Analysis.

Bodfish, J.W. & Madison, J.T. (1993). Diagnosis and fluoxetine treatment of compulsive behavior disorder of adults with mental retardation. *American Journal on Mental Retardation,* **98**, 360–7.

Borghgraef, M., Fryns, J.P., Van den Bergh, R., Ryck, K. & Van den Berghe, H. (1990). The post-pubertal Fra(X) male: a study of the intelligence and the psychological profile of 17 Fra(X) boys. In *Key Issues in Mental Retardation Research,* pp.94–105 (ed. W.I. Fraser). Routledge: London.

Borthwick-Duffy, S.A. (1994). Prevalence of destructive behaviors. In *Destructive Behavior in Developmental Disabilities: Diagnosis and Treatment,* pp.3–23 (ed. T. Thompson & D.B. Gray). Sage: Thousand Oaks.

Borthwick-Duffy, S.A., Eyman, R.K. & White, J.F. (1987). Client characteristics and residential placement patterns. *American Journal of Mental Deficiency,* **92**, 24–30.

Boyd, R.D. (1993). Neuroleptic malignant syndrome and mental retardation: Review and analysis of 29 cases. *American Journal on Mental Retardation,* **98**, 143–55.

Briggs, R. (1989). Monitoring and evaluating psychotropic drug use for persons with mental retardation: a follow-up report. *American Journal on Mental Retardation,* **93**, 633–9.

Bromley, J. & Emerson, E. (1993). *Rising to the Challenge? Needs and Responses to People with Learning Disabilities and Challenging Behaviours.* Hester Adrian Research Centre, University of Manchester: Manchester.

Bromley, J. & Emerson, E. (in press). Emotional reactions of care staff to challenging behaviour. *Journal of Intellectual Disability Research*

Browder, D.M. (1991). *Assessment of Individuals with Severe Disabilities.* Paul H
Brookes: Baltimore.

Bruininks, R.H., Olsen, K.M., Larson, S.A. & Lakin, K.C. (1994). Challenging behaviors
among persons with mental retardation in residential settings. In *Destructive
Behavior in Developmental Disabilities: Diagnosis and Treatment*, pp.24–48
(ed. T. Thompson & D.B. Gray). Sage: Thousand Oaks.

Buck, J.A. & Sprague, R.L. (1989). Psychotropic medication of mentally retarded
residents in community long-term care facilities. *American Journal on Mental
Retardation*, **93**, 618–23.

Bull, M. & Vecchio, F. (1978). Behavior therapy for a child with Lesch–Nyhan
syndrome. *Developmental Medicine and Child Neurology*, **20**, 368–75.

Bulmer, M (1982). *The Uses of Social Research.* Allen and Unwin: London.

Bulmer, M (1986). *Social Science and Social Policy.* Allen and Unwin: London.

Burgio, L.D., Whitman, T.L. & Reid, D.H. (1983). A participative management approach
for improving direct care staff performance in an institutional setting. *Journal of
Applied Behavior Analysis*, **16**, 37–53.

Campbell, R.V. & Lutzker, J.R. (1993). Using functional equivalence training to reduce
severe challenging behavior: a case study. *Journal of Developmental and Physical
Disabilities*, **5**, 203–16.

Carr, E.G. (1977). The motivation of self-injurious behavior: a review of some
hypotheses. *Psychological Bulletin*, **84**, 800–16.

Carr, E.G. (1988). Functional equivalence as a mechanism of response generalization.
In *Generalization and Maintenance: Life-Style Changes in Applied Settings* (ed.
R.H. Horner, G. Dunlap & R.L. Koegel). P.H. Brookes: Baltimore.

Carr, E.G. (1994). Emerging themes in the functional analysis of problem behavior.
Journal of Applied Behavior Analysis, **27**, 393–9.

Carr, E.G. & Carlson, J.I. (1993). Reduction of severe behavior problems in the
community using a multicomponent treatment approach. *Journal of Applied
Behavior Analysis*, **26**, 157–72.

Carr, E.G. & Durand, V.M. (1985*a*). Reducing behavior problems through functional
communication training. *Journal of Applied Behavior Analysis*, **18**, 111–26.

Carr, E.G. & Durand, V.M. (1985*b*). The social-communicative basis of severe behavior
problems in children. In *Theoretical Issues in Behavior Therapy* (ed. S. Reiss &
R.R. Bootzin). Academic Press: New York.

Carr, E.G. & Lovaas, O.I. (1983). Contingent electric shock as a treatment for severe
behavior problems. In *The Effects of Punishment on Human Behavior* (ed. S.
Axelrod & J. Apsche). Academic Press: New York.

Carr, E.G. & McDowell, J.J. (1980). Social control of self-injurious behavior of organic
etiology. *Behavior Therapy*, **11**, 402–9.

Carr, E.G. & Newsom, C.D. (1985). Demand-related tantrums: Conceptualization and
treatment. *Behavior Modification*, **9**, 403–26.

Carr, E.G., Levin, L., McConnachie, G., Carlson, J.I., Kemp, D.C. & Smith, C.E. (1993).
*Communication-Based Intervention for Problem Behavior: A User's Guide for
Producing Positive Change.* Brookes: Baltimore.

Carr, E.G., Newsom, C.D. & Binkoff, J.A. (1976). Stimulus control of self-destructive
behavior in a psychotic child. *Journal of Abnormal Child Psychology*, **4**, 139–53.

Carr, E.G., Newsom, C.D. & Binkoff, J.A. (1980). Escape as a factor in the aggressive behavior of two retarded children. *Journal of Applied Behavior Analysis*, **13**, 101–17.

Carr, E.G., Robinson, S. & Palumbo, L.W. (1990*a*). The wrong issue: aversive versus nonaversive treatment. The right issue: functional versus nonfunctional treatment. In *Current Perspectives in the Use of Nonaversive and Aversive Interventions with Developmentally Disabled Persons* (ed. A.C. Repp & N. Singh). Sycamore Press: Sycamore, IL.

Carr, E.G., Robinson, S., Taylor, J.C. & Carlson, J.I. (1990*b*). *Positive Approaches to the Treatment of Severe Behavior Problems in Persons with Developmental Disabilities*. The Association for Persons with Severe Handicaps: Seattle.

Carr, E.G., Taylor, J.C. & Robinson, S. (1991). The effects of severe behavior problems in children on the teaching behavior of adults. *Journal of Applied Behavior Analysis*, **24**, 523–35.

Cataldo, M.F. (1991). The effects of punishment and other behavior reducing procedures on the destructive behaviors of persons with developmental disabilities. In *Treatment of Destructive Behaviors in Persons with Developmental Disabilities* (ed. National Institute of Health). Department of Health and Human Services: Washington.

Cataldo, M.F. & Harris, C.J. (1982). The biological basis for self-injury in the mentally retarded. *Analysis and Intervention in Developmental Disabilities*, **2**, 21–39.

Chadsey-Rusch, J. & Sprague, R.L. (1989). Maladaptive behaviors associated with neuroleptic drug maintenance. *American Journal of Mental Retardation*, **93**, 607–17.

Chaney, R.H., Forbes, L. & Leve, L. (1989). Relationship of electroencephalographic rhythms to aggressive behavior in mentally retarded persons. *Brain Dysfunction*, **2**, 196–200.

Charlop, M.H., Kurtz, P.F. & Casey, F.G. (1990). Using aberrant behaviors as reinforcers for autistic children. *Journal of Applied Behavior Analysis*, **23**, 163–81.

Cipani, E. (1989). *The Treatment of Severe Behavior Disorders: Applied Behavior Analytic Approaches*. American Association on Mental Retardation: Washington, DC.

Clarke, A.M. & Clarke, A.D.B. (1974). Criteria and classification of subnormality. In *Mental Deficiency: The Changing Outlook* (ed. A.M. Clarke & A.D.B. Clarke). Methuen: London.

Cole, C.L., Gardner, W.I. & Karan, O.C. (1985). Self-management training of mentally retarded adults presenting severe conduct difficulties. *Applied Research in Mental Retardation*, **6**, 337–47.

Conway, J.B. & Butcher, B.D. (1974). Soap in the mouth as an aversive consequence. *Behavior Therapy*, **5**, 154–6.

Cook, E.H., Randall, R., Jaselskis, C. & Leventhal, B.L. (1992). Fluoxetine treatment of children and adults with autistic disorder and mental retardation. *Journal of the American Academy of Child and Adolescent Psychiatry*, **31**, 739–45.

Cooper, L.J., Wacker, D.P., Thursby, D., Plagmann, L.A., Harding, J., Millard, T. & Derby, M. (1992). Analysis of the effects of task preferences, task demands and adult attention on child behavior in outpatient and classroom settings. *Journal of Applied Behavior Analysis*, **25**, 823–40.

Cooper, S.J. & Dourish, C.T. (1990). *Neurobiology of Stereotyped Behaviour*. Oxford University Press: Oxford.

Corbett, J.A. & Campbell, H.J. (1980). Causes of self-injurious behavior. In *Frontiers of Knowledge in Mental Retardation Volume II – Biomedical Aspects*, pp.285–292 (ed. P. Mitler & J.M. de Jong). University Park Press: Baltimore.

Crawford, J., Brockel, B., Schauss, S. & Miltenberger, R.G. (1992). A comparison of methods for the functional assessment of stereotypic behavior. *Journal of the Association for Persons with Severe Handicaps*, **17**, 77–86.

Crews, W.D., Bonaventura, S., Rowe, F.B. & Bonsie, D. (1993). Cessation of long-term naltrexone therapy and self-injury: a case study. *Research in Developmental Disabilities*, **14**, 331–40.

Cross, A.J. & Owen, F. (1989). Dopamine receptors. In *Neurotransmitters, Drugs and Disease*, pp.126–142 (ed. R.A. Webster & C.C. Jordan). Blackwell: Oxford.

Cullari, S. & Ferguson, D.G. (1981). Individual behavior change: problems with programming in institutions for mentally retarded persons. *Mental Retardation*, **19**, 267–70.

Cullen, C. (1992). Staff training and management for intellectual disability services. In *International Review of Research in Mental Retardation, Vol. 18*, pp.225–245 (ed. N. Bray). New York: Academic Press.

Cullen, C., Burton, M., Watts, S. & Thomas, M. (1983). A preliminary report on the nature of interactions in a mental handicap institution. *Behaviour Research and Therapy*, **21**, 579–83.

Cullen, C., Hattersley, J. & Tennant, L. (1981). Establishing behaviour: the constructional approach. In *Applications of Conditioning Theory* (ed. G. Davey). Methuen: London.

Danforth, J.S. & Drabman, R.S. (1990). Community living skills. In *Handbook of Behavior Modification with the Mentally Retarded* (ed. J.L. Matson). Plenum: New York.

Darcheville, J.C., Rivière, V. & Wearden, J.H. (1993). Fixed-interval performance and self-control in infants. *Journal of the Experimental Analysis of Behavior*, **60**, 239–54.

Davidson, P.W., Cain, N.N., Sloane-Reeves, J.E., Speybroech, A., Segel, J., Gutkin, J., Quijano, L.E., Kramer, B.M., Porter, B., Shoham, I. & Goldstein, E. (1994). Characteristics of community-based individuals with mental retardation and aggressive behavioral disorders. *American Journal on Mental Retardation*, **98**, 704–16.

Davis, C.A., Brady, M.P., Williams, R.E. & Hamilton, R. (1992). Effects of high–probability requests on the acquisition and generalization and responses to requests in young children with behavior disorders. *Journal of Applied Behavior Analysis*, **25**, 905–16.

Davison, M. & McCarthy, D. (1988). *The Matching Law: A Research Review*. Lawrence Erlbaum and Associates: Hillsdale, NJ.

Day, R.M., Horner, R.H. & O'Neill, R.E. (1994). Multiple functions of problem behaviors: Assessment and intervention. *Journal of Applied Behavior Analysis*, **27**, 279–89.

Day, R.M., Johnson, W.L. & Schussler, N.G. (1986). Determining the communicative properties of self-injury: research, assessment and treatment implications. In *Advances in Learning and Behavioral Disabilities, Vol 5* (ed. K.D. Gadow). JAI Press: London.

Day, R.M., Rea, J.A., Schussler, N.G., Larsen, S.E. & Johnson, W.L. (1988). A functionally based approach to the treatment of self-injurious behavior. *Behavior Modification*, **12**, 565–89.

de Lissovoy, V. (1962). Head banging in early childhood. *Child Development*, **33**, 43–56.

de Lissovoy, V. (1963). Head banging in early childhood: a suggested cause. *Journal of*

Genetic Psychology, **102**, 109–14.

Department of Health (1989). *Needs and Responses.* Department of Health Leaflets Unit: Stanmore.

Department of Health (1993). *Services for People with Learning Disabilities and Challenging Behaviour or Mental Health Needs.* HMSO: London.

Derby, K.M., Wacker, D.P., Peck, S., Sasso, G., DeRaad, A., Berg, W., Asmus, J. & Ulrich, S. (1994). Functional analysis of separate topographies of aberrant behavior. *Journal of Applied Behavior Analysis,* **27**, 267–78.

Derby, K.M., Wacker, D.P., Sasso, G., Steege, M., Northup, J., Cigrand, K. & Asmus, J. (1992). Brief functional assessment techniques to evaluate aberrant behavior in an outpatient setting: a summary of 79 cases. *Journal of Applied Behavior Analysis,* **25**, 713–21.

Dickenson, A.H. (1989). 5-Hydroxytryptamine. In *Neurotransmitters, Drugs and Disease,* pp.143–155 (ed. R.A. Webster & C.C. Jordan). Blackwell: Oxford.

Diorio, M.S. & Konarski, E.A. (1989). Effects of a freely available response on the schedule performance of mentally retarded persons. *American Journal on Mental Retardation,* **93**, 373–9.

Doke, L., Woelry, M. & Sumberg, C. (1983). Treating chronic aggression: Effects and side-effects of response-contingent ammonia spirits. *Behavior Modification,* **7**, 531–56.

Donnellan, A.M. & LaVigna, G. (1990). Myths about punishment. In *Perspectives on the Use of Nonaversive and Aversive Interventions for People with Developmental Disabilities* (ed. A. C. Repp & N.N. Singh). Sycamore Publishing Co: Sycamore.

Donnellan, A.M., LaVigna, G.W., Negri-Shoultz, N. & Fassbender, L. L. (1988). *Progress Without Punishment: Effective Approaches for Learners with Behavior Problems.* Teachers College Press: New York.

Donnellan, A.M., Mirenda, P., Mesaros, R. & Fassbender, L. (1984). Analyzing the communicative functions of aberrant behavior. *Journal of the Association for Persons with Severe Handicaps,* **9**, 201–12.

Dorsey, M.F., Iwata, B.A., Ong, P. & McSween, T.E. (1980). Treatment of self-injurious behavior using a water mist: initial response suppression and generalisation. *Journal of Applied Behavior Analysis,* **13**, 343–53.

Dorsey, M., Iwata, B.A., Reid, D. & Davis, P. (1982). Protective equipment: Continuous and contingent application in the treatment of self-injurious behavior. *Journal of Applied Behavior Analysis,* **15**, 217–30.

Dossetor, D.R., Couryer, S. & Nicol, A.R. (1991). Massage for very severe self-injurious behaviour in a girl with Cornelia de Lange syndrome. *Developmental Medicine and Child Neurology,* **33**, 636–44.

Duker, P.C. & Rasing, E. (1989). Effects of redesigning the physical environment on self-stimulation and on-task behavior in three autistic-type developmentally disabled individuals. *Journal of Autism and Developmental Disorders,* **19**, 449–60.

Duker, P.C. & Seys, D.M. (1977). Elimination of vomiting in a retarded female using restitutional overcorrection. *Behavior Therapy,* **8**, 255–7.

Duker, P.C., Jol, K. & Palmen, A. (1991). The collateral decrease of self-injurious behavior with teaching communicative gestures to individuals who are mentally retarded. *Behavioral Residential Treatment,* **6**, 183–96.

Dunlap, G., dePerczel, M., Clarke, S., Wilson, D., Wright, S., White, R. & Gomez, A.

(1994). Choice making to promote adaptive behavior for students with emotional and behavioral challenges. *Journal of Applied Behavior Analysis*, **27**, 505–18.

Dunlap, G., Johnson, L.F. & Robbins, F.R. (1990). Preventing serious behavior problems through skill development and early interventions. In *Perspectives on the Use of Nonaversive and Aversive Interventions for Persons with Developmental Disabilities* (ed. A.C. Repp & N.N. Singh). Sycamore Publishing Company: Sycamore, ILL.

Dunlap, G., Kern–Dunlap, L., Clarke, S. & Robbins, F.R. (1991). Functional assessment, curricular revision and severe behavior problems. *Journal of Applied Behavior Analysis*, **24**, 387–97.

Dunlap, G., Kern, L., dePerczel, M., Clarke, S., Wilson, D., Childs, K.E., White, R. & Falk, G.D. (1993). Functional analysis of classroom responding for students with emotional and behavioral disorders. *Behavioral Disorders*, **18**, 275–91.

Durand, V.M. (1986). Self-injurious behavior as intentional communication. In *Advances in Learning and Behavioral Disabilities, Vol 5* (ed. K.D. Gadow). JAI Press: London.

Durand, V.M. (1990). *Severe Behavior Problems: A Functional Communication Training Approach*. Guilford Press: New York.

Durand, V.M. & Carr, E.G. (1987). Social influences on 'self-stimulatory' behavior: Analysis and treatment implications. *Journal of Applied Behavior Analysis*, **20**, 119–32.

Durand, V.M. & Carr, E.G. (1991). Functional communication training to reduce challenging behavior: maintenance and application in new settings. *Journal of Applied Behavior Analysis*, **24**, 251–64.

Durand, V.M. & Carr, E.G. (1992). An analysis of maintenance following functional communication training. *Journal of Applied Behavior Analysis*, **25**, 777–94.

Durand, V.M. & Crimmins, D.B. (1988). Identifying the variables maintaining self-injurious behavior. *Journal of Autism and Developmental Disorders*, **18**, 99–115.

Durand, V.M. & Crimmins, D. (1991). Teaching functionally equivalent responses as an intervention for challenging behaviour. In *The Challenge of Severe Mental Handicap: A Behaviour Analytic Approach* (ed. B. Remington). Wiley: Chichester.

Durand, V.M. & Crimmins, D.B. (1992). *The Motivation Assessment Scale*. Monaco & Associates: Topkepa, KS.

Durand, V.M. & Kishi, G. (1987). Reducing severe behavior problems among persons with dual sensory impairments: an evaluation of a technical assistance model. *Journal of the Association for Persons with Severe Handicaps*, **12**, 2–10.

Durand, V.M., Berotti, D. & Weiner, J.S. (1993). Functional communication training: factors affecting effectiveness, generalization and maintenance. In *Communicative Alternatives to Challenging Behavior*, pp.317–342 (ed. J. Reichle & D.P. Wacker). P. H. Brookes: Baltimore.

Durand, V.M., Crimmins, D., Caulfield, M. & Taylor, J. (1989). Reinforcer assessment I: using problem behavior to select reinforcers. *Journal of the Association for Persons with Severe Handicaps*, **14**, 113–26.

Dyer, K. (1987). The competition of autistic stereotyped behavior with usual and specially assessed reinforcers. *Research in Developmental Disabilities*, **8**, 607–26.

Dyer, K., Dunlap, G. & Winterling, V. (1990). Effects of choice making on the serious problem behaviors of students with severe handicaps. *Journal of Applied*

Behavior Analysis, **23**, 515–24.

Edelson, S.M., Taubman, M.T. & Lovaas, O.I. (1983). Some social contexts of self-destructive behavior. *Journal of Abnormal Child Psychology,* **11**, 299–312.

Egel, A.L. & Powers, M.D. (1989). Behavioral parent training: a view of the past and suggestions for the future. In *The Treatment of Severe Behavior Disorders* (ed. E. Cipani). American Association on Mental Retardation: Washington, DC.

Emerson, E. (1990). Designing individualised community based placements as alternatives to institutions for people with a severe mental handicap and severe problem behaviour. In *Key Issues in Mental Retardation* (ed. W. Fraser). Routledge: London.

Emerson, E. (1992). Self-injurious behaviour: an overview of recent developments in epidemiological and behavioural research. *Mental Handicap Research,* **4**, 49–81.

Emerson, E. (1993). Severe learning disabilities and challenging behaviour: Developments in behavioural analysis and intervention. *Behavioural and Cognitive Psychotherapy,* **21**, 171–98.

Emerson, E. & Bromley, J. (in press). The form and function of challenging behaviours. *Journal of Intellectual Disability Research*

Emerson, E. & Hatton, C. (1994). *Moving Out: The Effect of the Move from Hospital to Community on the Quality of Life of People with Learning Disabilities.* HMSO: London.

Emerson, E. & Howard, D. (1992). Schedule induced stereotypy. *Research in Developmental Disabilities,* **13**, 335–61.

Emerson, E. & McGill, P. (1989). Normalisation and applied behaviour analysis: values and technology in services for people with learning difficulties. *Behavioural Psychotherapy,* **17**, 101–17.

Emerson, E., Barrett, S. & Cummings, R. (1990). *Using Analogue Assessments.* South East Thames Regional Health Authority: Bexhill-on-Sea.

Emerson, E., Beasley, F., Offord, G. & Mansell, J. (1992). Specialised housing for people with seriously challenging behaviours. *Journal of Mental Deficiency Research,* **36**, 291–307.

Emerson, E., Cambridge, P. & Harris, P. (1991). *Evaluating the Challenge: A Guide to Evaluating Services for People with Learning Difficulties and Challenging Behaviour.* King's Fund: London.

Emerson, E., Cummings, R., Barrett, S., Hughes, H., McCool, C. & Toogood, A. (1988). Challenging behaviour and community services: 2. Who are the people who challenge services? *Mental Handicap,* **16**, 16–19.

Emerson, E., McGill, P. & Mansell, J. (1994). *Severe Learning Disabilities and Challenging Behaviours: Designing High Quality Services.* Chapman & Hall: London.

Emerson, E., Reeves, D., Thompson, S., Henderson, D. & Robertson, J. (in press*a*). Descriptive analysis of severe challenging behaviour: the application of lag-sequential analysis. *Journal of Intellectual Disability Research*

Emerson, E., Thompson, S., Reeves, D., Henderson, D. & Robertson, J. (in press*b*). Descriptive analysis of multiple response topographies of challenging behaviour. *Research in Developmental Disabilities*

Emerson, E., Thompson, S., Roberston, J. & Henderson, D. (in press*c*). Schedule-induced challenging behaviour? *Journal of Developmental and Physical Disabilities*

Endicott, O. (1988). This may hurt a bit. In *The Language of Pain: Perspectives on Behavior Modification* (ed G. Allen Roeher Institute). G. Allen Roeher Institute:

Downsview, Ont.

Epling, W.F. & Pierce, W.D. (1983). Applied behavior analysis: New directions from the laboratory. *The Behavior Analyst*, **6**, 27–37.

Espie, C. (1992). Optimal sleep-wake scheduling and profound mental handicap: potential benefits. *Mental Handicap*, **20**, 102–7.

Etzel, B.C., Hineline, P.N., Iwata, B.A., Johnston, J.M., Lindsley, O.R., McGrale, J.E., Morris, E.K. & Pennypacker, H.S. (1987). The ABA humanitarian awards for outstanding achievement in pursuit of the right to effective treatment. *The Behavior Analyst*, **10**, 235–7.

Evans, I.M. & Meyer, L.M. (1985). *An Educative Approach to Behavior Problems.* P.H. Brookes: Baltimore.

Evans, I.M. & Meyer, L.H. (1990). Toward a science in support of meaningful outcomes: a response to Horner *et al. Journal of the Association for Persons with Severe Handicaps*, **15**, 133–5.

Evans, I.M. & Meyer, L. (1993). One more with feeling: On the importance of moving forward. *Journal of the Association for Persons with Severe Handicaps*, **18**, 249–52.

Evans, I.M., Meyer, L.H., Kurkjian, J.A. & Kishi, G.S. (1988). An evaluation of behavioral interrelationships in child behavior therapy. In *Handbook of Behavior Therapy in Education*, pp.189–216 (ed. J.C. Witt, S.N. Elliott & F.N. Gresham). Plenum: New York.

Ewen, D. (1988). Aversive therapy. In *The Language of Pain: Perspectives on Behavior Modification* (ed G. Allen Roeher Institute). G. Allen Roeher Institute: Downsview, Ont. .

Eyman, R.K. & Call, T. (1977). Maladaptive behavior and community placement of mentally retarded persons. *American Journal of Mental Deficiency*, **82**, 137–44.

Eyman, R.K., Borthwick-Duffy, S.A. & Miller, C. (1981). Trends in maladaptive behavior of mentally retarded persons placed in community and institutional settings. *American Journal of Mental Deficiency*, **85**, 473–7.

Favell, J.E., McGimsey, J.F. & Schell, R.M. (1982). Treatment of self-injury by providing alternate sensory activities. *Analysis and Intervention in Developmental Disabilities*, **2**, 83–104.

Favell, J.E., McGimsey, J.F., Jones, M.L. & Cannon, P.R. (1981). Physical restraint as positive reinforcement. *American Journal of Mental Deficiency*, **85**, 425–32.

Fee, V.E. & Matson, J.L. (1992). Definition, classification and taxonomy. In *Self-injurious Behavior: Analysis, Assessment and Treatment*, pp.3–20 (ed. J.K. Luiselli, J.L. Matson & N.N. Singh). Springer-Verlag: New York.

Felce, D. (1991). Using behavioural principles in the development of effective housing services for adults with severe or profound handicap. In *The Challenge of Severe Mental Handicap: A Behaviour Analytic Approach* (ed. B. Remington). Wiley: Chichester.

Felce, D., Lowe, K. & de Paiva, S. (1994). Ordinary housing for people with severe learning disabilities and challenging behaviours. In *Severe Learning Disabilities and Challenging Behaviours: Designing High Quality Services*, pp.97–118 (ed. E. Emerson, P. McGill & J. Mansell). Chapman and Hall: London.

Felce, D., Repp, A., Thomas, M., Ager, A. & Blunden, R. (1991). The relationship of staff : client ratios, interactions, and residential placement. *Research in Developmental Disabilities*, **12**, 315–31.

Felce, D., Saxby, H., de Kock, U., Repp, A., Ager, A. & Blunden, R. (1987). To what behaviors do attending adults respond? A replication. *American Journal of Mental Deficiency*, **91**, 496–504.

Fenske, E.C., Zalenski, S., Krantz, P.J. & McClannahan, L.E. (1985). Age at intervention and treatment outcome for autistic children in a comprehensive intervention programme. *Analysis and Intervention in Developmental Disabilities*, **5**, 49–58.

Ferguson, D.L. & Ferguson, P.M. (1993). Postmodern vexations: a reply to Meyer and Evans. *Journal of the Association for Persons with Severe Handicaps*, **18**, 237–9.

Fielding, L.T., Murphy, R.J., Reagan, M.W. & Peterson, T.L. (1980). An assessment program to reduce drug use with the mentally retarded. *Hospital and Community Psychiatry*, **31**, 771–3.

Findholt, N.E. & Emmett, C.G. (1990). Impact of interdisciplinary team review on psychotropic drug use with persons who have mental retardation. *Mental Retardation*, **28**, 41–6.

Finney, J., Russo, D. & Cataldo, M. (1982). Reduction of pica in young children with lead poisoning. *Journal of Paediatric Psychology*, **7**, 197–207.

Fisher, W., Piazza, C.C., Bowman, L.G., Hagopian, L.P., Owens, J.C. & Slevin, I. (1992). A comparison of two approaches for identifying reinforcers for persons with severe and profound disabilities. *Journal of Applied Behavior Analysis*, **25**, 491–8.

Fisher, W.W., Piazza, C.C., Bowman, L.G., Kurtz, P.F., Sherer, M.R. & Lachman, S.R. (1994). A preliminary evaluation of empirically derived consequences for the treatment of pica. *Journal of Applied Behavior Analysis*, **27**, 447–57.

Fisher, W., Piazza, C., Cataldo, M., Harrell, R., Jefferson, G. & Conner, R. (1993). Functional communication training with and without extinction and punishment. *Journal of Applied Behavior Analysis*, **26**, 23–36.

Fixsen, D.L, & Blase, K.A. (1993). Creating new realities: program development and dissemination. *Journal of Applied Behavior Analysis*, **26**, 597–615.

Fleming, I. & Stenfert Kroese, B. (1993). *People with Learning Disability and Severe Challenging Behaviour: New Developments in Services and Therapy.* Manchester University Press: Manchester.

Forehand, R. & Baumeister, A.A. (1970). The effect of auditory and visual stimulation on stereotyped rocking behavior and general activity of severe retardates. *Journal of Clinical Psychology*, **26**, 426–9.

Forrest, J., Emerson, E., Cambridge, P. & Mansell, J. (1995). *Community Support Teams for People with Challenging Behaviour.* Tizard Centre, University of Kent at Canterbury: Canterbury.

Foster–Johnson, L., Ferro, J. & Dunlap, G. (1994). Preferred curricular activities and reduced problem behaviors in students with intellectual disabilities. *Journal of Applied Behavior Analysis*, **27**, 493–504.

Foxx, R.M. (1990). 'Harry': a ten year follow-up of the successful treatment of a self-injurious man. *Research in Developmental Disabilities*, **11**, 67–76.

Foxx, R.M. & Azrin, N.H. (1972). Restitution: a method of eliminating aggressive-disruptive behaviour of retarded and brain damaged patients. *Behaviour Research and Therapy*, **10**, 15–27.

Foxx, R.M. & Azrin, N.H. (1973). The elimination of autistic self-stimulatory behavior by overcorrection. *Journal of Applied Behavior Analysis*, **6**, 1–14.

Foxx, R.M. & Bechtel, D.R. (1983). Overcorrection: A review and analysis. In *The Effects of Punishment on Human Behavior* (ed. S. Axelrod & J. Apsche). Academic Press: New York.

Foxx, R.M. & Dufrense, D. (1984). 'Harry': the use of physical restraint as a reinforcer, time-out from restraint, and fading restraint in treating a self-injurious man. *Analysis and Intervention in Developmental Disabilities*, **4**, 1– 14.

Foxx, R.M. & Shapiro, S.T. (1978). The time-out ribbon: a nonexclusionary time-out procedure. *Journal of Applied Behavior Analysis*, **11**, 125–36.

Freagon, S. (1990). One educator's perspective on the use of punishment or aversives: advocating for supportive and protective systems. In *Perspectives on the Use of Nonaversive and Aversive Interventions for Persons with Developmental Disabilities*, pp.145–155 (ed. A.C. Repp & N.N. Singh). Sycamore: Sycamore, IL.

Fuqua, R.W. & Schwade, J. (1986). Social validation of applied behavioral research: a selective review and critique. In *Research Methods in Applied Behavior Analysis: Issues and Advances*, pp.265–292 (ed. A. Poling & R.W. Fuqua). Plenum: New York.

G. Allen Roeher Institute (1988). *The Language of Pain: Perspectives on Behavior Management*. G. Allen Roeher Institute: Downsview, Ont.

Gabler-Halle, D., Halle, J.W. & Chung, Y.B. (1993). The effects of aerobic exercise on psychological and behavioural variables of individuals with developmental disabilities: a critical review. *Research in Developmental Disabilities*, **14**, 359–86.

Gadow, K.D. & Poling, A.G. (1988). *Pharmacotherapy and Mental Retardation*. Little, Brown & Co.: Boston.

Gardner, W.I. & Cole, C.L. (1989). Self-management approaches. In *The Treatment of Severe Behavior Disorders: Behavior Analysis Approaches* (ed. E. Cipani). American Association on Mental Retardation: Washington, DC.

Gardner, W.I. & Cole, C.L. (1990). Aggression and related conduct disorders. In *Handbook of Behavior Modification with the Mentally Retarded* (ed. J.L. Matson). Plenum: New York.

Gardner, W.I., Clees, T.J. & Cole, C.L. (1983a). Self-management of disruptive verbal ruminations by a mentally retarded adult. *Applied Research in Mental Retardation*, **4**, 41–58.

Gardner, W.I., Cole, C.L., Berry, D.L. & Nowinski, J.M. (1983b). Reduction of disruptive behaviors in mentally retarded adults: a self-management approach. *Behavior Modification*, **7**, 76–96.

Gardner, W.I., Cole, C.L., Davidson, D.P. & Karan, O.C. (1986). Reducing aggression in individuals with developmental disabilities: an expanded stimulus control, assessment, and intervention model. *Education and Training of the Mentally Retarded*, **21**, 3–12.

Gardner, W.I., Karan, O.C. & Cole, C.L. (1984). Assessment of setting events influencing functional capacities of mentally retarded adults with behavior difficulties. In *Functional Assessment in Rehabilitation*, pp.171–185 (ed. A.S. Halpern & M.J. Fuhrer). P.H. Brookes: Baltimore.

Gary, L.A., Tallon, R.J. & Stangl, J.M. (1980). Environmental influences on self-stimulatory behavior. *American Journal of Mental Deficiency*, **85**, 171–5.

Gaylord-Ross, R., Weeks, M. & Lipner, C. (1980). An analysis of antecedent, response and consequence events in the treatment of self-injurious behavior. *Education and Training of the Mentally Retarded*, **15**, 35–42.

Gedye, A. (1989a). Extreme self-injury attributed to frontal lobe seizures. *American Journal on Mental Retardation*, **94**, 20–6.

Gedye, A. (1989b). Episodic rage and aggression attributed to frontal lobe seizures. *Journal of Mental Deficiency Research*, **33**, 369–79.

Gedye, A. (1990). Dietary increase in serotonin reduces self-injurious behaviour in a Down's syndrome adult. *Journal of Mental Deficiency Research*, **34**, 195–203.

Gedye, A. (1991). Buspirone alone or with serotonergic diet reduced aggression in a developmentally disabled adult. *Biological Psychiatry*, **30**, 88–91.

Gedye, A. (1993). Evidence of serotonergic reduction of self-injurious movements. *Habilitative Mental Health Newsletter*, **12**, 53–6.

Gold, M.W. (1980). *Try Another Way: Training Manual.* Research Press: Champaign, IL.

Goldiamond, I. (1974). Toward a constructional approach to social problems: Ethical and constitutional issues raised by applied behavior analysis. *Behaviorism*, **2**, 1–84.

Goldstein, M., Anderson, L.T., Reuben, R. & Dancis, J. (1985). Self-mutilation in Lesch–Nyhan disease is caused by dopaminergic denervation. *Lancet*, **i**, 338–9.

Gorman–Smith, D. & Matson, J.L. (1985). A review of treatment research for self-injurious and stereotyped responding. *Journal of Mental Deficiency Research*, **29**, 295–308.

Grace, N., Cowart, C. & Matson, J. (1988). Reinforcement and self–control for treating a chronic case of self-injury in Lesch–Nyhan syndrome. *Journal of the Multihandicapped Person*, **1**, 53–9.

Grant, G.W. & Moores, B. (1977). Resident characteristics and staff behavior in two hospitals for mentally retarded adults. *American Journal of Mental Deficiency*, **82**, 259–65.

Green, C.W., Gardner, S.M., Canipe, V.S. & Reid, D.H. (1994). Analyzing alertness among people with profound multiple disabilities: implications for provision of training. *Journal of Applied Behavior Analysis*, **27**, 519–31.

Green, C.W., Reid, D.H., Canipe, V.S. & Gardner, S.M. (1991). A comprehensive evaluation of reinforcer identification processes for persons with profound multiple handicaps. *Journal of Applied Behavior Analysis*, **24**, 537–52.

Green, C.W., Reid, D.H., White, L.K., Halford, R.C., Brittain, D.P. & Gardner, S.M. (1988). Identifying reinforcers for persons with profound handicaps: staff opinion versus systematic assessment of preferences. *Journal of Applied Behavior Analysis*, **21**, 31–43.

Griffin, J.C., Paisey, T.J., Stark, M.T. & Emerson, J.H. (1988). B. F. Skinner's position on aversive treatment. *American Journal on Mental Retardation*, **93**, 104–5.

Griffin, J.C., Ricketts, R.W. & Williams, D.E. (1986*a*). Reaction to Richmond *et al.*: propriety use of mechanical restraint and protective devices as tertiary techniques. In *Advances in Learning and Behavioural Disabilities, Vol 5* (ed. K.D. Gadow). JAI Press: London.

Griffin, J.C., Ricketts, R.W., Williams, D.E., Locke, B.J., Altmeyer, B.K. & Stark, M.T. (1987). A community survey of self-injurious behavior among developmentally disabled children and adolescents. *Hospital and Community Psychiatry*, **38**, 959–63.

Griffin, J.C., Williams, D.E., Stark, M.T., Altmeyer, B.K. & Mason, M. (1986*b*). Self-injurious behavior: A state-wide prevalence survey of the extent and circumstances. *Applied Research in Mental Retardation*, **7**, 105–16.

Griffith, R.G. (1989). Presidential address 1989. *Mental Retardation*, **27**, 289–95.

Groden, G. (1989). A guide for conducting a comprehensive behavioral analysis of a target behavior. *Journal of Behavior Therapy and Experimental Psychiatry*, **20**, 163–9.

Gross, A.M., Berler, E.S. & Drabman, R.S. (1982). Reduction of aggressive behavior in a retarded boy using a water squirt. *Journal of Behavior Therapy and Experimental Psychiatry,* **13**, 95–8.

Gross, E.J., Hull, H.G., Lytton, G.J., Hill, J.A. & Piersel, W.C. (1993). Case study of neuroleptic induced akathisia: important implications for individuals with Mental Retardation. *American Journal on Mental Retardation,* **98**, 156–64.

Grossman, H.J., Begab, M.J., Cantwell, D.P., Clements, J.D., Eyman, R. K., Meyers, C.E., Tarjan, G. & Warren, S.A. (1983). *Classification in Mental Retardation.* American Association on Mental Deficiency: Washington.

Gualtieri, C.T. & Schroeder, S.R. (1989). Pharmacotherapy of self-injurious behavior: Preliminary tests of the D1 hypothesis. *Psychopharmacology Bulletin,* **25**, 364–71.

Guess, D. & Carr, E.G. (1991). Emergence and maintenance of stereotypy and self-injury. *American Journal on Mental Retardation,* **96**, 299–319.

Guess, D., Helmstetter, H., Turnbull, H.R. & Knowlton, S. (1987). *Use of Aversive Procedures with Persons who are Disabled: An Historical Review and Critical Analysis.* The Association for Persons with Severe Handicaps: Seattle, WA.

Guess, D., Roberts, S., Siegel–Causey, E., Ault, M., Guy, B., Thompson, B. & Rues, J. (1993). Analysis of behavior state conditions and associated variables among students with profound handicaps. *American Journal on Mental Retardation,* **97**, 634–53.

Guess, D., Siegel-Causey, E., Roberts, S., Rues, J., Thompson, B. & Siegel– Causey, D. (1990). Assessment and analysis of behavior state and related variables among students with profoundly handicapping conditions. *Journal of the Association for Persons with Severe Handicaps,* **15**, 211–30.

Hagopian, L.P., Fisher, W.W. & Legacy, S.M. (1994). Schedule effects of noncontingent reinforcement on attention-maintained destructive behavior in identical quadruplets. *Journal of Applied Behavior Analysis,* **27**, 317–25.

Hall, S. & Oliver, C. (1992). Differential effects of severe self-injurious behaviour on the behaviour of others. *Behavioural Psychotherapy,* **20**, 355–65.

Halle, J.W. & Spradlin, J.E. (1993). Identifying stimulus control of challenging behavior. In *Communicative Alternatives to Challenging Behavior,* pp.83–112 (ed. J. Reichle & D.P. Wacker). P.H. Brookes: Baltimore.

Harchik, A.E. & Putzier, V.S. (1990). The use of high-probability requests to increase compliance with instructions to take medication. *Journal of the Association for Persons with Severe Handicaps,* **15**, 40–3.

Haring, T.G. & Kennedy, C.H. (1990). Contextual control of problem behaviors in students with severe disabilities. *Journal of Applied Behavior Analysis,* **23**, 235–43.

Harris, C.S., Bradley, R.J. & Titus, S.K. (1992). A comparison of the effects of hard rock and easy listening on the frequency of observed inappropriate behaviors: control of environmental antecedents in a large public area. *Journal of Music Therapy,* **29**, 6–17.

Harris, J.C. (1992). Neurobiological factors in self-injurious behavior. In *Self-injurious Behavior: Analysis, Assessment and Treatment,* pp.59–92 (ed. J.K. Luiselli, J.L. Matson & N.N. Singh). Springer–Verlag: New York.

Harris, P. (1993). The nature and extent of aggressive behaviour among people with learning difficulties (mental handicap) in a single health district. *Journal of Intellectual Disability Research,* **37**, 221–42.

Harris, S.L., Handleman, J.S., Gill, M.J. & Fong, P.L. (1991). Does punishment hurt? The impact of aversives on the clinician. *Research in Developmental Disabilities*, **12**, 17–24.

Hartmann, D.P. (1984). Assessment strategies. In *Single Case Experimental Designs: Strategies for Studying Behavior Change* (ed. D.H. Barlow & M. Hersen). Pergamon: Oxford.

Harvey, E.R. & Schepers, J. (1977). Physical control techniques and defensive holds for use with aggressive retarded adults. *Mental Retardation*, **15**, 29–31.

Hastings, R. (1993). *A Functional Approach to Care Staff Behaviour*. Unpublished PhD thesis. University of Southampton: Southampton.

Hastings, R. & Remington, B. (1993). "Is there anything on ... Why 'good' behavioural programmes fail?": A brief review. *Clinical Psychology Forum*, **55**, 9–11.

Hastings, R. & Remington, B. (1994a). Rules of engagement: toward an analysis of staff responses to challenging behavior. *Research in Developmental Disabilities*, **15**, 279–98.

Hastings, R. & Remington, B. (1994b). Staff behaviour and its implications for people with learning disabilities and challenging behaviour. *British Journal of Clinical Psychology*, **33**, 423–38.

Hatton, C., Emerson, E., Robertson, J., Henderson, D. & Cooper, J. (1994). *An Evaluation of the Quality and Costs of Services for Adults with Severe Learning Disabilities and Sensory Impairments*. Hester Adrian Research Centre, University of Manchester: Manchester.

Hayes, S.C. (1989). *Rule-Governed Behavior: Cognition, Contingencies and Instructional Control*. Plenum: New York.

Heal, L.W., Harner, C.J., Novak Amado, A.R. & Chadsey-Rusch, J. (1993). *Lifestyle Satisfaction Scale*. IDS: Worthington, OH.

Heidorn, S.D. & Jensen, C.C. (1984). Generalization and maintenance of the reduction of self-injurious behavior maintained by two types of reinforcement. *Behaviour Research and Therapy*, **22**, 581–6.

Helmstetter, E. & Durand, V.M. (1991). Nonaversive interventions for severe behavior problems. In *Critical Issues in the Lives of People with Severe Disabilities* (ed. L.H. Meyer, C.A. Peck, & L. Brown). P.H. Brookes: Baltimore.

Herman, B.H., Hammock, M.K., Arthur-Smith, A., Egan, J., Chatoor, I., Werner, A. & Zelnick, N. (1987). Naltrexone decreases self-injurious behavior. *Annals of Neurology*, **22**, 550–2.

Higgins-Hains, A. & Baer, D.M. (1989). Interaction effects in multielement designs: inevitable, desirable, and ignorable. *Journal of Applied Behavior Analysis*, **22**, 57–69.

Hile, M.G. & Vatterott, M.K. (1991). Two decades of treatment for self-injurious biting in individuals with mental retardation or developmental disabilities: a treatment focused review of the literature. *Journal of Developmental and Physical Disabilities*, **3**, 81–113.

Hill, B.K. & Bruininks, R.H. (1984). Maladaptive behavior of mentally retarded individuals in residential facilities. *American Journal of Mental Deficiency*, **88**, 380–7.

Hill, J. & Spreat, S. (1987). Staff injury rates associated with the implementation of contingent restraint. *Mental Retardation*, **25**, 141–5.

Hittner, J.B. (1994). Case study: the combined use of imipramine and behavior modification to reduce aggression in an adult male diagnosed as having autistic disorder. *Behavioral Interventions*, **9**, 123–39.

Hobbs, S.A. & Forehand, R. (1977). Important parameters in the use of time-out with children: a re-examination. *Journal of Behavior Therapy and Experimental Psychiatry*, **8**, 365–70.

Hogg, J. (1982). Reduction of self-induced vomiting in a multiply handicapped girl by 'lemon juice therapy' and concomitant changes in social behaviour. *British Journal of Clinical Psychology*, **21**, 227–8.

Hogg, J. & Mitler, P. (1987). *Staff Training in Mental Handicap*. Croom Helm: London.

Hogg, J. & Raynes, N. (1986). *Assessment in Mental Handicap*. Croom Helm: London.

Horner, R.D. (1980). The effects of an environmental 'enrichment' program on the behavior of institutionalized profoundly retarded children. *Journal of Applied Behavior Analysis*, **13**, 473–91.

Horner, R.H. (1991). The future of applied behavior analysis for people with severe disabilities: commentary I. In *Critical Issues in the Lives of People with Severe Disabilities*, pp.601–606 (ed. L.H. Meyer, C.A. Peck, & L. Brown). P.H. Brookes: Baltimore.

Horner, R.H. & Budd, C.M. (1985). Acquisition of manual sign use: Collateral reduction in maladaptive behavior and factors limiting generalisation. *Education and Training of the Mentally Retarded*, 39–47.

Horner, R.H. & Day, H.M. (1991). The effects of response efficiency on functionally equivalent competing behaviors. *Journal of Applied Behavior Analysis*, **24**, 719–32.

Horner, R.H., Day, H.M., Sprague, J.R., O'Brien, M. & Heathfield, L. T. (1991). Interspersed requests: a nonaversive procedure for reducing aggression and self-injury during instruction. *Journal of Applied Behavior Analysis*, **24**, 265–78.

Horner, R.H., Dunlap, G. & Koegel, R.L. (1988). *Generalization and Maintenance: Life-Style Changes in Applied Settings*. Paul H. Brookes: Baltimore.

Horner, R.H., Dunlap, G., Koegel, R.L., Carr, E.G., Sailor, W., Anderson, J., Albin, R.W. & O'Neill, R.E. (1990*a*). Toward a technology of 'nonaversive' behavioral support. *Journal of the Association of Persons with Severe Handicaps*, **15**, 125–32.

Horner, R.H., Sprague, J.R., O'Brien, M. & Heathfield, L.T. (1990*b*). The role of response efficiency in the reduction of problem behaviors through functional equivalence training: a case study. *Journal of the Association for Persons with Severe Handicaps*, **15**, 91–7.

Hutchinson, R.R. (1977). By-products of aversive control. In *Handbook of Operant Behavior* (ed. W.K. Honig & J.E.R. Staddon). Prentice-Hall: Englewood-Cliffs, NJ.

Intagliata, J. & Willer, B. (1982). Reinstitutionalization of mentally retarded persons successfully placed into family care and group homes. *American Journal of Mental Deficiency*, **87**, 34–9.

Isaacson, R.L. & Gispin, W.H. (1990). Neuropeptides and the issue of stereotypy in behaviour. In *Neurobiology of Stereotyped Behaviour* (ed. S.J. Cooper & C.T. Dourish). Oxford University Press: Oxford.

Iversen, I.H. & Lattal, K.A. (1991*a*). *Experimental Analysis of Behavior: Part 1*. Elsevier: Amsterdam.

Iversen, I.H. & Lattal, K.A. (1991*b*). *Experimental Analysis of Behavior: Part 2*. Elsevier: Amsterdam.

Iwata, B.A. (1988). The development and adoption of controversial default technologies. *The Behavior Analyst*, **11**, 149–57.

Iwata, B.A., Dorsey, M.F., Slifer, K.J., Bauman, K.E. & Richman, G.S. (1982). Toward a functional analysis of self-injury. *Analysis and Intervention in Developmental Disabilities,* **2**, 3–20.

Iwata, B.A., Pace, G.M., Cowdery, G.E. & Miltenberger, R.G. (1994*a*). What makes extinction work: an analysis of procedural form and function. *Journal of Applied Behavior Analysis,* **27**, 131–44.

Iwata, B., Pace, G.M., Dorsey, M.F., Zarcone, J.R., Vollmer, T.R., Smith, R.G., Rodgers, T.A., Lerman, D.C., Shore, B.A., Mazaleski, J.L., Goh, H-L., Cowdery, G.E., Kalsher, M.J., McCosh, K.C. & Willis, K.D. (1994*b*). The functions of self-injurious behavior: an experimental–epidemiological study. *Journal of Applied Behavior Analysis,* **27**, 215–40.

Iwata, B.A., Pace, G.M., Kalsher, M.J., Cowdery, G.E. & Cataldo, M. F. (1990*a*). Experimental analysis and extinction of self-injurious escape behavior. *Journal of Applied Behavior Analysis,* **23**, 11–27.

Iwata, B.A., Pace, G.M., Kissel, R.C., Nau, P.A. & Farber, J.M. (1990*b*). The Self-Injury Trauma (SIT) Scale: a method for quantifying surface tissue damage caused by self-injurious behavior. *Journal of Applied Behavior Analysis,* **23**, 99–110.

Iwata, B.A., Vollmer, T.R. & Zarcone, J.R. (1990*c*). The experimental (functional) analysis of behavior disorders: methodology, applications, and limitations. In *Perspectives on the Use of Nonaversive and Aversive Interventions for Persons with Developmental Disabilities* (ed. A.C. Repp & N.N. Singh). Sycamore Publishing Company: Sycamore, IL.

Jacobsen, J.W. (1992). Who is treated using restrictive behavioral procedures? *Journal of Developmental and Physical Disabilities,* **4**, 99–113.

Jacobsen, J.W., Silver, E.J. & Schwartz, A.A. (1984). Service provision in New York's group homes. *Mental Retardation,* **22**, 231–9.

Jansma, P. & Combs, C.S. (1987). The effects of fitness training and reinforcement on maladaptive behaviors of institutionalised adults classified as mentally retarded/ emotionally disturbed. *Education and Training of the Mentally Retarded,* **22**, 268–79.

Jensen, C.C. & Heidorn, S.D. (1993). Ten-year follow-up of a successful treatment of self-injurious behavior. *Behavioral Residential Treatment,* **8**, 263–80.

Johnson, K., Johnson, C.R. & Sahl, R.A. (1994). Behavioral and naltrexone treatment of self-injurious behavior. *Journal of Developmental and Physical Disabilities,* **6**, 193–202.

Johnson, W.L. & Day, R.M. (1992). The incidence and prevalence of self-injurious behavior. In *Self-Injurious Behavior: Analysis, Assessment and Treatment,* pp.21–58 (ed. J.K. Luiselli, J.L. Matson & N.N. Singh). Springer-Verlag: New York.

Jones, R.S.P. (1991). Reducing inappropriate behaviour using non–aversive procedures: evaluating differential reinforcement schedules. In *The Challenge of Severe Mental Handicap: A Behaviour Analytic Approach* (ed. B. Remington). Wiley: Chichester.

Jones, R.S.P., Williams, H. & Lowe, F. (1993). Verbal self-regulation. In *People with Leaning Disability and Severe Challenging Behaviour: New Developments in Services and Therapy* (ed. I. Fleming & B. Stenfert Kroese). Manchester University Press: Manchester.

Jones, R.S.P., Wint, D. & Ellis, N.C. (1990). The social effects of stereotyped behaviour. *Journal of Mental Deficiency Research,* **34**, 261–8.

Jordan, J., Singh, N.N. & Repp, A.C. (1989). An evaluation of gentle teaching and visual screening in the reduction of stereotypy. *Journal of Applied Behavior Analysis,* **22**, 9–22.

Kaiser, A.P. (1993). Understanding human behavior: Problems of science and practice. *Journal of the Association for Persons with Severe Handicaps,* **18**, 240–2.

Kantor, J.R. (1959). *Interbehavioral Psychology.* Principa Press: Chicago.

Kars, H., Broekema, W., Glaudemans-van Gelderen, I., Verhoeven, W.M.A. & van Ree, J.M. (1990). Naltrexone attenuates self-injurious behavior in mentally retarded subjects. *Biological Psychiatry,* **27**, 741–6.

Kazdin, A.E. & Matson, J.L. (1981). Social validation in mental retardation. *Applied Research in Mental Retardation,* **2**, 39–53.

Kearney, C.A. (1994). Interrater reliability of the motivation assessment scale: another, closer look. *Journal of the Association for Persons with Severe Handicaps,* **19**, 139–42.

Kennedy, C.H. (1994). Manipulating antecedent conditions to alter the stimulus control of problem behavior. *Journal of Applied Behavior Analysis,* **27**, 161–70.

Kennedy, C.H. & Haring, T.G. (1993). Teaching choice making during social interactions to students with profound multiple disabilities. *Journal of Applied Behavior Analysis,* **26**, 63–76.

Kennedy, C.H. & Itkonen, T. (1993). Effects of setting events on the problem behavior of students with severe disabilities. *Journal of Applied Behavior Analysis,* **26**, 321–7.

Kern, L., Koegel, R.L. & Dunlap, G. (1984). The influence of vigorous versus mild exercise on autistic stereotyped behaviors. *Journal of Autism and Developmental Disorders,* **14**, 57–67.

Kern, L., Koegel, R.L., Dyer, K., Blew, P.A. & Fenton, L.R. (1982). The effects of physical exercise on self-stimulation and appropriate responding in autistic children. *Journal of Autism and Developmental Disorders,* **12**, 399–419.

Kiely, M. & Lubin, R.A. (1991). Epidemiological methods. In *Handbook of Mental Retardation,* 586–602 (ed. J.L. Matson & J.A. Mulick). Pergamon: New York.

Kiernan, C. (1985). Behaviour modification. In *Mental Deficiency: The Changing Outlook* (4th Edition) (ed. A.M. Clarke, A.D.B. Clarke & J.M. Berg). Methuen: London.

Kiernan, C. (1991). Professional ethics: Behaviour analysis and normalization. In *The Challenge of Severe Mental Handicap: A Behaviour Analytic Approach* (ed. B. Remington). Wiley: Chichester.

Kiernan, C. (1993). *Research Into Practice? Implications of Research on the Challenging Behaviour of People with Learning Disabilities.* British Institute of Learning Disabilities: Kidderminster.

Kiernan, C. (1994). *Early Intervention and Challenging Behaviour.* Hester Adrian Research Centre, University of Manchester: Manchester.

Kiernan, C. & Alborz, A. (1994). *A Different Life: Parents Caring for Young Adults with Challenging Behaviours.* Hester Adrian Research Centre, University of Manchester: Manchester.

Kiernan, C. & Kiernan, D. (1994). Challenging behaviour in schools for pupils with severe learning difficulties. *Mental Handicap Research,* **7**, 117–201.

Kiernan, C. & Qureshi, H. (1993). Challenging behaviour. In *Research to Practice? Implications of Research on the Challenging Behaviour of People with Learning Disabilities,* pp.53–87 (ed. C. Kiernan). British Institute of Learning Disabilities: Kidderminster.

King, L. (1981). Comments on Adoption of innovations from applied behavioral research: 'Does anybody care?'. *Journal of Applied Behavior Analysis*, **14**, 507–11.

Knabe, R., Schulz, P. & Richard, J. (1990). Initial aggravation of self-injurious behavior in autistic patients receiving naltrexone treatment. *Journal of Autism and Developmental Disorders*, **20**, 591–2.

Koegel, R.L. & Frea, W.D. (1993). Treatment of social behavior in autism through the modification of pivotal social skills. *Journal of Applied Behavior Analysis*, **26**, 369–77.

Koegel, R.L. & Koegel, L.K. (1990). Extended reductions in stereotypic behavior of students with autism through a self-management treatment package. *Journal of Applied Behavior Analysis*, **23**, 119–27.

Koegel, L.K., Koegel, R.L., Hurley, C. & Frea, W.D. (1992). Improving social skills and disruptive behavior in children with autism through self-management. *Journal of Applied Behavior Analysis*, **25**, 341–53.

Konarski, E.A., Favell, J.E. & Favell, J.E. (1992). *Manual for the Assessment and Treatment of the Behavior Disorders of People with Mental Retardation*. Western Carolina Centre Foundation: Morganton, NC.

Konarski, E.A., Johnson, M.R., Crowell, C.R. & Whitman, T.L. (1981). An alternative approach to reinforcement for applied researchers: Response deprivation. *Behavior Therapy*, **12**, 653–66.

Korinek, L. (1991). Self management for the mentally retarded. In *Advances in Mental Retardation and Developmental Disabilities Vol 4* (ed. R.A. Gable). Jessica Kingsley: London.

Kraemer, G.W. & Clarke, H.S. (1990). The behavioral neurobiology of self-injurious behavior in rhesus monkeys. *Progress in Neuropsychopharmacology and Biological Psychiatry*, **14**, 141–68.

Krantz, P. & Risley, T.R. (1977). Behavioral ecology in the classroom. In *Classroom Management: The Successful Use of Behavior Modification* (ed. S.G. O'Leary & K.D. O'Leary). Pergamon: New York.

Krantz, P.J., MacDuff, M.T. & McClannahan, L.E. (1993). Programming participation in family activities for children with autism: parents' use of photographic activity schedules. *Journal of Applied Behavior Analysis*, **26**, 137–8.

Kratochwill, T.R. & Levin, J.R. (1992). *Single-Case Research Design and Analysis: New Directions for Psychology and Education*. Lawrence Erlbaum Associates: Hillsdale, New Jersey.

Lachiewicz, A.M., Spiridigliozzi, G.A., Gullion, C.M., Ransford, S.N. & Rao, K. (1994). Aberrant behaviors of young boys with Fragile X syndrome. *American Journal on Mental Retardation*, **98**, 567–79.

LaGrow, S.J. & Repp, A.C. (1984). Stereotypic responding: A review of intervention research. *American Journal of Mental Deficiency*, **88**, 595–609.

Lakin, K.C., Hill, B.K., Hauber, F.A., Bruininks, R.H. & Heal, L.W. (1983). New admissions and readmissions to a national sample of public residential facilities. *American Journal of Mental Deficiency*, **88**, 13–20.

Lalli, J.S. & Goh, H–L. (1993). Natural observations in community settings. In *Communicative Alternatives to Challenging Behavior*, pp.11–40 (ed. J. Reichle & D.P. Wacker). P.H. Brookes: Baltimore.

Lalli, J.S., Browder, D.M., Mace, F.C. & Brown, D.K. (1993). Teacher use of descriptive analysis data to implement interventions to decrease students' problem behaviors.

Journal of Applied Behavior Analysis, **26**, 227–38.

LaMendola, W., Zaharia, E.S. & Carver, M. (1980). Reducing psychotropic drug use in an institution for the retarded. *Hospital and Community Psychiatry,* **31**, 271–2.

Lancioni, G.E. & Hoogeveen, F.R. (1990). Non-aversive and mildly aversive procedures for reducing problem behaviours in people with developmental disorders: a review. *Mental Handicap Research,* **3**, 137–60.

Lancioni, G.E., Smeets, P.M., Ceccarani, P.S., Capodaglio, L. & Campanari, G. (1984). Effects of gross motor activities on the severe self-injurious tantrums of multihandicapped individuals. *Applied Research in Mental Retardation,* **5**, 471–82.

Langee, H.R. (1989). A retrospective study of mentally retarded patients with behavioral disorders who were treated with carbamazepine. *American Journal of Mental Deficiency,* **93**, 389–91.

Larson, J.L. & Miltenberger, R.G. (1992). The influence of antecedent exercise on problem behaviors in persons with mental retardation: a failure to replicate. *Journal of the Association for Persons with Severe Handicaps,* **17**, 40–6.

Larson, S.A. & Lakin, K.C. (1989). Deinstitutionalization of persons with mental retardation: behavioral outcomes. *Journal of the Association for Persons with Severe Handicaps,* **14**, 324–32.

LaVigna, G.W. & Donnellan, A.M. (1986). *Alternatives to Punishment: Solving Behavior Problems with Non-Aversive Strategies.* Irvington: New York.

Lawrenson, H.J. (1993). *Concurrent validity and inter-rater reliability analysis of the Motivation Assessment Scale.* MSc thesis, University of Manchester: Manchester.

Leland, H. (1991). Adaptive behavior scales. In *Handbook of Mental Retardation* (ed. J.L. Matson & J.A. Mulick). Pergamon: New York.

Lennox, D.B. & Miltenberger, R.G. (1989). Conducting a functional assessment of problem behavior in applied settings. *Journal of the Association for Persons with Severe Handicaps,* **14**, 304–11.

Lennox, D.B., Miltenberger, R.G., Spengler, P. & Erfanian, N. (1988). Decelerative treatment practices with persons who have mental retardation: a review of five years of the literature. *American Journal on Mental Retardation,* **92**, 492–501.

Lerman, D.C. & Iwata, B.A. (1993). Descriptive and experimental analysis of variables maintaining self-injurious behavior. *Journal of Applied Behavior Analysis,* **26**, 293–319.

Lerman, D.C., Iwata, B.A., Smith, R.G., Zarcone, J.R. & Vollmer, T. (1994). Transfer of behavioral function as a contributing factor in treatment relapse. *Journal of Applied Behavior Analysis,* **27**, 357–70.

Leudar, I., Fraser, W.I. & Jeeves, M.A. (1984). Behaviour disturbance and mental handicap: typology and longitudinal trends. *Psychological Medicine,* **14**, 923–35.

Lewis, M (1992). Neurobiological basis of stereotyped behavior: Non-human primate and clinical studies. Paper presented at the Gatlinburg Conference on Research and Theory in Mental Retardation and Developmental Disabilities, Gatlinburg TN.

Lewis, M.H. & Baumeister, A.A. (1982). Stereotyped mannerisms in mentally retarded persons: animal models and theoretical analyses. In *International Review of Research in Mental Retardation* (ed. N.R. Ellis). Academic Press: New York.

Lienemann, J. & Walker, F.D. (1989). Naltrexone for treatment of self-injury. *American Journal of Psychiatry,* **146**, 1639–40.

Linscheid, T.R. (1992). Aversive stimulation. In *Self-Injurious Behavior: Analysis,*

Assessment and Treatment (ed. J.K. Luiselli, J.L. Matson & N.N. Singh). Springer-Verlag: New York.

Linscheid, T.R., Iwata, B.A., Ricketts, R.W., Williams, D.E. & Griffin, J.C. (1990). Clinical evaluation of the self-injurious behavior inhibiting system (SIBIS). *Journal of Applied Behavior Analysis*, **23**, 53–78.

Linscheid, T.R., Pejeau, C., Cohen, S. & Footo-Lenz, M. (1994). Positive side-effects in the treatment of SIB using the self-injurious behavior inhibiting system (SIBIS): implications for operant and biochemical explanations of SIB. *Research in Developmental Disabilities*, **15**, 81–90.

Lovaas, O.I. (1982). Comments on self-destructive behaviors. *Analysis and Intervention in Developmental Disabilities*, **2**, 115–24.

Lovaas, O.I. (1987). Behavioral treatment and normal educational and intellectual functioning in young autistic children. *Journal of Consulting and Clinical Psychology*, **55**, 3–9.

Lovaas, O.I. (1993). The development of a treatment-research project for developmentally disabled and autistic children. *Journal of Applied Behavior Analysis*, **26**, 617–30.

Lovaas, O.I. & Simmons, J.Q. (1969). Manipulation of self-destructive behavior in three retarded children. *Journal of Applied Behavior Analysis*, **2**, 143–57.

Lovaas, O.I. & Smith, T. (1994). Intensive and long-term treatments for clients with destructive behaviors. In *Destructive Behavior in Developmental Disabilities: Diagnosis and Treatment*, pp.68–79 (ed. T. Thompson & D.B. Gray). Sage: Thousand Oaks.

Lovaas, O.I., Freitag, G., Gold, V.J. & Kassorla, I.C. (1965). Experimental studies in childhood schizophrenia: analysis of self-destructive behavior. *Journal of Experimental Child Psychology*, **2**, 67–84.

Lovaas, O.I., Newsom, C. & Hickman, C. (1987). Self-stimulatory behavior and perceptual reinforcement. *Journal of Applied Behavior Analysis*, **20**, 45–68.

Lowe, C.F. (1979). Determinants of human operant behavior. In *Reinforcement and the Organization of Behavior* (ed. M.D. Zeilor & P. Harjem). Wiley: Chichester.

Lowe, K. & Felce, D. (1994a). *Challenging Behaviour in the Community.* Welsh Centre for Learning Disabilities: Cardiff.

Lowe, K. & Felce, D. (1994b). The definition of challenging behaviour in practice. Manuscript submitted for publication.

Lowry, M.A. & Sovner, R. (1992). Severe behavior problems associated with rapid cycling bipolar disorder in two adults with profound mental retardation. *Journal of Intellectual Disability Research*, **36**, 269–81.

Luckasson, R., Coulter, D.L., Polloway, E.A., Reiss, S., Schalock, R. L., Snell, M.E., Spitalink, D.M. & Stark, J. (1992). *Mental Retardation: Definition, Classification, and Systems of Supports.* American Association on Mental Retardation: Washington, DC.

Luiselli, J.K. (1992a). Assessment and treatment of self-injury in a deaf–blind child. *Journal of Developmental and Physical Disabilities*, **4**, 219–26.

Luiselli, J.K. (1992b). Protective equipment. In *Self-Injurious Behavior: Analysis, Assessment and Treatment* (ed. J.K. Luiselli, J.L. Matson & N.N. Singh). Springer-Verlag: New York.

Luiselli, J.K., Beltis, J.A. & Bass, J. (1989). Clinical analysis of naltrexone in the treatment of self-injurious behavior. *Journal of the Multihandicapped Person*, **2**, 43–50.

Luiselli, J.K., Matson, J.L. & Singh, N.N. (1992). *Self-Injurious Behavior: Analysis, Assessment and Treatment.* Springer-Verlag: New York.

Luiselli, J.K., Myles, E., Evans, T.P. & Boyce, D.A. (1985). Reinforcement control of severe dysfunctional behavior of blind, multihandicapped students. *American Journal of Mental Deficiency,* **90**, 328–34.

Lundervold, D. & Bourland, G. (1988). Quantitative analysis of treatment of aggression, self-injury, and property destruction. *Behavior Modification,* **12**, 590–617.

Lutzker, J.R. (1978). Reducing self-injurious behavior by facial screening. *American Journal of Mental Deficiency,* **82**, 510–13.

McAfee, J.K. (1987). Classroom density and the aggressive behavior of handicapped children. *Education and Treatment of Children,* **10**, 134–45.

McBrien, J. & Felce, D. (1994). *Working with People Who Have Severe Learning Difficulty and Challenging Behaviour.* BILD Publications: Clevedon.

McClannahan, L.E. & Krantz, P.J. (1993). On systems-analysis in autism intervention programs. *Journal of Applied Behavior Analysis,* **26**, 589–96.

McDonnell, A., Dearden, B. & Richens, A. (1991). Staff training in the management of violence and aggression: 3. Physical restraint. *Mental Handicap,* **19**, 151–4.

McDowell, J.J. (1982). The importance of Herrnstein's mathematical statement of the law of effect for behavior therapy. *American Psychologist,* **37**, 771–9.

McDowell, J.J. (1988). Matching theory in natural human environments. *The Behavior Analyst,* **11**, 95–109.

McDowell, J.J. (1989). Two modern developments in matching theory. *The Behavior Analyst,* **12**, 153–66.

MacDuff, G.S., Krantz, P.J. & McClannahan, L.E. (1993). Teaching children with autism to use photographic activity schedules: maintenance and generalisation of complex response chains. *Journal of Applied Behavior Analysis,* **26**, 89–97.

McEachin, J.J., Smith, T. & Lovaas, O.I. (1993). Long-term outcome for children with autism who received early intensive behavioral treatment. *American Journal on Mental Retardation,* **97**, 359–72.

McGee, J.J. & Gonzalez, L. (1990). Gentle Teaching and the practice of human interdependence: a preliminary group study of 15 persons with severe behavioral disorders and their caregivers. In *Perspectives on the Use of Nonaversive and Aversive Interventions for Persons with Developmental Disabilities* (ed. A.C. Repp & N.N. Singh). Sycamore Publishing Company: Sycamore, Ill.

McGee, J.J., Menolascino, F.J., Hobbs, D.C. & Menousek, P.E. (1987). *Gentle Teaching: A Non-Aversive Approach to Helping Persons with Mental Retardation.* Human Sciences Press:

McGill, P. & Bliss, V. (1993). Staff training. In *Research to Practice? Implications of Research on the Challenging Behaviour of People with Learning Disabilities,* pp.53–87 (ed. C. Kiernan). British Institute of Learning Disabilities: Kidderminster.

McGill, P. & Emerson, E. (1992). Normalisation and applied behaviour analysis: values and technology in human services. In *Normalisation: A Reader for the 1990s* (ed. H. Brown & H. Smith). Routledge: London.

McGill, P. & Toogood, S. (1994). Organising community placements. In *Severe Learning Disabilities and Challenging Behaviours: Designing High Quality Services,* pp.119–156 (ed. E. Emerson, P. McGill & J. Mansell). Chapman and Hall: London.

McGill, P., Emerson, E. & Mansell, J. (1994). Individually designed residential provision for people with seriously challenging behaviours. In *Severe Learning Disabilities and Challenging Behaviours: Designing High Quality Services*, pp.119–156 (ed. E. Emerson, P. McGill & J. Mansell). Chapman and Hall: London.

McGimsey, J.F. & Favell, J.E. (1988). The effects of increased physical exercise on disruptive behavior in retarded persons. *Journal of Autism and Developmental Disorders*, **18**, 167–79.

McGonigle, J.J., Rojahn, J., Dixon, J. & Strain, P.S. (1987). Multiple treatment interference in alternating treatments design as a function of the intercomponent interval length. *Journal of Applied Behavior Analysis*, **20**, 171–8.

MacLean, W.E., Stone, W.L. & Brown, W.H. (1994). Developmental psychopathology of destructive behavior. In *Destructive Behavior in Developmental Disabilities: Diagnosis and Treatment*, pp.68–79 (ed. T. Thompson & D.B. Gray). Sage: Thousand Oaks.

MacMillan, D.L., Gresham, F.M. & Siperstein, G.N. (1993). Conceptual and psychometric concerns about the 1992 AAMR definition of mental retardation. *American Journal on Mental Retardation*, **98**, 325–35.

Mace, F.C. (1994*a*). Basic research needed for stimulating the development of behavioral technologies. *Journal of the Experimental Analysis of Behavior*, **61**, 529–50.

Mace, F.C. (1994*b*). The significance and future of functional analysis methodologies. *Journal of Applied Behavior Analysis*, **27**, 385–92.

Mace, F.C. & Belfiore, P. (1990). Behavioral momentum in the treatment of escape-motivated stereotypy. *Journal of Applied Behavior Analysis*, **23**, 507–14.

Mace, F.C. & Knight, D. (1986). Functional analysis and treatment of severe pica. *Journal of Applied Behavior Analysis*, **19**, 411–16.

Mace, F.C. & Lalli, J.S. (1991). Linking descriptive and experimental analyses in the treatment of bizarre speech. *Journal of Applied Behavior Analysis*, **24**, 553–62.

Mace, F.C. & Roberts, M.L. (1993). Factors affecting selection of behavioral interventions. In *Communicative Alternatives to Challenging Behavior*, pp.113–133 (ed. J. Reichle & D.P. Wacker). P. H. Brookes: Baltimore.

Mace, F.C., Hock, M.L., Lalli, J.S., West, B.J., Belfiore, P., Pinter, E. & Brown, B.D. (1988). Behavioral momentum in the treatment of noncompliance. *Journal of Applied Behavior Analysis*, **21**, 123–41.

Mace, F.C., Lalli, J.,S. & Lalli, E.P. (1991). Functional analysis and treatment of aberrant behavior. *Research in Developmental Disabilities*, **12**, 155–80.

Mace, F.C., Lalli, J.S. & Shea, M.C. (1992). Functional analysis and treatment of self-injury. In *Self-Injurious Behavior: Analysis, Assessment and Treatment*, pp.122–154 (ed. J.K. Luiselli, J.L. Matson & N.N. Singh). Springer-Verlag: New York.

Mace, F.C., Page, T.J., Ivancic, M.T. & O'Brien, S. (1986). Analysis of environmental determinants of aggression and disruption in mentally retarded children. *Applied Research in Mental Retardation*, **7**, 203–21.

Mace, F.C., Yankanich, M.A. & West, B. (1989). Toward a methodology of experimental analysis and treatment of aberrant classroom behaviors. *Special Services in the School*, **4**, 71–88.

Maisto, C.R., Baumeister, A.A. & Maisto, A.A. (1978). An analysis of variables related to self-injurious behavior among institutionalised retarded persons. *Journal of*

Mental Deficiency Research, **22**, 27–36.

Mansell, J. (1994). Specialized group homes for persons with severe or profound mental retardation and serious behavior problem in England. *Research in Developmental Disabilities*, **15**, 371–88.

Mansell, J., Cambridge, P., Forrest, J. & Emerson, E. (1994*a*). *Community Supports for People with Challenging Behavior.* Tizard Centre, University of Kent at Canterbury: Canterbury.

Mansell, J., Hughes, H. & McGill, P. (1994*b*). Maintaining local residential placements. In *Severe Learning Disabilities and Challenging Behaviours: Designing High Quality Services* (ed. E. Emerson, P. McGill & J. Mansell). Chapman & Hall: London.

Mansell, J., McGill, P. & Emerson, E. (1994*c*). Conceptualising service provision. In *Severe Learning Disabilities and Challenging Behaviours: Designing High Quality Services* (ed. E. Emerson, P. McGill & J. Mansell). Chapman & Hall: London.

Markowitz, P. (1992). Effect of fluoxetine on self-injurious behavior in the developmentally disabled: a preliminary study. *Journal of Clinical Psychopharmacology*, **12**, 27–31.

Marks, I.M. (1987). *Fears, Phobias and Rituals.* Oxford University Press: Oxford.

Martens, B.K. & Houk, J.L. (1989). The application of Herrnstein's Law of Effect to disruptive and on-task behavior of a retarded adolescent girl. *Journal of the Experimental Analysis of Behavior*, **51**, 17–27.

Martens, B.K., Lochner, D.G. & Kelly, S.Q. (1992). The effects of variable-interval reinforcement on academic engagement: a demonstration of matching theory. *Journal of Applied Behavior Analysis*, **25**, 143–51.

Matson, J.L. (1990). *Handbook of Behavior Modification with the Mentally Retarded.* Plenum: New York.

Matson, J.L. & DiLorenzo, T.M. (1984). *Punishment and its Alternatives.* Springer: New York.

Matson, J.L. & Taras, M.E. (1989). A 20 year review of punishment and alternative methods to treat problem behaviors in developmentally delayed persons. *Research in Developmental Disabilities*, **10**, 85–104.

Maurice, P. & Trudel, G. (1982). Self-injurious behavior: prevalence and relationships to environmental events. In *Life-threatening Behavior: Analysis and Intervention* (ed. J.H. Hollis & C.E. Meyers). American Association on Mental Deficiency: Washington, DC.

Mazaleski, J.L., Iwata, B.A., Rodgers, T.A., Vollmer, T.R. & Zarcone, J.R. (1994). Protective equipment as treatment for stereotypic hand mouthing: sensory extinction or punishment effects?. *Journal of Applied Behavior Analysis*, **27**, 345–55.

Meador, D.M. & Osborn, R.G. (1992). Prevalence of severe behavior disorders in persons with mental retardation and treatment procedures used in community and institutional settings. *Behavioral Residential Treatment*, **4**, 299–314.

Meinhold, P.M. & Mulick, J.A. (1990). Risks, choices and behavioral treatment. *Behavioral Residential Treatment*, **5**, 29–44.

Meisels, S.J. & Shonkoff, J.P. (1990). *Handbook of Early Childhood Intervention.* Cambridge University Press: Cambridge.

Meyer, L. & Evans, I.M. (1989). *Nonaversive Intervention for Behavior Problems: A Manual for Home and Community.* Teachers College Press: New York.

Meyer, L.H. & Evans, I.M. (1993*a*). Meaningful outcomes in behavioral intervention: evaluating positive approaches to the remediation of challenging behaviors. In

Communicative Alternatives to Challenging Behavior, pp.407–428 (ed. J. Reichle & D.P. Wacker). P.H. Brookes: Baltimore.

Meyer, L.H. & Evans, I.M. (1993*b*). Science and practice in behavioral intervention: meaningful outcomes, research validity, and usable knowledge. *Journal of the Association for Persons with Severe Handicaps*, **18**, 224–34.

Meyer, L.H. & Janney, R. (1989). User-friendly measures of meaningful outcomes: evaluating behavioral interventions. *Journal of the Association for Persons with Severe Handicaps*, **14**, 262–70.

Michael, J. (1980). Flight from behavior analysis. *The Behavior Analyst*, **3**, 1–21.

Michael, J. (1982). Distinguishing between discriminative and motivational functions of stimuli. *Journal of the Experimental Analysis of Behavior*, **37**, 149–55.

Michael, J. (1993). Establishing operations. *The Behavior Analyst*, **16**, 191–206.

Mithaug, D.E. & Mar, D.K. (1980). The relation between choosing and working prevocational tasks in two severely retarded young adults. *Journal of Applied Behavior Analysis*, **13**, 177–82.

Mittleman, G., Blaha, C.D. & Phillips, A.G. (1992). Pituitary-adrenal and dopaminergic modulation of schedule-induced polydipsia: behavioural and neurochemical evidence. *Behavioral Neuroscience*, **106**, 408–20.

Morris, E.K. (1993). Revise and resubmit. *Journal of the Association for Persons with Severe Handicaps*, **18**, 242–8.

Morris, E.K. & Midgley, B.D. (1990). Some historical and conceptual foundations of ecobehavioral analysis. In *Ecobehavioral Analysis and Developmental Disabilities* (ed. S.R. Schroeder). Springer-Verlag: New York.

Mudford, O.C. (1985). Treatment selection in behaviour reduction: gentle teaching versus the least intrusive treatment model. *Australia and New Zealand Journal of Developmental Disabilities*, **10**, 265–70.

Mulick, J.A. (1990). The ideology and science of punishment in mental retardation. *American Journal on Mental Retardation*, **95**, 142–56.

Mulick, J.A. & Meinhold, P.M. (1991). Evaluating models for the emergence and maintenance of stereotypy and self-injury. *American Journal on Mental Retardation*, **96**, 327–33.

Mulick, J.A., Hammer, D. & Dura, J.R. (1991). Assessment and management of antisocial and hyperactive behavior. In *Handbook of Mental Retardation* (ed. J.L. Matson & J.A. Mulick). Pergamon: New York.

Murphy, G. (1982). Sensory reinforcement in the mentally handicapped and autistic child: a review. *Journal of Autism and Developmental Disorders*, **12**, 265–78.

Murphy, G.H. (1986). Direct observation as an assessment tool in functional analysis and treatment. In *Assessment In Mental Handicap* (ed. J. Hogg & N. Raynes). Croom Helm: London.

Murphy, G. (1993). The use of aversive stimuli in treatment: The issue of consent. *Journal of Intellectual Disability Research*, **37**, 211–19.

Murphy, G. (1994). Understanding challenging behaviour. In *Severe Learning Disabilities and Challenging Behaviours: Designing High Quality Services*, pp.37–68 (ed. E. Emerson, P. McGill & J. Mansell). Chapman and Hall: London.

Murphy, G.H. & Oliver, C. (1987). Decreasing undesirable behaviours. In *Behaviour Modification for People with Mental Handicaps* (2nd edn) (ed. W. Yule & J. Carr). Croom Helm: London.

Murphy, G.H. & Wilson, B. (1980). Long–term outcome of contingent shock treatment for self-injurious behavior. In *Frontiers of Knowledge in Mental Retardation, Vol II - Biomedical Aspects* (ed. P. Mitler & J.M. de Jong). University Park Press: Baltimore.

Murphy, G.H., Hall, S. & Oliver, C. (1995). The early emergence of self-injury. Paper presented at AAMR Annual Conference, San Francisco, May 1995.

Murphy, G.H., Oliver, C., Corbett, J., Crayton, L., Hales, J., Head, D.,& Hall, S. (1993). Epidemiology of self-injury, characteristics of people with severe self-injury and initial treatment outcome. In *Research to Practice? Implications of Research on the Challenging Behaviour of People with Learning Disabilities*, pp.1–35 (ed. C. Kiernan). BILD: Kidderminster.

National Institute of Health (1991). *Treatment of Destructive Behaviors in Persons with Developmental Disabilities*. US Department of Health and Human Services: Washington.

Neef, N.A., Mace, F.C. & Shade, D. (1993). Impulsivity in students with serious emotional disturbance: the interactive effects of reinforcer rate, delay and quality. *Journal of Applied Behavior Analysis*, **26**, 37–52.

Neef, N.A., Mace, F.C., Shea, M. & Shade, D.B. (1992). Effects of reinforcer rate and reinforcer quality on time allocation: extension of matching theory to educational settings. *Journal of Applied Behavior Analysis*, **25**, 691–9.

Neri, C.L. & Sandman, C. (1992). Relationship between diet and self-injurious behavior: a survey. *Journal of Developmental and Physical Disabilities*, **4**, 189–94.

Newsom, C., Favell, J.E. & Rincover, A. (1983). Side effects of punishment. In *The Effects of Punishment on Human Behavior* (ed. S. Axelrod & J. Apsche). Academic Press: New York.

Newton, T.S., Ard, W.R. & Horner, R.H. (1993). Validating predicted activity preferences of individuals with severe disabilities. *Journal of Applied Behavior Analysis*, **26**, 239–45.

Newton, J.T. & Sturmey, P. (1991). The Motivation Assessment Scale: inter-rater reliability and internal consistency in a British sample. *Journal of Mental Deficiency Research*, **35**, 472–4.

Nihira, K., Leland, H. & Lambert, N. (1993). *Adaptive Behavior Scale – Residential and Community (2nd edn)*. Pro-Ed: Austin, TX.

Nordquist, V.M., Twardosz, S. & McEvoy, M.A. (1991). Effects of environmental reorganization in classrooms for children with autism. *Journal of Early Intervention*, **15**, 135–52.

Northup, J., Wacker, D.P., Berg, W., Kelly, L., Sasso, G. & DeRaad, A. (1994). The treatment of severe behavior problems in school settings using a technical assistance model. *Journal of Applied Behavior Analysis*, **27**, 33–47.

Northup, J., Wacker, D.P., Sasso, G., Steege, M., Cigrand, K., Cook, J. & DeRaad, A. (1991). A brief functional analysis of aggressive and alternative behavior in an out-clinic setting. *Journal of Applied Behavior Analysis*, **24**, 509–22.

Nyhan, W.L. (1994). The Lesch–Nyhan disease. In *Destructive Behavior in Developmental Disabilities: Diagnosis and Treatment*, pp.181–197 (ed. T. Thompson & D.B. Gray). Sage: Thousand Oaks.

O'Brien, F. (1989). Punishment for people with developmental disabilities. In *The Treatment of Severe Behavior Disorders* (ed. E. Cipani). AAMR: Washington.

O'Brien, J. (1991). Against pain as a tool in professional work on people with severe disabilities. *Disability, Handicap and Society,* **6**, 81–90.

O'Brien, S. & Repp, A.C. (1990). Reinforcement-based reductive procedures: a review of 20 years of their use with persons with severe or profound mental retardation. *Journal of the Association for Persons with Severe Handicaps,* **15**, 148–59.

Oliver, C. (1991). The application of analogue methodology to the functional analysis of challenging behaviour. In *The Challenge of Severe Mental Handicap: A Behaviour Analytic Approach* (ed. B. Remington). Wiley: Chichester.

Oliver, C. (1993). Self-injurious behaviour: from response to strategy. In *Research to Practice? Implication of Research on the Challenging Behaviour of People with Learning Disabilities,* pp.135–188 (ed. C. Kiernan). Clevedon: British Institute of Learning Disabilities.

Oliver, C. & Head, D. (1990). Self-injurious behaviour in people with learning disabilities: determinants and interventions. *International Review of Psychiatry,* **2**, 101–16.

Oliver, C., Murphy, G.H. & Corbett, J.A. (1987). Self-injurious behaviour in people with mental handicap: a total population survey. *Journal of Mental Deficiency Research,* **31**, 147–62.

O'Neill, R.E., Horner, R.H., Albin, R.W., Storey, K., Sprague, J.R. (1990). *Functional Analysis of Problem Behavior: A Practical Assessment Guide.* Sycamore: Sycamore, IL.

Overskeid, G. (1992). Is any human behavior schedule-induced? *Psychological Record,* **42**, 323–40.

Pace, G.M., Ivancic, M.T., Edwards, G.L., Iwata, B.A. & Page, T.J. (1985). Assessment of stimulus preference and reinforcer value with profoundly retarded individuals. *Journal of Applied Behavior Analysis,* **18**, 249–55.

Pace, G.M., Iwata, B.A., Edwards, G.L. & McCosh, K.C. (1986). Stimulus fading and transfer in treatment of self-restraint and self-injurious behavior. *Journal of Applied Behavior Analysis,* **19**, 381–9.

Pace, G.M., Iwata, B.A., Cowdery, G.E., Andree, P.J. & McIntyre, T. (1993). Stimulus (instructional) fading during extinction of self-injurious behavior. *Journal of Applied Behavior Analysis,* **26**, 205–12.

Paisey, T.J.H., Whitney, R.B. & Hislop, P.M. (1991). Non–intrusive operant analysis of aggressive behavior in persons with mental retardation. *Behavioral Residential Treatment,* **6**, 51–64.

Paisey, T.J.H., Whitney, R.B. & Moore, J. (1989). Person-treatment interactions across nonaversive response–deceleration procedures for self-injury: a case study of effects and side effects. *Behavioral Residential Treatment,* **4**, 69–88.

Parrish, J.M. & Roberts, M.L. (1993). Interventions based on covariation of desired and inappropriate behavior. In *Communicative Alternatives to Challenging Behavior* (ed. J. Reichle & D.P. Wacker). Brookes: Baltimore.

Parrish, J.M., Cataldo, M.F., Kolko, D.J., Neef, N.A. & Egel, A.L. (1986). Experimental analysis of response covariation among compliant and inappropriate behaviors. *Journal of Applied Behavior Analysis,* **19**, 241–54.

Parsons, M.B. & Reid, D.H. (1990). Assessing food preferences among persons with profound mental retardation. *Journal of Applied Behavior Analysis,* **23**, 183–95.

Parsons, M.B., Reid, D.H. & Green, C.W. (1993). Preparing direct-care staff to teach people with severe disabilities: a comprehensive evaluation of an effective and acceptable training programme. *Behavioral Residential Treatment*, **8**, 163–85.

Parsons, M.B., Reid, D.H., Reynolds, J. & Bumgarner, M. (1990). Effects of chosen versus assigned jobs on the work performance of persons with severe handicaps. *Journal of Applied Behavior Analysis*, **23**, 253–8.

Pary, R. (1993). Psychoactive drugs used with adults and elderly adults who have mental retardation. *American Journal on Mental Retardation*, **98**, 121–7.

Pierce, K.L. & Schreibman, L. (1994). Teaching daily living skills to children with autism in unsupervised settings through pictorial self-management. *Journal of Applied Behavior Analysis*, **27**, 471–81.

Pierce, W.D. & Epling, W.F. (1980). What happened to the analysis in applied behavior analysis?. *The Behavior Analyst*, **3**, 1–9.

Podboy, J.W. & Mallery, W.A. (1977). Caffeine reduction and behavior change in the severely retarded. *Mental Retardation*, **15**, 40.

Poling, A. & Fuqua, R.W. (1986). *Research Methods in Applied Behavior Analysis*. Plenum: New York.

Pratt, M.W., Luszcz, M.A. & Brown, M.E. (1980). Measuring the dimensions of the quality of care in small community residences. *American Journal of Mental Deficiency*, **85**, 188–94.

Premack, D. (1959). Toward empirical behavior laws: I. Positive reinforcement. *Science*, **136**, 255–7.

Pyles, D.A.M. & Bailey, J.S. (1990). Diagnosing severe behavior problems. In *Perspectives on the Use of Nonaversive and Aversive Interventions for Persons with Developmental Disabilities* (ed. A. C. Repp & N.N. Singh). Sycamore Publishing Company: Sycamore, Ill.

Quine, L. & Pahl, J. (1985). Examining the causes of stress in families with mentally handicapped children. *British Journal of Social Work*, **15**, 501–17.

Qureshi, H. (1992). Young adults with learning difficulties and challenging behavior: parents' views of services in the community. *Social Work and Social Services Review*, **3**, 104–23.

Qureshi, H. (1994). The size of the problem. In *Severe Learning Disabilities and Challenging Behaviours: Designing High Quality Services* (ed. E. Emerson, P. McGill & J. Mansell). Chapman & Hall: London.

Qureshi, H. & Alborz, A. (1992). The epidemiology of challenging behaviour. *Mental Handicap Research*, **5**, 130–45.

Rachman, S.J. (1990). The determinants and treatment of simple phobias. *Advances in Behaviour Research and Therapy*, **12**, 1–30.

Rast, J., Johnston, J.M. & Drum, C. (1984). A parametric analysis of the relationship between food quantity and rumination. *Journal of the Experimental Analysis of Behavior*, **41**, 125–34.

Rast, J., Johnston, J.M., Drum, C. & Conrin, J. (1981). The relation of food quantity to rumination behavior. *Journal of Applied Behavior Analysis*, **14**, 121–30.

Ratey, J., Sovner, R., Parks, A. & Rogentine, K. (1991). Buspirone treatment of aggression and anxiety in mentally retarded patients: a multiple-baseline, placebo lead-in study. *Journal of Clinical Psychiatry*, **52**, 159–62.

Realon, R.E. & Konarski, E.A. (1993). Using decelerative contingencies to reduce the self-injurious behavior of people with multiple handicaps: the effects of response satiation? *Research in Developmental Disabilities*, **14**, 341–57.

Reese, R.M., Sherman, J.A. & Sheldon, J. (1984). Reducing agitated–disruptive behavior of mentally retarded residents of community group homes: the role of self-recording and peer prompted self-recording. *Analysis and Intervention in Developmental Disabilities*, **4**, 91–107.

Reichle, J. & Wacker, D.P. (1993). *Communicative Alternatives to Challenging Behavior*. P.H. Brookes: Baltimore.

Reichle, J., Sigafoos, J. & Piché, L. (1989). Teaching an adolescent with blindness and severe disabilities: a correspondence between requesting and selecting preferred objects. *Journal of the Association for Persons with Severe Handicaps*, **14**, 75–80.

Reid, A.H., Naylor, G.J. & Kay, D.S.G. (1981). A double-blind, placebo controlled crossover trial of carbamazepine in overactive severely mentally handicapped patients. *Psychological Medicine*, **11**, 109–13.

Reid, D.H. & Green, C.W. (1990). Staff training. In *Handbook of Behavior Modification with the Mentally Retarded* (ed. J.L. Matson). Plenum: New York.

Reid, D.H., Parsons, M.B. & Green, C.W. (1989*a*). *Staff Management in Human Services: Behavioral Research and Application*. Charles C. Thomas: Springfield, IL.

Reid, D.H., Parsons, M.B. & Green, C.W. (1989*b*). Treating aberrant behavior through effective staff management: a developing technology. In *The Treatment of Severe Behavior Disorders: Behavior Analysis Approaches* (ed. Cipani, E.). American Association on Mental Retardation: Washington, DC.

Remington, B. (1991*a*). *The Challenge of Severe Mental Handicap: A Behaviour Analytic Approach*. Wiley: Chichester.

Remington, B. (1991*b*). Behaviour analysis and severe mental handicap: the dialogue between research and application. In *The Challenge of Severe Mental Handicap: A Behaviour Analytic Approach* (ed. B. Remington). Wiley: Chichester.

Repp, A.C. & Felce, D. (1990). A micro-computer system used for evaluative and experimental behavioural research in mental handicap. *Mental Handicap Research*, **3**, 21–32.

Repp, A.C. & Karsh, K.G. (1994a). Laptop computer systems for data recording and contextual analysis. In *Destructive Behavior in Developmental Disabilities: Diagnosis and Treatment*, pp.83–101 (ed. T. Thompson & D.B. Gray). Sage: Thousand Oaks.

Repp, A.C. & Karsh, K.G. (1994*b*). Hypothesis-based interventions for tantrum behaviors of persons with developmental disabilities in school settings. *Journal of Applied Behavior Analysis*, **27**, 21–31.

Repp, A.C. & Singh, N.N. (1990). *Perspectives on the Use of Nonaversive and Aversive Interventions for Persons with Developmental Disabilities*. Sycamore Publishing Company: Sycamore, IL.

Repp, A.C., Felce, D. & Barton, L.E. (1988). Basing the treatment of stereotypic and self-injurious behaviors on hypotheses of their causes. *Journal of Applied Behavior Analysis*, **21**, 281–9.

Richmond, G., Schroeder, S.R. & Bickel, W. (1986). Tertiary prevention of attrition related to self-injurious behaviors. In *Advances in Learning and Behavioral Disabilities, Vol 5* (ed. K.D. Gadow). JAI Press: London.

Ricketts, R.W., Ellis, C.R., Singh, Y.N. & Singh, N.N. (1993). Opioid antagonists II: clinical effects in the treatment of self-injury in individuals with developmental disabilities. *Journal of Developmental and Physical Disabilities*, **5**, 17–28.

Ricketts, R.W., Goza, A.B. & Matese, M. (1992). Case study: effects of naltrexone and SIBIS on self-injury. *Behavioral Residential Treatment*, **7**, 315–26.

Rincover, A. & Devany, J. (1982). The application of sensory extinction procedures to self-injury. *Analysis and Intervention in Developmental Disabilities*, **2**, 67–81.

Rincover, A., Cook, A., Peoples, A. & Packard, D. (1979*a*). Sensory extinction and sensory reinforcement principles for programming multiple adaptive behavior change. *Journal of Applied Behavior Analysis*, **12**, 221–33.

Rincover, A., Newsom, C.D. & Carr, E.G. (1979*b*). Use of sensory extinction procedures in the treatment of compulsive-like behavior of developmentally disabled children. *Journal of Consulting and Clinical Psychology*, **47**, 695–701.

Rojahn, J. (1986). Self-injurious and stereotypic behavior of noninstitutionalized mentally retarded people: prevalence and classification. *American Journal of Mental Deficiency*, **91**, 268–76.

Rojahn, J. (1994). Epidemiology and topographic taxonomy of self-injurious behavior. In *Destructive Behavior in Developmental Disabilities: Diagnosis and Treatment*, pp.49–67 (ed. T. Thompson & D.B. Gray). Sage: Thousand Oaks.

Rojahn, J. & Marshburn, E.C. (1992). Facial screening and visual occlusion. In *Self-Injurious Behavior: Analysis, Assessment and Treatment* (ed. J.K. Luiselli, J.K. Matson & N.N. Singh). Springer-Verlag: New York.

Rojahn, J. & Sisson, L.A. (1990). Stereotyped behavior. In *Handbook of Behavior Modification with the Mentally Retarded* (ed. J.L. Matson). Plenum: New York.

Rojahn, J., Schroeder, S.R. & Mulick, J.A. (1980). Ecological assessment of self-protective devices in three profoundly retarded adults. *Journal of Autism and Developmental Disorders*, **10**, 59–66.

Rolider, A. & Van Houten, R. (1990). The role of reinforcement in reducing inappropriate behavior: some myths and misconceptions. In *Perspectives on the Use of Nonaversive and Aversive Interventions for Persons with Developmental Disabilities* (ed. A. C. Repp & N.N. Singh). Sycamore: Sycamore, IL.

Romanczyk, R.G. (1986). Self-injurious behavior: conceptualization, assessment, and treatment. In *Advances in Learning and Behavioral Disabilities*, Vol 5 (ed. K.D. Gadow). JAI Press: London.

Romanczyk, R.G., Lockshin, S. & O'Connor, J. (1992). Psychophysiology and issues of anxiety and arousal. In *Self-Injurious Behavior: Analysis, Assessment and Treatment*, pp.93–121 (ed. J.K. Luiselli, J.L. Matson & N.N. Singh). Springer-Verlag: New York.

Rosine, L.P.C. & Martin, G.L. (1983). Self-management training to decrease undesirable behavior of mentally handicapped adults. *Rehabilitation Psychology*, **28**, 195–205.

Rudrud, E.H., Ziarnik, J.P. & Coleman, G. (1984). Reduction of tongue protrusion of a 24-year-old woman with Down Syndrome through self-monitoring. *American Journal of Mental Deficiency*, **88**, 647–52.

Rusch, F.R. & Hughes, C. (1989). Overview of supported employment. *Journal of Applied Behavior Analysis*, **22**, 351–63.

Rusch, R.G., Hall, J.C. & Griffin, H.C. (1986). Abuse provoking characteristics of institutionalized mentally retarded individuals. *American Journal of Mental Deficiency*, **90**, 618–24.

Russell, P. (1995). *Children with Severe Learning Difficulties and Challenging Behaviour*. Mental Health Foundation: London.

Russo, D.C., Cataldo, M.F. & Cushing, P.J. (1981). Compliance training and behavioral covariation in the treatment of multiple behavior problems. *Journal of Applied Behavior Analysis*, **14**, 209–22.

Ryan, E.P., Helsel, W.J., Lubetsky, M.J., Miewald, B.K., Hersen, M. & Bridge, J. (1989). Use of naltrexone in reducing self-injurious behavior: a single case analysis. *Journal of the Multihandicapped Person*, **2**, 295–309.

Sackett, G.P. (1978). *Observing Behavior: Data Collection and Analysis Methods.* University Park Press: Baltimore.

Sackett, G.P. (1979). The lag sequential analysis of contingency and cyclicity in behavioral interaction research. In *Handbook of Infant Development* (ed. J.D. Osofsky). Wiley: New York.

Sackett, G.P. (1987). Analysis of sequential social interaction data: Some issues, recent developments, and a causal inference model. In *Handbook of Infant Development.* 2nd edn (ed. J.D. Osofsky). Wiley: New York.

Sajwaj, T., Libet, J. & Agras, S. (1974). Lemon-juice therapy: the control of life threatening rumination in a six month old infant. *Journal of Applied Behavior Analysis*, **1**, 557–63.

Sajwaj, T., Twardosz, S. & Burke, M. (1972). Side effect of extinction procedures in a remedial playschool. *Journal of Applied Behavior Analysis* **5**, 163–75.

Sandman, C.A. (1990/1991). The opiate hypothesis in autism and self-injury. *Journal of Child and Adolescent Psychopharmacology*, **1**, 237–48.

Sandman, C. & Barron, J.L. (1992). Paradoxical response to sedative/hypnotics in patients with self-injurious behavior and stereotypy. *Journal of Developmental and Physical Disabilities*, **4**, 307–16.

Sandman, C.A., Barron, J.L. & Colman, H. (1990*a*). An orally administered opiate blocker, naltrexone, attenuates self-injurious behavior. *American Journal on Mental Retardation*, **95**, 93–102.

Sandman, C.A., Barron, J.L., Chicz-DeMet, A. & DeMet, E.M. (1990*b*). Plasma β-endorphin levels in patients with self-injurious behavior and stereotypy. *American Journal on Mental Retardation*, **95**, 84–92.

Sasso, G.M., Reimers, T.M., Cooper, L.J., Wacker, D., Berg, W., Steege, M., Kelly, L. & Allaire, A. (1992). Use of descriptive and experimental analyses to identify the functional properties of aberrant behavior in school settings. *Journal of Applied Behavior Analysis*, **25**, 809–21.

Saunders, R.R., Saunders, M.D. & Saunders, J.L. (1994). Data collection with bar code technology. In *Destructive Behavior in Developmental Disabilities*, pp.102–116 (ed. T. Thompson & D.B. Gray). Sage: Thousand Oaks.

Schalock, R.L. (1990). *Quality of Life: Perspectives and Issues.* American Association on Mental Retardation: Washington, DC.

Schalock, R.L. & Kieth, K.D. (1993). *Quality of Life Questionnaire.* IDS: Worthington, OH.

Schalock, R.L., Harper, R.S. & Genung, T. (1981). Community integration of mentally retarded adults: community placement and program success. *American Journal of Mental Deficiency*, **85**, 478–88.

Schalock, R.L., Stark, J.A., Snell, M.E., Coulter, D.L., Polloway, E. A., Luckasson, R., Reiss, S. & Spitalink, D.M. (1994). The changing conception of mental retardation: implications for the field. *Mental Retardation*, **32**, 181–93.

Schlosser, R.W. & Goetze, H. (1992). Effectiveness and treatment validity of interventions addressing self-injurious behavior: from narrative reviews to meta-analyses. *Advances in Learning and Behavioral Disabilities*, **7**, 135–76.

Schroeder, S.R. (1991). Self-injury and stereotypy. In *Handbook of Mental Retardation* (ed. J.L. Matson & J.A. Mulick). Pergamon: New York.

Schroeder, S.R. & Luiselli, J.K. (1992). Self-restraint. In *Self-Injurious Behavior: Analysis, Assessment and Treatment*, pp.3–20 (ed. J.K. Luiselli, J.L. Matson & N.N. Singh). Springer-Verlag: New York.

Schroeder, S.R. & MacLean, W. (1987). If it isn't one thing it's another: experimental analysis of covariation in behavior management data of severe behavior disturbances. In *Living Environments and Mental Retardation* (ed. S. Landesman & P. Vietze). American Association on Mental Retardation: Washington, DC.

Schroeder, S.R. & Schroeder, C.S. (1989). The role of the AAMR in the aversives controversy. *Mental Retardation* 27(3), iii–v.

Schroeder, S.R. & Tessel, R. (1994). Dopaminergic and serotonergic mechanisms in self-injury and aggression. In *Destructive Behavior in Developmental Disabilities: Diagnosis and Treatment* (ed. T. Thompson & D.B. Gray). Sage: Thousand Oaks.

Schroeder, S.R., Bickel, W.K. & Richmond, G. (1986). Primary and secondary prevention of self-injurious behaviors: a lifelong problem. In *Advances in Learning and Behavioral Disabilities*, Vol 5 (ed. K.D. Gadow). Little, Brown & Co.: Boston.

Schroeder, S.R., Kanoy, R.C., Mulick, J.A., Rojahn, J., Thios, S.J., Stevens, M. & Hawk, B. (1982). Environmental antecedents which affect management and maintenance of programs for self-injurious behavior. In *Life-Threatening Behavior: Analysis and Intervention* (ed. J.H. Hollis & C.E. Meyers). American Association on Mental Deficiency: Washington, DC.

Schroeder, S.R., Oldenquist, A. & Rojahn, J. (1990a). A conceptual framework for judging the humaneness and effectiveness of behavioral treatment. In *Perspectives on the Use of Nonaversive and Aversive Interventions for People with Developmental Disabilities* (ed. A.C. Repp & N.N. Singh). Sycamore Publishing Co: Sycamore, IL.

Schroeder, S.R., Rojahn, J., Mulick, J.A. & Schroeder, C.S. (1990b). Self-injurious behavior. In *Handbook of Behavior Modification with the Mentally Retarded* (2nd edn) (ed. J.L. Matson). Plenum: New York.

Schroeder, S.R., Rojahn, J. & Oldenquist, A. (1991). Treatment of destructive behaviors among people with mental retardation and developmental disabilities: Overview of the problem. In *Treatment of Destructive Behaviors in Persons with Developmental Disabilities* (ed. National Institute of Health). US Department of Health and Human Services: Washington. DC.

Schroeder, S.R., Schroeder, C.S., Smith, B. & Dalldorf, J. (1978). Prevalence of self-injurious behaviors in a large state facility for the retarded: a three year follow-up. *Journal of Autism and Childhood Schizophrenia*, **8**, 261–9.

Schutz, R., Wehman, P., Renzaglia, A. & Karan, O. (1978). Efficacy of contingent social disapproval on inappropriate verbalisation of two severely retarded males. *Behavior Therapy*, **9**, 657–62.

Schwartz, I.S. & Baer, D.M. (1991). Social validity assessments: Is current practice state of the art?. *Journal of Applied Behavior Analysis*, **24**, 189–204.

Scotti, J.R., Evans, I., Meyer, L. & DiBenedetto, A. (1991a). Individual repertoires as behavioural systems: implications for program design and evaluation. In *The*

Challenge of Severe Mental Handicap: A Behaviour Analytic Approach (ed. B. Remington). Wiley: Chichester.

Scotti, J.R., Evans, I.M., Meyer, L.H. & Walker, P. (1991*b*). A meta-analysis of behavioral research with problem behavior: treatment validity and standards of practice. *American Journal of Mental Retardation*, **93**, 233–56.

Severence, L.J. & Gastrom, L.L. (1977). Effects of the label 'mentally retarded' on causal explanations for success and failure outcomes. *American Journal on Mental Deficiency*, **81**, 547–55.

Seys, D. & Duker, P. (1988). Effects of staff management on the quality of residential care for mentally retarded individuals. *American Journal on Mental Retardation*, **93**, 290–9.

Shapiro, E.S. & Browder, D.M. (1990). Behavioral Assessment. In *Handbook of Behavior Modification with the Mentally Retarded* (ed. J.L. Matson). Plenum: New York.

Sidman, M. (1986). Functional analysis of emergent verbal classes. In *Analysis and Integration of Behavioral Units* (ed. T. Thompson & M.D. Zeilor). Lawrence Erlbaum Associates: Hillsdale, NJ.

Sidman, M. (1989). *Coercion and its Fallout*. Authors Cooperative: Boston.

Sigafoos, J. & Dempsey, R. (1992). Assessing choice making among children with multiple disabilities. *Journal of Applied Behavior Analysis*, **25**, 747–55.

Sigafoos, J, & Kerr, M. (1994). Provision of leisure activities for the reduction of challenging behavior. *Behavioral Interventions*, **9**, 43–53.

Sigafoos, J., Kerr, M. & Roberts, D. (1994). Interrater reliability of the Motivation Assessment Scale: failure to replicate with aggressive behavior. *Research in Developmental Disabilities*, **15**, 333–42.

Singer, G.H.S., Singer, J. & Horner, R.H. (1987). Using pretask requests to increase the probability of compliance for students with severe disabilities. *Journal of the Association for Persons with Severe Handicaps*, **12**, 287–91.

Singh, N.N. & Aman, M.G. (1990). Ecobehavioral assessment of pharmacotherapy. In S. Schroeder (ed.) *Ecobehavioral Analysis in Developmental Disabilities*. New York: Springer-Verlag.

Singh, N.N. & Repp, A.C. (1989). The behavioural and pharmacological management of problem behaviours in people with mental retardation. *Irish Journal of Psychology*, **9**, 264–85.

Singh, N.N., Donatelli, L.S., Best, A., Williams, D.E., Barrera, F.J., Lenz, M.W., Landrum, T.J., Ellis, C.R. & Moe, T.L. (1993*a*). Factor structure of the motivation assessment schedule. *Journal of Intellectual Disability Research*, **37**, 65–74.

Singh, N.N., Singh, Y.N. & Ellis, C.R. (1992). Psychopharmacology of self-injury. In *Self-Injurious Behavior: Analysis, Assessment and Treatment*, pp.307–351 (ed. J.K. Luiselli, J.L. Matson & N.N. Singh). Springer-Verlag: New York.

Singh, N.N, Watson, J.E. & Winton, A.S.W. (1986). Treating self-injury: water mist spray versus facial screening or forced arm exercise. *Journal of Applied Behavior Analysis*, **19**, 403–10.

Singh, N.N., Winton, A.S.W. & Dawson, M.J. (1982). Suppression of anti-social behavior by facial screening using multiple baseline and alternating treatments designs. *Behavior Therapy*, **13**, 511–20.

Singh, Y.N., Ricketts, R.W., Ellis, C.R. & Singh, N.N. (1993*b*). Opioid antagonists I:

pharmacology and rationale for use in treating self-injury. *Journal of Developmental and Physical Disabilities*, **5**, 5–16.

Skinner, B.F. (1953). *Science and Human Behavior.* MacMillan: New York.

Skinner, B.F. (1966). An operant analysis of problem solving. In *Problem Solving: Research, Methods and Theory* (ed. B. Klienmuntz). Wiley: New York.

Skinner, B.F. (1971). *Beyond Freedom and Dignity.* Knopf: New York.

Skinner, B.F. (1977). Herrnstein and the evolution of behaviorism. *American Psychologist*, **32**, 1006–12.

Slifer, K.J., Ivancic, M.T., Parrish, J.M., Page, T.J. & Burgio, L. (1986). Assessment and treatment of multiple behavior problems exhibited by a profoundly retarded adolescent. *Journal of Behavior Therapy and Experimental Psychiatry*, **17**, 203–13.

Smith, M.D. (1985). Managing the aggressive and self-injurious behavior of adults disabled by autism. *Journal of the Association for Persons with Severe Handicaps*, **10**, 228–32.

Smith, M.D. & Coleman, D. (1986). Managing the behavior of adults with autism in the job setting. *Journal of Autism and Developmental Disorders*, **16**, 145–54.

Smith, R.G., Iwata, B.A., Vollmer, T.R. & Pace, G.M. (1992). On the relationship between self-injurious behavior and self-restraint. *Journal of Applied Behavior Analysis*, **25**, 433–45.

Smith, R.G., Iwata, B.A., Vollmer, T.R. & Zarcone, J.R. (1993*a*). Experimental analysis and treatment of multiply controlled self-injury. *Journal of Applied Behavior Analysis*, **26**, 183–96.

Smith, T., McEachin, J.J. & Lovaas, O.I. (1993*b*). Comments on replication and evaluation of outcome. *American Journal on Mental Retardation*, **97**, 385–91.

Solnick, J.V., Rincover, A. & Peterson, C.R. (1977). Some determinants of the reinforcing and punishing effects of timeout. *Journal of Applied Behavior Analysis*, **10**, 415–24.

Sovner, R., Fox, C.J., Lowry, M.J. & Lowry, M.A. (1993). Fluoxetine treatment of depression and associated self-injury in two adults with mental retardation. *Journal of Intellectual Disability Research*, **37**, 301–11.

Spain, B., Hart, S.A. & Corbett, J. (1984). The use of appliances in the treatment of severe self-injurious behaviour. *Occupational Therapy*, 353–57.

Special Development Team (1988). *Annual Report 1988.* University of Kent: Canterbury.

Sprague, J.R. & Horner, R.H. (1992). Covariation within functional response classes: implications for treatment of severe problem behavior. *Journal of Applied Behavior Analysis*, **25**, 735–45.

Sprague, R.L. & Werry, J.S. (1971). Methodology of psychopharmacological studies with the retarded. In *International Review of Research in Mental Retardation*, 5 (ed. N. Ellis). Academic Press: New York.

Spreat, S., Lipinski, D., Hill, J. & Halpin, M.E. (1986). Safety indices associated with the use of contingent restraint procedures. *Applied Research in Mental Retardation*, **7**, 475–81.

Staddon, J.E.R. (1977). Schedule-induced behavior. In *Handbook of Operant Behavior* (ed. W.K. Honig & J.E.R. Staddon). Prentice Hall: Englewood Cliffs, NJ.

Stahmer, A. & Schreibman, L. (1992). Teaching children with autism appropriate play in unsupervised settings using a self-management treatment package. *Journal of Applied Behavior Analysis*, **25**, 447–59.

Steege, M.W., Wacker, D.P., Berg, W.K., Cigrand, K.K. & Cooper, L. J. (1989). The use of behavioral assessment to prescribe and evaluate treatments for severely handicapped children. *Journal of Applied Behavior Analysis*, **22**, 23–33.

Steege, M.W., Wacker, D.P., Cigrand, K.C., Berg, W., Novak, C.G., Reimers, T.M., Sasso, G.M. & DeRaad, A. (1990). Use of negative reinforcement in the treatment of self-injurious behavior. *Journal of Applied Behavior Analysis*, **23**, 459–67.

Steen, P.L. & Zuriff, G.E. (1977). The use of relaxation in the treatment of self-injurious behavior. *Journal of Behavior Therapy and Experimental Psychiatry*, **8**, 447–8.

Stenfert-Kroese, B. & Fleming, I. (1993). Prevalence and persistency of challenging behaviour in children. In *People with Learning Disability and Severe Challenging Behaviour: New Developments in Services and Therapy* (ed. I. Fleming & B. Stenfert Kroese). Manchester University Press: Manchester.

Stolz, S. (1981). Adoption of innovations from applied behavioral research: 'Does anybody care?'. *Journal of Applied Behavior Analysis*, **14**, 491–505.

Stone, R.K., Alvarez, W.F., Ellman, G., Hom, A.C. & White, J.F. (1989). Prevalence and prediction of psychotropic drug use in California Developmental Centers. *American Journal of Mental Deficiency*, **93**, 627–32.

Sturmey, P., Carlsen, A., Crisp, A.G. & Newton, J.T. (1988). A functional analysis of multiple aberrant responses: a refinement and extension of Iwata et al's methodology. *Journal of Mental Deficiency Research*, **32**, 31–46.

Suen, H.K. & Ary, D. (1989). *Analyzing Quantitative Behavioral Observation Data*. Lawrence Erlbaum Associates: Hillsdale, NJ.

Talkington, L. & Riley, J. (1971). Reduction diets and aggression in institutionalized mentally retarded patients. *American Journal of Mental Deficiency*, **76**, 370–2.

Tanner, B. & Zeiler, M. (1975). Punishment of self-injurious behavior using aromatic ammonia as the aversive stimulus. *Journal of Applied Behavior Analysis*, **8**, 53–7.

Tate, B.G. (1972). Case study: control of chronic self-injurious behavior by conditioning procedures. *Behavior Therapy*, **3**, 72–83.

Tate, B.G. & Baroff, G.S. (1966). Aversive control of self-injurious behavior in a psychotic boy. *Behaviour Research and Therapy*, **4**, 281–7.

Tausig, M. (1985). Factors in family decision making about placement for developmentally disabled adults. *American Journal of Mental Deficiency*, **89**, 352–61.

Taylor, D.V., Hetrick, W.P., Neri, C.L., Touchette, P., Barron, J.L. & Sandman, C.A. (1991). Effect of naltrexone on self-injurious behavior, learning and activity: a case study. *Pharmacology Biochemistry and Behavior*, **40**, 79–82.

Taylor, D.V., Rush, D., Hetrick, W.P. & Sandman, C. (1993*a*). Self-injurious behavior within the menstrual cycle of women with mental retardation. *American Journal on Mental Retardation*, **97**, 659–64.

Taylor, D.V., Sandman, C.A., Touchette, P., Hetrick, W.P. & Barron, J.L. (1993*b*). Naltrexone improves learning and attention in self-injurious individuals with developmental disabilities. *Journal of Developmental and Physical Disabilities*, **5**, 29–42.

Taylor, J.C. & Carr, E.G. (1993). Reciprocal social influences in the analysis and intervention of severe challenging behavior. In *Communicative Alternatives to Challenging Behavior*, pp.63–82 (ed. J. Reichle & D.P. Wacker). P.H. Brookes: Baltimore.

Taylor, J.C. & Carr, E.G. (1994). Severe problem behaviors of children with developmental disabilities: reciprocal social influences. In *Destructive Behavior in Developmental Disabilities*, pp.274–291 (ed. T. Thompson & D.B. Gray). Sage: Thousand Oaks.

Taylor, J.C. & Romanczyk, R.G. (1994). Generating hypotheses about the function of student problem behavior by observing teacher behavior. *Journal of Applied Behavior Analysis*, **27**, 251–65.

Thompson, T., Egli, M., Symons, F. & Delaney, D. (1994*a*). Neurobehavioral mechanisms of drug action in developmental disabilities. In *Destructive Behavior in Developmental Disabilities: Diagnosis and Treatment*, pp.133–180 (ed. T. Thompson & D.B. Gray). Sage: Thousand Oaks.

Thompson, T., Hackenberg, T. & Schaal, D. (1991). Pharmacological treatments for behavior problems in developmental disabilities. In *Treatment of Destructive Behaviors in Persons with Developmental Disabilities*, pp.343–445 (ed. US Department of Health and Human Services). National Institutes of Health: Bethesda, MD.

Thompson, T., Hackenberg, T., Cerutti, D., Baker, D. & Axtell, S. (1994*b*). Opioid antagonist effects on self-injury in adults with mental retardation: response form and location as determinants of medication effects. *American Journal on Mental Retardation*, **99**, 85–102.

Thompson, S. & Emerson, E. (in press). Inter-informant agreement on the Motivation Assessment Scale. *Mental Handicap Research*

Timberlake, W. (1980). A molar equilibrium theory of learned performance. In *The Psychology of Learning and Motivation* (Vol 14), pp.1–58 (ed. G. Bower). Academic Press: New York.

Tomporowski, P. & Ellis, N.R. (1984). Effects of exercise on the physical fitness, intelligence and adaptive behavior of institutionalized mentally retarded adults. *Applied Research in Mental Retardation*, **5**, 329–37.

Tomporowski, P. & Ellis, N. (1985). The effects of exercise on the health, intelligence, and adaptive behavior of institutionalized severely and profoundly mentally retarded adults. *Applied Research in Mental Retardation*, **6**, 465–73.

Touchette, P.E., MacDonald, R.F. & Langer, S.N. (1985). A scatter plot for identifying stimulus control of problem behavior. *Journal of Applied Behavior Analysis*, **18**, 343–51.

Tröster, H. (1994). Prevalence and functions of stereotyped behaviors in non-handicapped children in residential care. *Journal of Abnormal Child Psychology*, **22**, 79–97.

Ullman, L. & Krasner, L. (eds.) (1965). *Case Studies in Behavior Modification*. Holt, Rinehart and Winston: New York.

Van Houten, R., Axelrod, S., Bailey, J.S., Favell, J.E., Foxx, R.M., Iwata, B.A. & Lovaas, O.I. (1988). The right to effective behavioral treatment. *Journal of Applied Behavior Analysis*, **21**, 381–4.

Van Houten, R., Rolider, A. & Houlihan, M. (1992). Treatments of self-injury based on teaching compliance and/or brief physical restraint. In *Self-Injurious Behavior: Analysis, Assessment and Treatment* (ed. J.K. Luiselli, J.L. Matson & N.N. Singh). Springer-Verlag: New York.

Voeltz, L.M. & Evans, I.M. (1982). Behavioral interrelationships in child behavior therapy. *Behavioral Assessment*, **4**, 131–65.

Vollmer, T.R. (1994). The concept of automatic reinforcement: implications for behavioral research in developmental disabilities. *Research in Developmental*

Disabilities, **15**, 187–207.

Vollmer, T.R. & Iwata, B.A. (1991). Establishing operations and reinforcement effects. *Journal of Applied Behavior Analysis,* **24**, 279–91.

Vollmer, T.R., Iwata, B.A., Zarcone, J.R., Smith, R.G. & Mazaleski, J.L. (1993). The role of attention in the treatment of attention-maintained self-injurious behavior: noncontingent reinforcement and differential reinforcement of other behavior. *Journal of Applied Behavior Analysis,* **26**, 9–21.

Vollmer, T.R., Marcus, B.A. & LeBlanc, L. (1994). Treatment of self-injury and hand mouthing following inconclusive functional analysis. *Journal of Applied Behavior Analysis,* **27**, 331–44.

Wacker, D.P., Berg, W.K., Wiggins, B., Muldoon, M. & Cavanaugh, J. (1985). Evaluation of reinforcer preferences for profoundly handicapped students. *Journal of Applied Behavior Analysis,* **18**, 173–8.

Wacker, D., McMahon, C., Steege, M., Berg, W., Sasso, G. & Melloy, K. (1990*a*). Applications of sequential alternating treatments design. *Journal of Applied Behavior Analysis,* **23**, 333–9.

Wacker, D.P., Steege, J.N., Sasso, G., Berg, W., Reimers, T., Cooper, L., Cigrand, K. & Donn, L. (1990*b*). A component analysis of functional communication training across three topographies of severe behavior problems. *Journal of Applied Behavior Analysis,* **23**, 417–29.

Wacker, D.P., Wiggins, B., Fowler, M. & Berg, W.K. (1988). Training students with profound or multiple handicaps to make requests via microswitches. *Journal of Applied Behavior Analysis,* **21**, 331–43.

Wahler, R.G. (1975). Some structural aspects of deviant child behavior. *Journal of Applied Behavior Analysis,* **8**, 27–42.

Wahler, R.G. (1980). The insular mother: her problems in parent–child treatment. *Journal of Applied Behavior Analysis,* **13**, 207–17.

Wahler, R.G. & Fox, J.J. (1981). Setting events in applied behavior analysis: Toward a conceptual and methodological expansion. *Journal of Applied Behavior Analysis,* **14**, 327–38.

Wahler, R.G. & Graves, M.G. (1983). Setting events in social networks: ally or enemy in child behavior therapy?. *Behavior Therapy,* **14**, 19–36.

Wahler, R.G., Sperling, K.A., Thomas, M.R., Teeter, N.C. & Luper, H.L. (1970). The modification of childhood stuttering: some response–response relationships. *Journal of Experimental Child Psychology,* **9**, 411–28.

Walters, A.S., Barrett, R.P., Feinstein, C., Mercurio, A. & Hole, W.T. (1990). A case report of naltrexone treatment of self-injury and social withdrawal in autism. *Journal of Autism and Developmental Disorders,* **20**, 169–76.

Weeks, M. & Gaylord-Ross, R. (1981). Task difficulty and aberrant behavior in severely handicapped students. *Journal of Applied Behavior Analysis,* **14**, 449–63.

Weiss, C.H. (1979). The many meanings of research utilization. *Public Administration Review,* **39**, 426–31.

Weiss, C.H. & Bucuvalas, M. (1980). *Social Science Research and Decision Making.* Columbia University Press: New York.

Weiss, N.R. (1992). *The Application of Aversive Procedures to Individuals with Developmental Disabilities: A Call to Action.* Weiss: Baltimore.

Werry, J.S., Carlielle, J. & Fitzpatrick, J. (1983). Rhythmic motor activities (stereotypies) in children under five: etiology and prevalence. *Journal of the American Academy of Child Psychiatry,* **22**, 329–36.

Westlake, C.R. & Kaiser, A.P. (1991). Early childhood services for children with severe disabilities: research, values, policy and practice. In *Critical Issues in the Lives of People with Severe Disabilities* (ed. L.H. Meyer, C.A. Peck, & L. Brown). P.H. Brookes: Baltimore.

Whitman, T.L. (1990). Self-regulation and mental retardation. *American Journal on Mental Retardation,* **94**, 347–62.

Wieseler, N.A., Hanson, R.H., Chamberlain, T.P. & Thompson, T. (1985). Functional taxonomy of stereotypic and self-injurious behavior. *Mental Retardation,* **23**, 230–4.

Willems, E.P. (1974). Behavioral technology and behavioral ecology. *Journal of Applied Behavior Analysis,* **7**, 151–65.

Williams, D.E., Kirkpatrick–Sanchez, S. & Crocker, W.T. (1994). A long-term follow-up of treatment for severe self-injury. *Research in Developmental Disabilities,* **15**, 487–501.

Williams, D.E., Kirkpatrick-Sanchez, S. & Iwata, B.A. (1993*a*). A comparison of shock intensity in the treatment of longstanding and severe self-injurious behavior. *Research in Developmental Disabilities,* **14**, 207–19.

Williams, L., Ellis, C.R., Ickowicz, A., Singh, N.N. & Singh, Y.N. (1993*b*). Pharmacotherapy of aggressive behavior in individuals with mental retardation and mental illness. *Journal of Developmental and Physical Disabilities,* **5**, 87–94.

Windahl, S.I. (1988). Self-injurious behavior in a time perspective. 8th Congress of the International Association for the Scientific Study of Mental Deficiency, Dublin.

Winnett, R.A. & Winkler, R.C. (1972). Current behavior modification in the classroom: be still, be quiet, be docile. *Journal of Applied Behavior Analysis,* **5**, 499–504.

Winterling, V., Dunlap, G. & O'Neill, R.E. (1987). The influence of task variation on the aberrant behaviors of autistic students. *Education and Treatment of Children,* **10**, 105–19.

Wise, R.A. (1982). Neuroleptics and operant behavior: the ahedonia hypothesis. *Behavioral and Brain Sciences,* **5**, 39–53.

Wolf, M.M. (1978). Social validity: the case for subjective measurement, or how applied behavior analysis is finding its heart. *Journal of Applied Behavior Analysis,* **11**, 203–14.

Wolf, M.M., Risley, T.R. & Mees, H.L. (1964). Application of operant conditioning procedures to the behavior problems of an autistic child. *Behaviour Research and Therapy,* **1**, 305–12.

Wolfensberger, W. (1972). *The Principle of Normalization in Human Services.* National Institute on mental retardation: Toronto.

Wolfensberger, W. (1975). *The Origin and Nature of Our Institutional Models.* Human Policy Press: Syracuse.

Wolfensberger, W. & Thomas, S. (1983). PASSING: *Program Analysis of Service Systems Implementation of Normalization Goals.* National Institute on Mental Retardation: Toronto.

Zangwill, O.L. (1980). *Behaviour Modification: Report of a Joint Working Party to Formulate Ethical Guidelines.* HMSO: London.

Zarcone, J.R., Iwata, B.A., Smith, R.G., Mazaleski, J.L. & Lerman, D.C. (1994). Reemergence and extinction of self-injurious escape behavior during stimulus (instructional) fading. *Journal of Applied Behavior Analysis,* **27**, 307–16.

Zarcone, J.R., Iwata, B.A., Vollmer, T.R., Jagtiani, S., Smith, R.G. & Mazaleski, J.L. (1993). Extinction of self-injurious escape behavior with and without instructional fading. *Journal of Applied Behavior Analysis,* **26**, 353–60.

Zarcone, J.R., Rodgers, T.A., Iwata, B.A., Rourke, D.A. & Dorsey, M.F. (1991). Reliability analysis of the motivation assessment scale: a failure to replicate. *Research in Developmental Disabilities,* **12**, 349–60.

Zarkowska, E. & Clements, J. (1994). *Severe Problem Behaviour: The STAR Approach.* Chapman & Hall: London.

Zeigob, L., Klukas, N. & Junginger, J. (1978). Reactivity of self-monitoring procedures with retarded adolescents. *American Journal of Mental Deficiency,* **83**, 156–63.

Zingarelli, G., Ellman, G., Hom, A., Wymore, M., Heidorn, S. & Chicz-DeMet, A. (1992). Clinical effects of naltrexone on autistic behavior. *American Journal on Mental Retardation,* **97**, 57–63.

INDEX